Despite the Best Intentions

TRANSGRESSING BOUNDARIES
Studies in Black Politics and Black Communities
Cathy Cohen and Fredrick Harris, Series Editors

Despite the Best Intentions

*How Racial Inequality Thrives
in Good Schools*

AMANDA E. LEWIS AND
JOHN B. DIAMOND

OXFORD
UNIVERSITY PRESS

OXFORD
UNIVERSITY PRESS

Oxford University Press is a department of the University of
Oxford. It furthers the University's objective of excellence in research,
scholarship, and education by publishing worldwide.

Oxford   New York
Auckland   Cape Town   Dar es Salaam   Hong Kong   Karachi
Kuala Lumpur   Madrid   Melbourne   Mexico City   Nairobi
New Delhi   Shanghai   Taipei   Toronto

With offices in
Argentina   Austria   Brazil   Chile   Czech Republic   France   Greece
Guatemala   Hungary   Italy   Japan   Poland   Portugal   Singapore
South Korea   Switzerland   Thailand   Turkey   Ukraine   Vietnam

Oxford is a registered trademark of Oxford University Press
in the UK and certain other countries.

Published in the United States of America by
Oxford University Press
198 Madison Avenue, New York, NY 10016

© Oxford University Press 2015

Cataloging-in-Publication data is on file at the Library of Congress
ISBN 978-0-19-534272-7

9 8 7 6 5 4 3 2 1
Printed in the United States of America
on acid-free paper

Contents

Acknowledgments

Over the course of this project, from the data collection phase through the writing of the book, both of us have gone through a number of major life events, including childbirth, job changes, multiple cross-country moves, and significant personal and family health challenges. Thus, this book has taken somewhat longer to come to fruition than we had ever imagined, but in many ways we believe it is better for it. We had the time to talk through ideas, work and rework them, and puzzle through the pieces.

We must, of course, begin our acknowledgments with our deepest appreciation to the Riverview community. Though we began this work out of an invitation from a school administrator, doing it well required a great number of community members being willing to have sometimes difficult conversations with us about the good work they are doing and the challenges they continue to face. We are also very grateful to the institutions that helped fund parts of the research and writing, including The Spencer Foundation, the Riverview School District, The University of Illinois at Chicago (Office of Social Science Research, Departments of Sociology and African American Studies), Emory University, The University of Wisconsin—Madison, the Harvard Graduate School of Education, the Milton Fund at Harvard University, and the Minority Student Achievement Network.

In addition, we thank the multiple institutions that we have worked for or who have supported research leaves for one or both of us through this process—University of Illinois at Chicago (Institute for Research on Race and Public Policy, Institute for Government and Public Affairs), Emory University, Harvard Graduate School of Education, University of Wisconsin (Madison and Milwaukee), Northwestern University School of Education and Social Policy, the Radcliffe Institute for Advanced Study at Harvard, and Stanford's Center for the Advanced Studies of Behavioral Sciences.

We are immensely grateful to the many current and former graduate and undergraduate students who have assisted us with the research and manuscript development. Thanks to Nana Akua Anyidoho, Carole Ayanlaja, Heather Benjamin, Geoffrey Banks, Kristy Cooper, Tomas Garrett, Lamont Gordon, R. Michelle Green, Mosi Ifatunji, Grace Kim, Douglas Knecht, Julia Noveske Kobulsky, Van Lac, Myosha McAfee, Briana Perry, Sherry Reddick, Matthew Rodriguez, Erin Starkey, Katherine Swanson, Dyan Watson, and Sun Young Yoon. An especially huge thanks to Michelle Manno, who has played an important role throughout this process, helping with everything from tracking down respondents to setting up interviews to cleaning interview transcripts to proofreading footnotes to providing substantive feedback on chapters. We are grateful that she was willing to direct her smarts and her attention to detail to polishing this manuscript not just once but at several points in the process. Another special thank you goes to James Huguley, who played a critical role in the quantitative analysis and reporting in Chapter 2. His work and collaboration on this project have been invaluable. Sybil Madison-Boyd was an early collaborator in thinking about the research project and played an important role in working through the project design.

The book has benefited from feedback from a number of colleagues. In January of 2013 we were honored to be able to bring together several very smart colleagues to read and comment on a complete draft of the manuscript. William Darity, Tyrone Forman, Heather Beth Johnson, and Carla O'Connor all gave us two days out of their busy lives and a number of really useful suggestions. We used these along with the great comments from several anonymous reviewers to do the final revising and polishing. Barbara Lewis provided an invaluable and careful copyediting of these draft chapters. If there is anything graceful in our prose, it is thanks to her keen eye. Other colleagues read drafts of parts of chapters and helped in the process of developing our ideas. These include Antwi Akom, Bill

Ayers, Ron Ferguson, Maria Krysan, Annette Lareau, Garvey Lundy, Omar McRoberts, Jerome Morris, Dina Okamoto, and Beth Richie.

The book has also benefited from the questions and comments we received while presenting earlier versions of the chapters in a number of venues, including the following: Center for the Study of Race and Social Problems at University of Pittsburgh's School of Social Work, Stanford Center for Opportunity Policy in Education, Duke University's Department of Sociology, Department of Educational Studies—Emory University, Northwestern University Department of Sociology, University of Pennsylvania School of Education (UPENN), University of Wisconsin – Madison School of Education, Minority Student Achievement Network, Delaware Valley Consortium for Excellence & Equity at UPENN, Harvard Achievement Gap Initiative, Oakland Michigan Public Schools, Boston Public Schools, Madison Metropolitan School District, University of Michigan's School of Education, and the Racial Attitudes and Identity Network. Students at Harvard and the University of Wisconsin also read and commented on chapters during courses, and members of Carl Grant's Multicultural Education Working Group also provided valuable feedback.

Many thanks to the editorial and production staff at Oxford University Press. Special thanks to David McBride at Oxford for his patience and faith in the book throughout this journey, series editors Cathy Cohen and Fred Harris for their early interest and support, and Sarah Rosenthal for marshaling us through the editorial process.

We must also take a moment to each personally acknowledge those friends and family members who have provided needed sustenance, care, and reassurance throughout.

John:

I have always found a deep well of support from my family and friends. John and Barbara Diamond, my parents, continue to give me an example of love, strength, commitment, and resilience to live by. My sister, Kim, has always laid a path of integrity and perseverance for me to follow. My second set of parents, Allen and Patricia Peterson, have blessed me with unconditional love and support. Other family members who have provided various forms of support include Beverly Holmes, Henrietta Baylor, Lincoln Berry, and Lincoln Allen, as well as the ancestors from whom I draw strength.

Many other friends and colleagues also deserve thanks for their various contributions. My colleagues at the University of Wisconsin–Madison Departments of Educational Leadership and Policy Analysis and Educational Policy Studies have provided a wonderful intellectual home. Particular thanks go to Rich Halverson, Jerlando Jackson, Rochelle Winkle-Wagner, Julie Mead, Carolyn Kelly, Clif Conrad, Linn Posey-Maddox, Bianca Baldridge, Michael Fultz, and Gloria Ladson Billings.

Other colleagues who have provided various forms of support include Walter Allen, Wendy Angus, Curtis Askew, Phil Bowman, William Branch, Prudence Carter, Dorinda Carter Andrews, Thomas Cook, Laura Cooper, Bruce Carruthers, David Deming, James Earl Davis, Richard Elmore, Wendy Espeland, Madeline M. Hafner, Nancy Hill, Andrew Ho, James Honan, Janice Jackson, Jane Kamensky, Michele Lamont, Sara Lawrence-Lightfoot, Daphne Layton, Bridget Terry Long, Vivian Louie, Carlos Manjarrez, Karen Mapp, Kathy McCartney, Aldon Morris, Gary Orfield, Charles Payne, Robert Peterkin, Mica Pollock, Leah Price, Julie A. Reuben, James Spillane, Bernice Stokes, Francesca Trivellato, Frank Tuittt, Natasha Warikoo, Mark Warren, Rick Weissbourd, Ken White, Charles Willie, William Julius Wilson, and Dorsey Yearly.

My son Baylor Holmes Diamond was born near the beginning of this project. He is an inspiration for me every day and for this project. He wakes up every morning with a smile and approaches each day with optimism. He has taught me a lot through his resilience, strength, and compassion for others. Lydia Diamond has been with me for most of my adult life. We have grown up together and she has taught me valuable life lessons. Our many conversations about the dynamics of race, class, sex, and inequality have undoubtedly made their way into this book. Thank you for supporting me along this journey.

Amanda:

Over the last few years, good friends and family have listened to me talk about and struggle with both the substance and the writing/logistics of this book with patience, encouragement, and sometimes even deep interest. First, much gratitude to my parents, Robert and Barbara Lewis. Robert reminded me to always keep my eye on the prize and to literally and metaphorically prioritize the things that matter. My mother, Barbara, gave her brain power to reading each and every chapter and has always been that source of unconditional support and encouragement that helps sustain me when I'm not sure I've got anything interesting to say. My sister Rebecca was a regular sounding board for both ideas and stress about how to juggle many competing life demands. Other members of my family who have kept me going throughout the process include Chris, Charlie, and Nico Kanelopoulos, Josh, Lisa, Joey, and Charlotte Lewis, and Elizabeth Van Deusen Macleod. I feel lucky to have a group of friends who are more like family who have supported me in innumerable ways throughout this process. Some of them have read drafts, many of them have fed me or helped with childcare when I needed to work, some of them have just reminded me that the work is important and thus worth the effort, and others have provided spontaneous dance parties at just the right moment. They include Beth Richie, Cathy Cohen, and Ella Cohen-Richie, Regine, Mitchell, and Nathaniel Jackson, Katani Ostine-Franklin, Naimah Oladuwa-Frame and Suriyah, Sanaa, and Oman Frame, Cynthia Blair, Barbara Ransby, Peter Sporn Janice Bloom, Eduardo Bonilla-Silva and Mary Hovsepian Dorothy Steele, Donna Troka, Mosi Ifatunji, Parna Sengupta, Valerie Character, Kim Hall, Maggie Hagerman, Moon-Kie Jung, Maria Krysan, Laurie Schaffner, Lorena Garcia, Merida Rua, Michelle Boyd, Michael and Karen Owens, the Davis-McRoberts family (Shelley, Omar, Naimah, & Sage), Tom Guglielmo, and Liza Vertinsky. I also have an extended network of colleagues who I don't see often enough but who I learn from regularly. I can't name them all here but big thanks to Gianpaolo Baiocchi, Chip Gallagher, Prudence Carter, Karolyn Tyson, David Embrick, David Brunsma, Tanya Golash-Boza, Lawrence Bobo, Alford Young, and Monica McDermott. Also, even though I may get mocked for it, I must give a shoutout to my Crossfit coaches and friends (e.g., Robin, Nicole, Chad, Matt, and Emily), who might not have always realized it but were immensely helpful throughout key moments of this journey; big thanks especially to Ben Benson, who passed along Will Smith's advice to focus on "one brick at a time." Two important mentors passed away while I was working on this book and I owe both of them a debt of gratitude for the encouragement and wisdom they shared with me over the years. Donald R. Deskins Jr. and Linda Levine are dearly missed.

In the last eight years I have been lucky to be a part of several different writing accountability groups that have provided support and a gentle push when needed. I am very grateful to all the individuals from these writing groups who reminded me that while writing can be a lonely process, we are never in it alone: Beth Richie, Maria Krysan, Omar McRoberts, Merida Rua, Lorena Garcia, Mari Castaneda, David Embrick, Andy Clarno, Ainsworth Clarke, Helen Jun, David Stovall, Badia Ahad, Michelle Boyd, Dennis Condron, Beth Griffiths, and Tyrone Forman.

Nyla Lewis Forman was not yet born when this project started, but she has blossomed into a funny and lovely child in the intervening years and has tried to be patient with me when work has pulled me away. She was often in the back of my mind as I worked on this book and was a strong inspiration to get it right. I have learned a great deal from her bold, beautiful, and unapologetic way of moving through the world. She is fierce in a way I cannot begin to capture. Tyrone Forman has always pushed me to be better and do better even when I have wanted to settle for "good enough." This book is smarter thanks to his insights and I am a better scholar, writer, and person thanks to his encouragement and support. Even if I don't remember to say so on a daily basis, I continue to be ever so grateful to have him as my partner and best friend.

Prologue

It all started with a phone call. We were busy with beginning-of-the-semester activity, when the phone rang. It was Maurice Webber, an assistant principal at Riverview High School, reaching out. Riverview is a comprehensive high school in the suburbs of Metro, a large Midwestern city. Mr. Webber had spent the entirety of his career there—30-plus years spanning his time from brand-new instructor to celebrated teacher, from teacher to dean, from dean to assistant principal. He was nearing retirement and was frustrated, he said—thoroughly dissatisfied with all the explanations of why black students, in his district and elsewhere, were not doing as well in school as white students. From where he sat, Riverview seemed to have everything going for it. Unlike popular images of failing urban public schools, it was a highly resourced suburban school in a liberal community. His colleagues, he believed, were well-meaning and highly skilled. How, then, to explain the disparity in achievement between white and black students even at Riverview?

Maurice Webber wasn't the only person at Riverview to be concerned. Closing what is referred to here and elsewhere as the "racial achievement gap" had been an explicit goal of Riverview teachers and staff members for a number of years, without transformative results. Their failure to make headway was deeply troubling. Why weren't the district's resources and faculty's good intentions enough? On the cusp of retirement, Maurice Webber was calling us to ask if we might speak to some of the low-achieving black students and help him understand what was going on.

We accepted Mr. Webber's request not only because of our mutual concern for these students' outcomes, but also because we recognized that Riverview offered a kind of best-case scenario for exploring these issues. It is an award-winning suburban school that enjoys strong financial support, the recipient of abundant goodwill within a community that has prioritized public schooling. The town's schools have been voluntarily desegregated for decades; many families opt to live there precisely because the schools are diverse.[1] Black families there tend to be much better off financially than those living in nearby municipalities such as Metro City. Riverview seems to have everything going for it.

The high school serves about 3,500 students, approximately 90 percent of them white or black, in equal measure, with the remaining percentage comprised of Latina/os and a small but growing Asian population. About 30 percent of the students are low income.[2] While the majority of the teachers are white, the teaching staff has become more racially diverse over the past few decades. African American teachers made up less than 5 percent of the staff in the late 1960s, but by the academic year 2005–2006 they comprised almost 20 percent of the school's faculty.

Riverview is a well-resourced school district. In 2006–2007, it spent more than $18,000 per student, twice as much as the state average and nearly twice as much as nearby Metro City. More than 80 percent of its teachers hold master's degrees (again, about twice as many as in Metro City). The high school is also impressive physically. Its assets include multiple swimming pools and gymnasiums, and modern facilities for science, art, and vocational training. In many ways the school has the feel of a small college campus. Athletic facilities stretch out at the rear of the building, and a large, well-manicured grass lawn leads to the main entrance. On warm days, students play Frisbee in the school's courtyard, sit and read on the front lawn, and a few even stand in the student parking lot across the street from the main buildings to smoke cigarettes during break periods or at lunchtime.

Riverview itself is a largely middle-class community with a median yearly household income of nearly $70,000, high owner-occupancy rates, and low poverty rates.[3] To be sure, while all groups in Riverview are on average far better off than their peers in the neighboring city, there are still real racial differentials in resources favoring whites over blacks and

Latina/os. Still, median family incomes for all groups are above national averages, while poverty rates are well below. The community has a thriving commercial district, significant arts and cultural facilities and events, abundant historical architecture, well-maintained parks, and numerous town-supported recreational activities. For the many reasons apparent to those who spend time there, a national magazine recently named Riverview as one of the most desirable places in the country to live. It is a self-described "diverse" and "progressive" community—a liberal city.

On paper, Riverview seems like a place where all students should have ample opportunities to succeed academically and thrive personally. Put differently, Riverview presents a "least likely case" in which to find deep racial divisions in educational outcomes. In many ways, the school is a picture of racial integration and high student achievement (e.g., all groups are outperforming their peers in the city next door). There are numerous good reasons why parents want to send their children to Riverview schools and to Riverview High in particular.

Given Riverview's many resources—well-trained teachers, high-quality facilities, abundant financial support from local property taxes—it is not surprising that the school's academic accomplishments are impressive. The graduation rate for the district's racial subgroups is higher than for their counterparts in the state as a whole. And when those students graduate from Riverview, between 75 and 80 percent attend college.[4] Many Riverview graduates qualify as National Merit Scholars, and national magazines regularly name Riverview as one of the top high schools in the state. In this racially diverse school, students report significant cross-race interaction. When asked to identify the racial composition of their six closest friends in a 2001 survey, 80 percent of black, Latina/o, white, and Asian students reported that either some or most of their friends were of a different race than themselves.[5] Such levels of interaction are an important accomplishment in a society where many schools remain segregated.[6]

In 2002, when we started spending significant time at the school, Riverview High School appeared to have achieved long-term, stable integration. The larger community was a place people moved to for the schools and for its diversity. While several nearby suburban communities have highly ranked high schools, what differentiates Riverview from those places is its racial demographics—those other schools are attended primarily by white students. Thus, Riverview schools are not just good schools but good, diverse schools.

Unfortunately, as Mr. Webber's call indicated, Riverview's good schools do not serve all students equally well. Descriptions of Riverview schools as "integrated" are perhaps overstated. While clearly desegregated, evidence of the schools' real integration is wanting. As Dr. Martin Luther King Jr. stated more than 40 years ago:

> Although the terms *desegregation* and *integration* are often used interchangeably, there is a great deal of difference between the two. In the context of what our community needs, desegregation alone is empty and shallow. We must always be aware of the fact that our ultimate goal is integration, and that desegregation alone is only a first step on the road to the good society.[7]

In the case of Riverview, a first foray into the school's hallways certainly conveys an image of an integrated space, as bustling interracial crowds of teenagers move through the corridors on their way to cafeterias, classrooms, gymnasiums, and administrative offices. And yet, students' classroom destinations belie the image of integration. Whether they are on the move toward American history, biology, or geometry class, black, Latina/o, and white students are more often than not heading in different directions. In fact, one key manifestation of the "achievement gap" at Riverview that Mr. Webber worried about is the quite different racial demographics of the school's "high" and "low" academic tracks, with white students far overrepresented in the school's "top" tracks (honors and advanced placement) and black and Latina/o students similarly overrepresented in the school's lower academic tracks.

While Riverview students often attend the same classes during the early elementary grades, their classes become differentiated along racial lines as they move toward the upper elementary and middle school years.[8] Riverview high school has essentially three instructional levels in all subjects—basic, honors, and advanced placement (AP). In a school with less than 50 percent white students, almost 90 percent of AP-class students are white, as are almost 80 percent of honors-class students. In contrast, two-thirds of the students taking basic-level classes are black or Latina/o.[9] As Karolyn Tyson writes, whereas the original movements that led to desegregation in districts like Riverview embodied a hope that "black and white students would come together as equals ... the movement toward integration ... was interrupted" before it was ever achieved.[10]

Achievement differentials are apparent not just in academic tracks. For example, multiple datasets show cumulative grade point averages of white and Asian students to be a full point higher than the average for black and Latina/o students.[11] Test score outcomes also follow racial patterns. On the 2006 ACT exam, the mean composite score for white students was about 26, while the score for African American and Latina/o students was about 18.[12]

Finally, while black and Latina/o Riverview graduates are much more likely than their peers in nearby Metro City to attend college, white Riverview graduates are far more likely than their black and Latina/o peers to attend four-year colleges (more than 90 percent for whites versus closer to 60 percent for blacks and Latina/os). While only 5 percent of white Riverview graduates end up in two-year colleges, 30 percent of black graduates and 40 percent of Latina/o graduates do so. Thus, while Riverview graduates' overall college attendance rates are high, the institutions that they attend are stratified by race and ethnicity. These numbers in part highlight why black and Latina/o parents might choose to send their children to Riverview—Riverview students' outcomes are better than those of students in other nearby districts. However, these figures also highlight that even within schools like Riverview, which are considered to be very good, significant racial gaps exist in students' educational outcomes.

The central question we tackle in this book is "Why?" In concrete terms, we ask, Why is it that when you walk into one of the high-track classes at Riverview, you see almost all white faces? Why are the "regular" or "basic" classes predominantly black? Why do we continue to think of places like Riverview as good schools, if not great ones, when they produce such stark inequalities? Beyond "Why," we wonder "How?" How do Riverview students, faculty, and staff make sense of these stark racial realities? How do well-meaning people—skilled and caring educators, liberal white parents, and middle-class black parents—come to live with these patterns on a daily basis? These questions drive this book's two central goals.

Our first objective is to provide a fuller account of what is *racial* about "racial achievement gaps"—an account that goes beyond the individual characteristics of students and peer culture to understand what is going on within the institution of school that contributes to unequal outcomes. How does race matter? Second, and more broadly, we seek to use this close examination of Riverview to shed light on a wider paradox in the post–civil-rights United States. Many if not most Americans today express support for diversity and claim to be color-blind and largely beyond race, yet we find deeply seated racial inequality on almost every social and economic indicator we can name. How does this inequality persist long after the explicit and deliberate racist policies of the past have been formally outlawed? What are the mechanisms and processes that contribute to racial inequality today, decades after the triumphs of the civil rights movement? In this way, we believe that the racial dynamics at Riverview and places like it are not unique. Rather, we can see that they capture something larger about the way race works in the United States today.

In search of answers to our questions, we began collecting data in 2003, shortly after our early conversations with Maurice Webber. We started exactly where he asked us to, by interviewing low-achieving black students. After interviewing 23 students, we then reached out to their parents and interviewed as many of them as we could.[13] After examining that data, we sought out additional resources to do what clearly needed to be done: Conduct a broader examination of the experiences of individuals across the school. With additional research support from the universities where we worked and the Spencer Foundation, in 2006 we then expanded the project to interview a wider group of black, white, and Latina/o Riverview students, along with their parents. We also interviewed teachers and staff from departments and units across Riverview. In total, between 2003 and 2007, we interviewed just over 170 members of the Riverview community.[14] During this period we also spent regular time at the school, taking on various formal and informal roles. For part of the time, one of us worked for an external organization that had a collaborative relationship with the district and was housed in the school building. We also worked with the school in different roles, including conducting workshops, consulting formally and informally with personnel, and working with different classroom teachers. Our own regular participation in and around the school undoubtedly helped us secure participation in the research from a wide cross-section of the school community. To supplement this observational and interview data, we also drew on survey data collected in Riverview and 14 similar districts.[15]

While it has taken us longer than we had hoped to answer Maurice Webber's request for help, we have taken substantial time, energy, and care to conduct a thorough examination of what is going on in Riverview. Assistant Principal Webber is not the only one who needs an answer. We share in his feeling of urgency precisely because we think the stakes are so high. In the chapters that follow, we argue that race has a key role in producing achievement differentials, but not in the ways we typically assume. Importantly, while contemporary patterns of racial inequality are similar to those of the past, the mechanisms that produce them are different. Race still operates on multiple levels—shaping how we think about and interact with one another, shaping the resources we have available as we move through the world, and shaping how institutions like schools reward those resources. Many of the hourly and daily practices and processes that are the substance of what we think of as "school" are racially inflected. What is different is that even as these school policies and practices are operating to create advantages for some groups and put others at a disadvantage, they simultaneously appear to be "race-neutral." Their apparent "nonracialness" is crucial; at the same time that their enactment contributes to inequities, their surface "neutrality" helps to provide legitimacy to the differential outcomes they help to produce.[16] To be sure, today they are generally not designed to or even intended to produce discrepant outcomes. Yet good intentions do not mitigate the results. However intended, these patterns still reinforce racial hierarchies and dominant racial belief systems. It is, we argue, in the daily interaction among school policy, everyday practice, racial ideology, and structural inequality that contradictions emerge between good intentions and bad outcomes.

Despite the Best Intentions represents our best effort to answer Maurice Webber's call to shed light on how racial disparities persist in Riverview. We turn now to what is for us an essential piece of telling this story thoroughly and well—gaining a fuller understanding of how exactly racial dynamics shape educational experience in places like Riverview.

1

Introduction

Dawn, Renee, Miles, Nico, Maria, and Patrick are all students at Riverview High School. They are 15, 16, athletic, artistic, witty, clumsy, tall, medium, goal-oriented, and not. They describe themselves as regular, hard-working, friendly, and shy. They plan to go to Stanford, work for their uncle, play in the NBA, become a lawyer. They are beloved children, annoying siblings, adolescents through and through. They are trying to make their way through the world as best they can with the tools they have. They attend a school that is funded better than many, in a city that is more liberal than most—a school where Mr. Michaels, Ms. Jackson, Ms. Grace, Mr. Fell, and Mr. Bettencourt all work hard every day to help them succeed. And yet, as with most schools, not all of them are successful. That there is variation in student achievement would not be noteworthy if not for that fact that that variation has a racial cast to it—often referred to as "the racial achievement gap." Riverview High School is like many schools nationally in which student outcomes vary significantly along racial lines. This book is our attempt to contribute to an ongoing set of conversations about why that is. We explore how factors inside schools sometimes play a role in these young people's unfolding trajectories. As we explain in the prologue, while a phone call from Riverview High School assistant principal Maurice Webber initially spurred us into action, we had both been concerned about race and educational outcomes for some time.

Mr. Webber's and our concern about racial differences in academic outcomes is not unique—it is mirrored in a wealth of recent attention focused on the "racial achievement gap."[1] Generally, the term *racial achievement gap* refers to the disparities in test scores, grade point averages, and/or high school and college completion rates between white students and black and/or Latina/o students.[2] As at Riverview, on each of these measures nationally, the average white student outperforms their typical black and Latina/o peers.[3] For example, major gaps exist on a range of standardized tests, including the National Assessment of Education Progress (NAEP), often referred to as the national school report card, and the SAT. In 2006 black students averaged 434 on their verbal SAT scores, Latina/os averaged 457, and whites averaged 527. A similar pattern existed in mathematics, with blacks scoring 429, Latina/os 463, and whites 536.[4]

Differences also exist in high school grade point averages, graduation rates, and placement in gifted programs in lower grades, and honors or advanced placement (AP) educational tracks in upper grades (especially in desegregated schools).[5] Resulting differences in educational attainment (which is influenced by scores and grades) have major implications for one's chances of getting ahead in life. For example, in 2011, college graduates earned nearly $30,000 more per year than high school graduates and about $40,000 a year more than those without a high school diploma.[6] As we show in Table 1.1, over a lifetime, those with college degrees will earn about $1 million more than high school graduates and about $1.5 million more than those without a high school diploma.

When we began this work, the "achievement gap" had been getting a great deal of attention, but the scholarly explanations of what led to the gap had stalled somewhat. Studies using nationally representative survey data, controlling for individual-level measures such as family background and the skills students begin school with, had been unable to fully explain the variance in student performance across race.[7] There was also growing evidence that school-based processes were strongly contributing to the growth in achievement gaps over time. For example, research by scholars such as economists Roland Fryer and Steven Levitt highlighted the fact that black students fell further behind the longer they stayed in school.[8] Thus, while factors outside of school, particularly socioeconomic status and family resources, clearly matter a great deal for educational outcomes, a growing number of scholars had begun to call for a different kind of work. They suggested that in trying to understand why some groups of students continued to underperform, we still did not know enough about what was happening inside school buildings and classrooms. For example,

TABLE 1.1. Synthetic Work-Life Earnings by Educational Attainment[a]

Educational attainment	Synthetic work-life earnings[b]	Margin of error[c]
None to 8th grade	936,000	7,000
9th to 12th grade	1,099,000	7,000
High school graduate	1,371,000	3,000
Some college	1,632,000	5,000
Associate's degree	1,813,000	9,000
Bachelor's degree	2,422,000	8,000
Master's degree	2,834,000	13,000
Professional degree	4,159,000	33,000
Doctorate degree	3,525,000	29,000

[a] Listed in dollars. Source: US Census Bureau, 2011 American Community Survey.
[b] Synthetic work-life earnings represent expected earnings over a 40-year period for the population aged 25–64 who maintain full-time, year-round employment on median annual earnings. Calculations are based on median annual earnings from a single point in time for eight five-year age groups and multiplied by 5.
[c] The margin of error can be interpreted roughly as providing a 90-percent probability that the interval defined by the estimate minus the margin of error and the estimate plus the margin of error (the lower and upper confidence bounds) contains the true value.

as Vincent Roscigno and James Ainsworth-Darnell put it, much research on school achievement had "overlooked important micropolitical processes that occur in schools and classrooms."[9] Or, as Dennis Condron expressed it, we need far more "rich detail on processes occurring between and within schools."[10] These holes in our understanding existed partly because of the kind of research that had been done. For example, while nationally representative survey data had given us an overall picture of individual student performance and attitudes, it could not provide much insight into everyday school processes that shape school outcomes.[11] While a number of studies had examined racial achievement gaps, most had been conducted in urban schools.[12] This existing work typically discussed African American students as a monolithic group, failing to attend to variations in students' achievement levels, the social class differences that are becoming increasingly important within the black community, or the growing reality of black suburbanization.[13]

Holes in our understanding also resulted from problems in how much of the research on "achievement gaps" conceptualized (or underconceptualized) race. What is "racial" about "racial achievement gaps"? Why is Riverview students' whiteness or blackness relevant to their school performance? Like too much educational research in general, research on achievement gaps had often treated race as a variable, showing that it had statistical significance in examinations of test scores but not explaining how or why it mattered. In this kind of work, "race" is left to stand in as a proxy for an implied something "else."[14] However, race cannot be the "cause" of achievement or of good or bad SAT scores.[15] Race is a social and political category.[16] It marks the way that bodies have historically become "racialized"—meaning how bodies have been assigned to socially con-structed "races" and how racial categories have emerged and unfolded—the way elite Englishmen, Dutch settlers, Italian peasants, and Jewish refugees became "white," the way that Chippewa and Choctaw and Iroquis tribe members became "Indians," and the way that members of diverse African ethnic groups (e.g., Yoruba, Igbo, and Hausa) became "black." Despite his-toric arguments to the contrary, "race" is not a biological category.[17] Racial categories, their boundaries, and which bodies are understood to belong to which category have not been stable across time, nor across space or geography.[18] While it is crucial to understand that "race" is not a natural or biological category, it is also important to recognize that it can still be socially "real," having fundamentally shaped the organization of social life in the United States for centuries.[19] To paraphrase historian W. I. Thomas, when people define situations as real, they are real in their consequences.

This discussion of what "race" is, what it does and does not mean, complicates discussions of how race matters for school outcomes.[20] If those identified or racialized as black at Riverview High School are collectively per-forming in school differently than those identified or racialized as "white," it is not because these groups are fundamentally different in some underly-ing genetic way. Instead, we must examine the multiple historic and current consequences of racialization—what happened to and continues to happen to people once they were/are placed within particular categories, including the historic and current operation of racism and racial discrimination. In the next sections, we dig deeper into the full and broad consequences of these racialization processes for schooling. What does race have to do with it?

RACE "MATTERS" ON MANY LEVELS

Too often today people continue to talk about race and its consequences in shallow terms—as merely a set of ideas or identities or attitudes. As his-torian Thomas Guglielmo put it, "It is, to be sure, all of these things—but also much more. It is … very much about power and resources (or lack thereof)."[21] While clearly race has consequences for our individual understandings of self and other, it matters much more—with deep and broad consequences for the very organization of social institutions. In societies like the United States, where race has been a fundamental organizing principle since before the country's founding, racialization led not only to the formation of entrenched cultural belief systems that suggested some people were essentially different (and better) than others, but also led to the development of complex hierarchies in which those racialized bodies were *treated differently* in social, legal, political, and economic realms.

Over time the exact organization of these hierarchies has evolved, along with the belief systems that accompany them. From slavery to Jim Crow to what many now label the "post–civil rights era," how we think about race, and how race organizes our lives, has changed dramatically. And yet, contrary to popular claims that we are in a "post-racial" moment, we are not witnessing the slow demise of the relevance of race. Current shifts are a matter of changes in the form of racial dynamics (e.g., *de jure* segregation being replaced by *de facto* segregation). When rain turns to snow as the seasons change, we might well need different clothing, but we are getting wet just the same.

The challenge for understanding what is "racial" about "racial achievement gaps" comes in part from the challenge of keeping the larger history of race in mind when we are trying to understand daily processes. This is the challenge of paying attention simultaneously to the very bigness and the very smallness of its effects and to the connections between the two. As Matthew Hughey argues in his work *White Bound*, "Dominant meanings of race organize our social relations … [and] this social order works to reproduce racist schema and racial inequality through the mundane activities of everyday life."[22] When racial categories are (even subconsciously) assigned in daily interactions, entrenched cultural belief systems get primed, cultural belief systems that emerged and evolved across long histories. Thus, if blacks or whites or Latina/os or Asians at Riverview or elsewhere are thought of as more or less criminal, more or less intelligent, more or less athletically inclined, more or less trustworthy, it is because of how racial thinking and our ideas about different groups developed and evolved across time.[23] How we keep track of and make sense of connections between our daily living and this larger structure and history of race is no small task. Sociologist C. Wright Mills wrote of this challenge over 50 years ago in his call for the "sociological imagination":

> . . . men do not usually define the troubles they endure in terms of historical change and institutional contradiction. The well-being they enjoy, they do not usually impute to the big ups and downs of the societies in which they live. Seldom aware of the intricate connection between the patterns of their own lives and the course of world history, ordinary men do not usually know what this connection means for the kinds of men they are becoming and for the kinds of history-making in which they might take part. They do not possess the quality of mind essential to grasp the interplay of man and society, of biography and history, of self and world.[24]

This "quality of mind" is rare because making these connections between daily life and "world history" is not simple or straightforward.

Our racial history is part of our present, it is in our structures, its legacies can be felt in the ways schools are organized, in how neighborhoods are laid out, in the composition of our family trees, in the unconscious stereotypes that get primed when we mentally sort people along racial lines. We walk around with it, and while it is never the only dynamic in the room, it matters. For example, the long history of degrading black and brown bodies and black and brown minds, of characterizing black and brown people as "less than," as dangerous, or "just" deviant is in the room when a teacher perceives a black student's questions as combative or threatening and a white student's as inquisitive.

Clearly, no individual's or student's life and experiences are solely determined by their racial categorization. But the history and present realities of race shape the parameters within which we operate. Our long racial history has resulted in both entrenched material inequalities and entrenched cultural belief systems. In addition to providing ways of making sense of abstract and distant hierarchies, these belief systems also play out in daily interactions. Research in social psychology shows, for example, that these belief systems attach status or value to distinguishing attributes such as race.[25] Resulting *race-based status beliefs* shape how we understand others and ourselves, how we make sense of the racial landscape in which we operate, and how we act and interact. Ridgeway and Erickson define status beliefs as "widely shared cultural beliefs that people who belong to one social group are more esteemed and competent than those who belong to another social group."[26] Status beliefs both construct and justify social inequality between categories of people.[27] Thus, long histories of racial stratification shape opportunities, shifting racial ideologies set a context for how we understand racial difference, cultural belief systems influence how we interact and respond to one another. Even if not over-determining, all of these dynamics set the context for action.

So, when we ask, "How do you make sense of an award-winning public high school that is known for its rigor, diversity, and quality in which white and black students are so internally academically segregated?," we must think of the question within the larger context of racial contradictions and ironies. How do you make sense of a society founded on principles of justice and liberty for all, which has since its founding formally and informally disenfranchised large swaths of the population? Particularly in a context like the United States, founded on principals of equality, we understand that ways of making *sense* of entrenched racial hierarchies are key to their continuation.[28]

NEW RACISM AND SCHOOLING—STRUCTURAL, INSTITUTIONAL, AND IDEOLOGICAL DYNAMICS

While we seem to be fixated on the "racial achievement gap" now, there have always been "achievement gaps" in the United States between black and white and Latina/o and white children. During the very long period of our country's history, spanning the several centuries of slavery and almost 100 years of Jim Crow, there were large collective gaps between the academic skills and access of blacks and whites. While whites at the time might have understood those gaps to be a result of the inherent intellectual inferiority of blacks, the gaps were ensured and enforced first by laws limiting if not outlawing African Americans' access to education and then by laws permitting access only to separate and unequal schooling. Segregated and unequal schooling was also the norm throughout the Southwest, ensuring that Mexican-American children would remain available to serve as low-wage labor.[29] It would be absurd to characterize the educational situation during those earlier historic moments as "achievement gaps." As James Anderson argues, "It made no sense . . . to focus on test score gaps during the periods when African American [and Latina/o] students were denied basic access to elementary and secondary schools."[30]

It is also a mistake today to try to understand current "achievement gaps" without paying attention to the real "opportunity gaps" or "curriculum gaps" that persist between the schooling we provide to different groups of students.[31] While the mechanisms that structure schooling have changed, there remain deep and persistent quality differences between the schools that average white and black/Latina/o students attend. These inequalities have been well documented and seem to point us toward places like Riverview as an answer—if only children could attend well-resourced "integrated" schools, we could eliminate the "gaps."

And yet, although the formal and legalized structures for maintaining separate schools ended decades ago, they were never replaced by a truly integrated educational system that could provide high-quality educational opportunities to all. There was no time in the history of Riverview schools—in the history of American public schools—when they were segregated or since they have been "desegregated," when they served all students equally and well. As we try to understand the dynamics in a school like Riverview, it is essential to avoid historical amnesia and instead to uncover the important connections between the history of racial stratification and the realities of racial inequality today, in order to understand what has changed—how race works differently today—and what remains the same.

A number of social scientists have captured how, in the current moment, racism has shifted, become much more subtle and implicit. Whether labeling this new form "new racism," "color-blind racism," "laissez-faire racism," "symbolic racism," "racial apathy," or "aversive racism," scholars agree that while racism persists, the way it works has changed.[32] In the post–civil rights era, the practices that sustain racial inequality (and ultimately white supremacy) have not gone away but simply grown more elusive. The move from legalized and rigidly enforced racial exclusion to much more subtle processes means that racial dynamics and the mechanisms of racial exclusion are now harder to see and thus harder to challenge.

As we show in the chapters that follow, today, rather than functioning through overt processes, contemporary racial patterns are supported by *structural inequalities, institutional practices*, and *racial ideologies* that mutually reinforce each other but appear to be largely "nonracial." This is how race works today at Riverview and elsewhere. Such dynamics are masked by widespread beliefs that our society functions as a meritocracy where "people get ahead or behind based on what they earn and deserve rather than what circumstances they were born into."[33] As Heather Beth Johnson discusses in her book *The American Dream and the Power of Wealth*, "a system of meritocracy ... justifies inequality" through the implicit widespread assumption that any inequality of outcomes results from personal failing to achieve in what is a fair competition.[34]

While almost every social and economic indicator shows that persistent racial inequality continues, these patterns are justified today through a new racial common sense.[35] This new "logic" includes the assertion that most people do not see or notice race today (are "color-blind"), that racism is a thing of the past, and that any inequality that persists is the result of individuals or groups not taking full advantage of existing opportunities.[36] Racial inequalities in educational outcomes are reproduced at multiple levels by these same structural inequalities, institutional practices, and racial ideologies. By *structural inequalities*, we refer primarily to political and economic hierarchies that are patterned by racial group membership. In Riverview, for example, political and economic power and resources reside with whites. While the school board has consistently included black representatives, it has always had a large white majority; whites also dominate parent-teacher organizations and wield substantial power over school and district decision making.

Moreover, whites in Riverview possess more economic resources. In this overwhelmingly middle-class community, racial differences in income and wealth persist. For instance, while the median family income for African Americans and Latinos is well over $40,000, the same figure for whites is closer to $80,000.[37] Riverview whites are also more likely to own their homes (which are between two and three times as valuable as homes owned by blacks and Latina/os), and residential segregation among whites, blacks, and Latina/os is pervasive.[38] Thus, because of the continued implications of race, comparisons of social class across racial groups must acknowledge the stark racial inequalities within social class categories.[39] As Rosa, an 11th-grade Riverview student, said in her interview: "Most of the white kids have really big houses that they live in by the river—which are sort of like mansions. Us, the Mexicans, yeah, we have our house or whatever, but it's not as big as theirs." While there are class differences among families, and family background matters for school outcomes, past research shows that black-white achievement gaps cannot be explained entirely by family background.[40] Moreover, even those resources black families have do not pay off in the same way in school as they do for white families (see Chapter 4 for fuller discussion). White families' superior political and economic resources also combine with residential segregation to infuse white social networks with greater power, better access to and influence over school officials, and more information about the schools.[41] In other words, as a result of structural inequalities, whites not only have more economic resources but also possess greater social, cultural, and symbolic capital with which to help their children navigate the schools.

These structural inequalities result in widespread differences between the quality of *schools* that typical white students attend and those that black and Latino students end up in; moreover, they also affect the quality of *experience* that black and Latino students have even when they are in the same schools as white students. Racial dynamics inside desegregated spaces like Riverview are perhaps more complicated but no less potent.

As we will show in the pages that follow, the racial inequality that exists broadly in the United States and in the Riverview community is replicated more narrowly within schools like Riverview. As Roslyn Mickelson noted, "So long as race confers privileges outside schools, it is hard to imagine it does not do the same within schools."[42] The structural advantages possessed by white families are converted into school-based advantages through *institutional* practices—school practices that systematically create institutional advantages for some groups (i.e., whites) and disadvantages for other groups (i.e., blacks and Latina/os) by differentially responding to and rewarding parents' and students' social and cultural resources. For example, as has been shown in other desegregated communities such as Shaker Heights, Ohio; Berkeley, California; and Charlotte-Mecklenburg, North Carolina,[43] school practices result in white students being vastly overrepresented in the most advantaged locations for learning and black and Latina/o students being concentrated in the least advantaged locations. White students are disproportionately located in gifted and talented programs in early grades and in honors and advanced placement classes during high school. Because of these patterns, they are also taught by the most qualified teachers and have greater access to the school's highest quality instructional resources.

Of course, discriminatory institutional practices are deeply connected to from *racial ideologies* and the cultural belief systems that inform and shape behavior. For when we think about how, exactly, race works in our lives, it is important to keep in mind that it operates simultaneously on multiple levels.[44] It is a part of formal structures and institutions and a part of mundane everyday exchanges. With regard to the latter, for example, recent research in social psychology has shown that race is one of few "primary categories" (others include gender and age) that are "used so frequently as to be processed quickly and automatically without the need for conscious thought."[45] In daily interactions, primary categories result in those present in the exchange being automatically mentally placed into categories (being assigned a racial identity). As esteemed social psychologist Cecilia Ridgeway explains, that placement also involves a subconscious process whereby "shared cultural stereotypes associated with the categories" are brought to the fore.[46] Once race has been primed, these shared cultural stereotypes or *race-based status beliefs* become available and begin to unconsciously shape judgments and behavior. The fact that race is a primary category is an historic artifact. While some might argue that categorizing or sorting in general is an automatic and natural part of social life, sorting along *racial* lines in particular and the cultural belief systems that coincide with this sorting are not natural or inevitable. Race is an historical construction and at other points in time it was not a part of social sorting and categorizing. But it is now, and that social sorting and categorizing is not neutral.

Race-based status beliefs reinforce inequality in self-fulfilling ways in school by shaping everyday interactions and heightening performance pressures on students of color.[47] One powerful set of status beliefs are stereotypes about black and Latina/o students' intellectual ability that influence how they are perceived and treated in daily interaction. As Aronson and Steele summarize:

> By middle-childhood, most American children have learned that blacks and Latina/os are less intelligent than whites ... not everyone believes the stereotypes, but most people in the culture are aware of them, targets and nontargets alike. ... knowledge of their content alone can bias perceptions of stereotype targets.[48]

These broader beliefs are part of the racial common sense in places like Riverview. As research by Grace Kao shows, adolescents are aware of these prevalent stereotypes about different groups' academic abilities.[49] Gabe, a white junior from Riverview observed, "Usually the perception is ... that black people are dumber than white people and Hispanics are not as smart as everyone else." We show how such beliefs lead to what we call *everyday discrimination*—conscious and unconscious ways of thinking and interacting that reinforce racial hierarchies. Such everyday discrimination is reflected in lower *performance expectations* for black and Latina/o students (what George W. Bush referred to as "the soft bigotry of low expectations"[50]) and in behaviors like more aggressive monitoring of black and Latina/o students' conduct in comparison to whites', and differential responses to parents' efforts to intervene in their children's education.[51]

Related to race-based status beliefs, collective narratives about racial hierarchies manifest in *racial ideologies* that also shape students' school experiences in multiple ways. First and foremost, they play an important role in explaining and justifying (and sometimes challenging) race-based structural and institutional inequalities.[52] If race-based status beliefs generate hierarchy through producing discrepancies in treatment for different youth, racial ideologies explain away and normalize the resulting differential outcomes. We document the explanations that local actors put forward to explain the stark inequalities in school opportunities and outcomes in Riverview and to show how they use widely held status beliefs to naturalize racial patterns and minimize the importance of race in explaining racial inequality. These local explanations resonate with broader, post–civil-rights-era racial ideologies in suggesting that the United States is an open society in which individual behaviors, values, and responsibility are more important for explaining racial achievement gaps than external structures of inequality, school practices that have racial implications, or day-to-day racial dynamics in the school and community.

We further show how, on a daily basis, blacks and Latina/os must contend with and manage the implications of such status beliefs and ideologies. The power of status beliefs, in part, is that "both groups come to agree, as a matter of social reality, that one group is socially evaluated as better than the other."[53] The group held in lower esteem must expend psychic energy to deal with negative stereotypes such as low expectations.[54] This can make students vulnerable to what Claude Steele calls *stereotype threat*—the fear that one's performance on an academic task will reinforce negative stereotypes about the person's stigmatized group—and depress performance.[55] We detail the implications of racial spotlighting,[56] stereotype threat, and performance expectations for black and Latina/o students at Riverview. Black and Latina/o students must manage others' impressions of them in the local context.[57] This was brought home to us early in our study when one black female student sat for an interview. She explained that every semester she approached the teachers in her mostly honors classes to let them know she was a serious student, because she assumed they would hold low expectations of her. Prior to the interview, she had placed her honor roll certificate on the table in a very deliberate fashion, perhaps sending us researchers a signal similar to the one she sends her teachers.

Importantly, the emphasis on institutional discrimination and racial ideology helps us to understand how those in places like Riverview, who are operating with the best of intentions, can produce less than optimal results. It is, we argue, in the daily interaction among school policy, everyday practice, and racial ideology that contradictions emerge between good intentions and school outcomes. One helpful way of thinking about how such contradictions emerge and become tolerated comes from the work of scholars studying organizational dynamics.

Schools (and all organizations) function partly through the operation of organizational routines. These routines include all of the collective daily practices that people engage in to get things done. We can think about the typical morning ritual at a school (e.g., Pledge of Allegiance, morning announcements, circle time, student advisory meetings), the changes of class on the hour, and teacher lunch breaks and faculty meetings as organizational routines. These routines also include discipline practices like the teacher referral process and the way that students are dealt with through discipline procedures. There are also the routines for class placement, which involve multiple related processes (e.g., test taking, teacher recommendations, counselor referrals, parental appeals) associated with tracking. These routines do not always function like they are supposed to.

Research in organizational studies has identified two key parts or "aspects" of organizational routines—the *ostensive aspect* (the ideal of the routine) and the *performative aspect* (the routine as practiced).[58] As Sherer explains: "The ostensive aspect is the idea of the routine—the ideal or schematic form of a routine. It is the abstract or generalized idea of the routine," or the narrative in the organization about how things *should* be done.[59] "The performative aspect of the routine consists of specific actions, by specific people, in specific places and times."[60] It consists of how the routine is *actually* performed in everyday practice. The performative aspect of a routine may be highly aligned with the ostensive aspect or it may diverge dramatically. Attending to the distinction between the ostensive and performative aspects of organizational routines is critical because "without making this distinction, the parts—either the ostensive or the performative—can be mistaken for the whole. The most common mistake is to take the ostensive for the performative, or to mistake the summary of the way tasks [should be] performed for the ways the tasks are *actually* performed" (emphasis added).[61]

Attention to the divergence between aspects of organizational routines is helpful for understanding schools like Riverview, where everyday educational practices seem to diverge from the school's expressed values and goals. The ostensive aspect of organizational routines might well be aligned with the expressed values and mission of the school even as the performative aspects of routines are not. In fact, as we will describe in detail in the following chapters, there is real divergence at Riverview between the seemingly race-neutral ostensive aspects of school routines and the racialized performance of those routines. The racialized performance of the routines contributes to racialized achievement outcomes, but the school's role in producing such outcomes is masked by the existence of the ostensive routines, which present an image of the school as operating solely on fair, "race-neutral" terms. The divergence between ostensive and performative aspects of organizational routines might seem to raise significant organizational contradictions—things are not done as they are supposed to be. Importantly, however, as we will show, the availability of the ostensibly fair and race-neutral official story of the organizational practice (the ostensive aspect) serves as "cover" for the divergent performative aspect. The ostensive aspect protects the organization's legitimacy and provides a ready narrative for community members to use to explain "how things work." The contradictions or divergence between aspects of the organizational routine are, then, not so much a "problem" as a "solution" for the organization, to the extent that the existence of the "fair" narrative or ostensive aspect is crucial to the legitimacy of the system.

Overall, we argue that when we try to understand what is "racial" about "racial achievement gaps" we need to keep the larger history of race with its multiple penetrations and reverberations in the present in mind. That history is still a part of daily processes, often in forms that are so automatic or "common sense" that we aren't consciously aware of them (e.g., racial stereotypes). These reverberations are both "big" (wealth gaps) and "small" (minor daily exchanges that convey performance expectations). They feed into contemporary forms of often apparently "race-neutral" dynamics or policies that have decidedly racial effects, creating cumulative advantages for white students and cumulative disadvantages for black and Latina/o students. With regard to academic and disciplinary organizational routines, the racialized performance of those routines (race-neutral school policy notwithstanding) contributes to racialized achievement outcomes. Thus, through a combination of the structural, institutional, and ideological forces and despite the best intentions of most of those who work in, attend, and participate in the school, racial stratification gets reproduced in places like Riverview.

WHAT IS TO COME

In the next chapter we examine some popular explanations for racial achievement gaps to see if they have any salience in Riverview.[62] This will be the only part of the book that will focus on the theory popularly known as the "oppositional culture" or "acting white hypothesis"—the idea that black students don't do well in school because they reject school success as a white thing and feel peer pressure from other black students to disengage.[63] Like a number of other scholars whose work we will review in Chapter 2, we examine this theory carefully and do not find it to be useful for explaining the reality of school outcomes in Riverview. Yet we give it some attention in order to try to understand why it lives on long beyond what the scholarly support would justify. There are many complicated reasons for its persistence in the popular imagination, not least of which is that, like other victim-blaming narratives, it underplays the importance of structural inequalities and requires almost no adjustment to the way schools are currently organized.[64] As James Anderson and others have pointed out recently, "Being blamed for one's own subordination is a cross that African Americans have borne for centuries, and it is somewhat disturbing to witness the reemergence of this burden as a means to rationalize the unfulfilled promise of *Brown v. Board of Education*" in the 21st century.[65]

Chapter 3 focuses on disciplinary routines at Riverview. Here we show how racial dynamics play a part in both (a) who gets selected for discipline, and (b) how punishment gets processed, with black and Latina/o students being disciplined more often and differently than white students. Moreover, we show how race shapes disciplinary outcomes in ways that school personnel not only did not intend but mostly did not want. The disciplinary routines at Riverview are important in multiple ways—not least because they communicate key messages to students about who is a full citizen within the school context and have consequences for whether students feel valued, respected, and cared for at school.

In Chapter 4 we turn to the academic achievement gaps at Riverview and focus specifically on racialized academic hierarchies. We examine the role school organizational practices and policies play in producing uneven outcomes and the ways in which racial dynamics are a part of these processes. Here, we find that Riverview students, teachers, administrators, and parents discuss an environment where black (and Latina/o) students are seen as less capable than their white peers and where school personnel hold lower performance expectations of these black and brown students. The racialized academic hierarchy (embodied in tracking) reinforces the very stereotypes and status beliefs that contributed to its creation in the first place. While track placements are justified as "race-neutral" embodiments of meritocratic differences, we outline how the actual performances of tracking routines are, in fact, deeply racialized.

Chapter 5 tackles the question of why, despite the community's general commitment to equity and awareness on the part of key community members of troubling racial patterns in the school, the problematic structures and policies we discuss in previous chapters have mostly remained in place. We argue that historically, efforts to address the black/white achievement gap have often focused on some version of the question "What's going on with the black kids?" However, to understand why some aspects of educational outcomes at Riverview are so entrenched, we instead must ask, "What role do white parents play here?" We show that while white families reported choosing to live in Riverview because they wanted their children to be educated in a diverse community, these same parents' concerns about making sure their children have every educational advantage mean they are often deeply ambivalent about if not explicitly hostile to changing the rules and practices that benefit their children (and disadvantage others). We show that at least one consequence of their cumulative behavior is to reproduce their racial advantage. Finally, in the Conclusion, we review the overall patterns and discuss key interventions necessary to begin addressing the racial realities in schools like Riverview and beyond.

2

Race, Oppositional Culture, and School Outcomes

*Are We Barking Up the Wrong Tree?**

> *[C]hildren can't learn unless we raise their expectations and turn off the television and eradicate the slander that says a black youth with a book is acting white.*
>
> Barack Obama, 2004 Democratic National Convention

Over the last several decades, one of the most common narratives raised in discussions of racial achievement gaps is one that suggests that black students underachieve because of negative peer pressure.[1] Similar to the above quote from then Illinois State senator Obama, such storylines regularly appear in prominent national media citing as fact that black students face a "burden of acting white"—pervasive, racialized feedback from their friends that trying to do well in school entails trying to "act white" and thus entails disloyalty to blackness. For example, Bob Herbert from *The New York Times* wrote:

> Some African-American students . . . have adopted the incredibly stupid tactic of harassing fellow blacks who have the temerity to take their studies seriously. According to the poisonous logic of the harassers, any attempt at acquiring knowledge is a form of "acting white," and that, of course is to be shunned at all costs.[2]

* with James P. Huguley

Or, also from *The New York Times*, Tamar Lewin states:

> Inevitably, as students notice that honors classes are mostly white and lower-level ones mostly black, they develop a corrosive sense that behaving like honors students is "acting white," while "acting black" demands they emulate lower-level students.[3]

This storyline has become an almost taken-for-granted explanation for the black-white achievement gap, for those both inside and outside schools,[4] showing up frequently not only in research literature but also in newspapers, magazines, and even in the political discourse. It was at his famous speech at the 2004 Democratic National Convention that Barack Obama argued for the need to "eradicate the slander that says a black youth with a book is acting white."

Related to the "acting white" narrative is a broader set of understandings that suggest that black students do not do well in school because they inherit a general opposition to the educational system from their families and communities. This idea has been heavily influenced by John Ogbu, and his writing on the cultural-ecological model (CEM), which he uses to explain "minority" achievement patterns in the United States. Ogbu and his associates[5] argued that in order to account for the unequal educational outcomes of different racial minorities in US schools, we must distinguish between "involuntary minorities" and "voluntary minorities." They believed that involuntary minorities who were historically forcibly incorporated into the United States through colonization and slavery would have very different relationships to dominant institutions like schools than voluntary minorities who come to the United States through their own free will. While voluntary minorities tend to favorably compare their situation in the United States to their former condition in their homeland, involuntary minorities compare their status to whites and understand that their opportunities are constrained along a number of dimensions. With an understanding of the many social, economic, political, and institutional barriers members of their group face when trying to succeed, Ogbu hypothesized that involuntary minorities would develop an oppositional culture and limit the effort they put forth to succeed in dominant institutions. Ogbu's original theory thus envisaged a complex relationship between *structural constraints* and *cultural responses*, imagining a tightly linked reciprocal relationship between involuntary minorities' experience of limited opportunity and what he predicted to be their negative personal and collective attitudes toward schooling.[6] Essentially, Ogbu suggests that experiences with structural exclusion and discrimination undermine the black communities' commitment to mainstream institutions like school.

Building on this general theory, Signithia Fordham and John Ogbu[7] studied youth in a predominantly black high school in Washington, DC, and argued that a part of the general pattern of "oppositional culture" was a phenomenon of "the burden of acting white." Specifically, they argued that African Americans define a whole set of behaviors, styles, and symbols as "white," including doing well in school. Therefore, the authors suggested, African Americans generally reject school as a "white domain" and, related to that, individual African American students feel pressure from their peers not to work hard on certain school-related activities lest they be accused of "acting white."

Since the middle 1980s, the "acting white" hypothesis and the related oppositional culture argument has captured scholarly and popular imagination in discussions of educational achievement.[8] The "acting white" hypothesis and the correlate explanation that black students underperform in school because their peers discourage them from achieving has taken on a life of its own in popular culture as arguably *the* explanation for black-white achievement gaps.[9] In fact, between 1984 and 2004 more than 150 articles in newspapers and popular magazines featured the concept of "acting white" in discussions of educational achievement.[10] When written about in the press, these explanations highlight adolescent behaviors but downplay or ignore the structures of inequality that the scholarly work suggests give rise to these cultural responses. So, for example, Bob Herbert wrote in a *New York Times* editorial that "some African-American students . . . have adopted the incredibly stupid tactic of harassing fellow blacks who have the temerity to take their studies seriously,"[11] but says nothing about the structures of inequality that Fordham and Ogbu see as antecedents to these peer dynamics. This perspective is also popular among teachers, who often use it to explain racial disparities in students' outcomes.[12]

Despite its popularity in the press and among the lay public, recent research challenges the idea that black students either possess an oppositional orientation toward education or reject school as a "white thing."[13] For example, black students want to attend college at the same rate,[14] spend about the same amount of time (or more time) on homework,[15] and have similar rates of absenteeism when compared to whites of the same social class.[16] Likewise, African American students who do well in school appear to be among the most popular with their peers, and black students generally possess more pro-school attitudes than whites.[17] Other work suggests that ultimately, racial differences in these academic orientations, even when favoring African Americans, may be so inconsequential that they make practically zero contribution to actual achievement disparities.[18] With regard to black parents, research demonstrates that while they expect their children to experience racial discrimination, they place more value on education, have higher expectations for their children than white parents, and are just as involved in their education.[19]

Qualitative studies also fail to find consistent support for the acting white hypothesis.[20] Karolyn Tyson and her colleagues found that black students were achievement-oriented and experienced very little race-based negative peer pressure related to academic achievement. In fact, they found strong similarities in the experiences of high-achieving black and white adolescents, suggesting that negative peer pressure is not unique to black students or more prevalent among them, but is instead a more general pattern faced by both black and white students.

While oppositional culture does not seem to be a powerful explanation for racial achievement disparities in general, some suggest that it may be important in integrated schools like Riverview.[21] For example, Karolyn Tyson argues that while only a small percentage of students face the accusation of acting white (about 20 percent), the few who do experience this accusation are likely to be found in schools with racialized educational tracks in which white students are disproportionately found in higher-level classes than black students—schools like Riverview.[22] In his study of the affluent Cleveland suburb of Shaker Heights, John Ogbu argued that black students' educational disengagement was a key ingredient in the black-white achievement gap found there.[23] Roland Fryer and his colleagues argue that black and Latina/o students in integrated schools like Riverview pay a "popularity penalty" for high achievement.[24] However, among black students, this pattern only exists in schools where blacks make up less than 80 percent of the student population and not in predominantly black schools or in private schools. This suggests that if we expect to find oppositional culture among black students, integrated schools like Riverview might be the place to look. In other words, there may be something about the structural characteristics of schools that shape the existence of the acting white phenomenon.[25] So, while current work challenges major tenets of the oppositional culture explanation,[26] other work suggests that race-based oppositional culture might emerge among some students in racially integrated schools in which achievement hierarchies exist.

For this reason, we decided we should examine whether there is a culture of opposition among black students at Riverview. Do they experience the "burden of acting white" and thus disengage from school? In order to answer these questions, we focus on the different aspects of the oppositional culture framework. Figure 2.1 provides a conceptual overview of the components of the oppositional culture model as we discuss it in this chapter. In this model, race and status are thought to influence experiences within the opportunity structure (including in schools, communities, labor markets, and society as a whole). Ogbu refers to these as school and societal forces, which are a precursor to the development of community forces. Community forces include the perception among African Americans that they will have limited opportunities because of their race. Such perceptions are imagined, in turn, to lead to a number of responses, including differences in educational orientations (e.g., doubts about the value of education or negative peer pressure). The final link is between

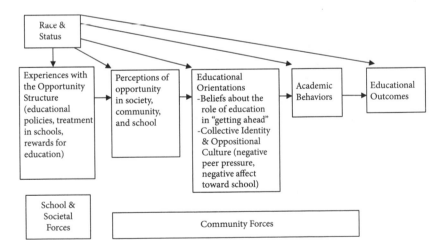

FIGURE 2.1. Conceptual Model of the Oppositional Culture Argument Discussed in This Chapter

Note: This figure draws from Harris (2011) and Ogbu (2008). In discussing his cultural-ecological model, Ogbu (2008) details five distinct "community forces" that result from group responses to school and societal forces. Here, we highlight the two community forces that are most relevant to our discussion. These are beliefs about the role of education in getting ahead and "collective identity," which is where Ogbu argues that the oppositional culture argument fits in his broader cultural-ecological model.

these community forces and actual schooling behaviors. Oppositional culture theory predicts that in an effort to maintain status with their peers, young people purposefully engage in behaviors that ultimately undermine their academic success. This leads to reduced educational achievement and helps explain racial differences in educational outcomes.[27]

To make sense of the argument and assess its relevance for explaining the patterns in educational outcomes we witnessed at Riverview, we review its components one step at a time. First, we look at societal and school forces by examining research on how racial discrimination continues to impact the lives of African Americans in the United States across a number of dimensions of social well-being. Related to this, we then examine students' (and to a lesser extent parents') beliefs about race and opportunity in the United States as well as within their own school and community. Next we discuss students' educational orientations with a particular focus on their beliefs about the role of education in getting ahead in life, their experiences with negative and positive peer pressure, and their affect toward their schools. Finally, we look at students' academic behaviors. More specifically, we explore the extent to which students' reported educational orientations are consistent with their reported academic behaviors.

To examine students' orientations, we draw on both interview and survey data.[28] In analyzing the survey data, we identified five hypotheses based on the oppositional culture framework (see Table 2.1). If the oppositional culture argument was to be supported, we would expect that in comparison to white students, black students would (1) have lower educational expectations, (2) experience more negative peer pressure, (3) experience less positive peer pressure, (4) have more negative affect toward schools, and (5) engage in less achievement-related behavior. While our survey contained many indicators related to these hypotheses, we highlight findings for those that were linked to students' actual educational outcomes. These appear in bold text in Table 2.1.[29]

We demonstrate that there is virtually no support for the oppositional culture argument in our data. Like recent work using national and even international data, we conclude that educational researchers have been barking up the wrong tree in a quest to find oppositional culture among black students.[30] Instead, we argue that in order to understand racial differences in educational outcomes we need to shift our focus, which we will do in the chapters that follow.

TABLE 2.1. Five Hypotheses Related to Oppositional Culture and Their Corresponding Survey Questions

Hypotheses	Survey questions
Hypothesis 1: Black students have lower educational aspirations than white students.	1. "How far do you think you'll go in school?" 2. **"How important is it to you to go to one of the best colleges?"**
Hypothesis 2: Black students have less favorable affect toward school than white students.	1. "I like the books and plays we read in English." 2. "I enjoy doing math problems." 3. **"I am happy to be at this school."**
Hypothesis 3: Black students perceive more opposition to educational achievement and achievement-related behaviors from their peers than white students (negative peer pressure).	1. "My friends make fun of people who do well in school." 2. "My friends think it's not cool to study hard for tests and quizzes." 3. "Studying a lot tends to make you less popular." 4. "In this school, getting better grades than others tends to make you less popular." 5. "I didn't try as hard as I could because I was worried about what my friends might think." 6. **At times when I didn't study last year it was because my friends wanted me to do something else.**
Hypothesis 4: Black students experience (or perceive) less support for school achievement than white students (positive peer pressure).	1. **"My friends want me to study harder than I do."** 2. "How important do your friends think it is to study hard and get good grades?" 3. **"How important do your friends think it is to participate actively in class?** 4. "How important do your friends think it is to continue their education past high school?" 5. "When you work really hard, which of the following reasons are most important for you?" (Odds ratio for selecting "My friends put pressure on me" and "I want to keep up with my friends")
Hypothesis 5: Black students exhibit less achievement-related behavior than white students.	1. **"On weekdays, how many hours per week do you spend on studying and doing homework?"** 2. **"How often do you really pay attention in class?"** 3. "How many hours do you typically study for an end of marking period exam in History?"

STUDENTS' PERCEPTIONS OF RACE AND OPPORTUNITY IN THE CONTEMPORARY UNITED STATES

As we discussed in the previous chapter, race remains a major factor in the life chances of people in the United States. For example, on almost every measure of social well-being, blacks lag behind whites. While the mere existence of inequality does not mean that discrimination is the cause, research demonstrates that contemporary discrimination has a powerful impact on racial disparities across a number of domains, including returns to education and access to employment.[31] For example, blacks earn less money than whites with comparable education, have higher unemployment levels, and continue to face labor market discrimination.[32] But as research has recently documented, much of this discrimination operates in much more subtle forms than were true historically. One compelling study of labor market discrimination conducted by Devah Pager and her colleagues used field testers (who were matched pairs of trained black, Latina/o, and white job candidates with identical credentials and demeanor) to examine experiences applying for entry-level jobs. When these field testers were sent on job interviews, black and Latina/o applicants were called back for interviews only half as often as white applicants. Moreover, white applicants who reported just being released from prison were more likely to be called back than black applicants with no criminal records.[33] Another recent study examined employer responses to resumes. Bertrand and Mullainathan attached white- and black-sounding names to randomly selected resumes sent to employers in Boston and Chicago. Callbacks were 50 percent higher for applicants with white-sounding names in comparison to those with black-sounding names. These findings occurred regardless of employer size, occupational category, and industry.[34] But explicit discrimination was not required in either case. Blacks and Latina/os were not discouraged from applying. As Bonilla-Silva suggests, while privilege was [historically] achieved through overt and usually explicit racial practices, "today . . . it is accomplished through institutional, subtle, and apparently nonracial means."[35] The coupling of more subtle forms of discrimination with a color-blind discourse on racial inequality has made it more difficult for people to know when discriminatory practices are at work.

But the oppositional culture argument depends (at least to some extent) on members of the black community perceiving racial discrimination to be a real problem. Do young people in Riverview still believe that racism is a problem in the contemporary United States? Do they think that their race will be a liability in getting ahead? Work on oppositional culture suggests that when students believe that racial discrimination will limit their life chances, they become skeptical about the payoff to education and adopt oppositional orientations toward schooling.

In national surveys, a majority of blacks believe that racial inequality is "mainly due to discrimination."[36] In 2009 85 percent of blacks felt that racism in society was a problem, with 44 percent of those believing it was a "big problem."[37] Likewise, the majority of blacks believe that they do not have equal access to homes they can afford, jobs they are qualified for, or equal treatment from police or at local businesses.[38] Finally, 74 percent of blacks report having been discriminated against, and some research suggests that this number is even higher.[39]

Young blacks also feel that discrimination is a problem. According to data from the Black Youth Project at the University of Chicago, 61 percent of young African Americans believe that "it is hard for young black people to get ahead because they face so much discrimination" and 54 percent believe that black youth receive a poorer education than white youth.[40] These findings suggest that among adults and youth in the black community, racial discrimination is seen as a problem that limits community members' chances of getting ahead in life.

As with this broader survey data, the vast majority of the African American students and parents we interviewed in Riverview believe that race limits their chances of "getting ahead" in life. Black students expected to experience discrimination. For example, Tyrone, a low-achieving student, stated that being black would "make it more difficult" for him "because as a black person, [I'm] part of the minority groups, and minority groups have a tough time getting ahead." Keisha, a black student who also struggles in school, argued that "I think it'll be difficult [for me] because like black people probably have to work harder to be whatever they want to be." Such beliefs were not limited to low-achieving students. Many of the high-achieving black students also expressed concerns about discrimination. For instance, Tammy, a high-achieving student, echoed the belief that race would impact her future, arguing that "black people, in general just have to work harder than everyone else to get recognized . . . They have to work harder I feel like."

Black students expected to face discrimination in the future, but many also believe that such discrimination affects them in the present in their community and school. Tracey, for example, contends that "In a way just in the world that we live in, right, being black it's . . . always gonna be hard just because of the color of your skin. No matter where you go, you say [this] isn't a racist city or country; it's always gonna be hard being black. Point blank." Each of these students maintains that because of racial discrimination, they will face challenges getting ahead in life. As Tracey argues, racism will exist "no matter where you go." It is something that is a given that must be overcome.

Students seemed to reach these conclusions about discrimination from their own experiences and the experiences of their parents and other relatives. In his discussion of the implications of race, Julius (a black junior with a 4.1 weighted GPA)[41] talks about an older cousin whom he looks up to because he overcame poverty and racial discrimination:

> He lived in a 10x 10 foot shack in the middle of nowhere—no running water. He went to school, and there was a lot of racism, and he got called, "Nigger this, Nigger that." Basically, he ended up becoming captain of [a college] basketball team. He had the chance to get drafted into the pros, but he chose to go into the work world. Then he worked at [major beverage company] and all these other companies. Then he got an MBA. Then he ended up becoming the CEO of [major appliance company]. Then he was the CEO of [a national athletic company]. I think he was the first black member of [a historic golf club]. Now he's got his own start-up company, I think. I talk to him a lot. He's really, really successful.

David, another high-achieving student, also discusses being sensitized to discrimination through discussions with his father about his work environment. When we asked David if he thought being black would affect his life chances, he said:

> DAVID: I'm a practical guy. I know racism is never ever going to go away. Of course, it's gotten a lot better. But it's not going to go away. So I sit back and see the stuff my parents go through—which is not like terrible stuff. It's just like little stuff that they get every day on the job.

INTERVIEWER: For example?

DAVID: My dad is a manager of [a local] company, which is equivalent to vice president. There's not many African American figures in the same position as him. Whenever he meets with people, sometimes when he walks into meetings with other companies and stuff, just like the expressions on people's faces, like, "Oh, hello." Sometimes, he'll go to like cocktail parties and stuff and people will think he's like the waiter. Just little stuff like that.

In addition to black students at Riverview feeling that they would face discrimination at some point in the labor market and/or other areas of their life, many also reported a belief that they were treated differently at school. Because we were interested in students' perceptions of race and opportunity in general and also at Riverview, we asked them if they thought all students were treated the same at the high school. While we did not ask specifically about race, many students reported perceiving that white and black students were treated differently at the school level. One difference these students identified was their perception that school officials believed that white students were smarter and better behaved than black students. For example, several black students like Daryl argued that being a black male was likely the biggest obstacle to his getting ahead in life:

> Cause I mean that's who I am, that's how they gon' look at me; and they don't expect much from black males, like you know—cause like I was looking at the percentage of our grades and stuff, the black males, we're like at the bottom. Our grades are the lowest. They don't expect nothing of us.

Daryl believed that expectations for students like him were low. Patterns of lower overall black student GPAs were, for him, evidence of those low expectations. Tammy, a sophomore with a 3.9 grade point average, argued that, when it came to grading, some teachers treated black and white students differently in their classes:

> I think there's more leeway for white kids. . . . You have to work way harder as a black kid in honors class than white kids. You just . . . It's like an automatic grade for white kids just for doing the work. But they look for things to mark you down on, some teachers.

Echoing what we heard from black students and parents, white students also reported that some of their black friends felt mistreated because of race. One white female student argued that expectations for black students make access to upper-level classes more difficult for them: "I've heard from minority students in my . . . homeroom or just in general that they've been discouraged or it's been hard, their parents have to call the school in order to get them into higher-level classes."

While black students at Riverview seem to believe that racial discrimination is a problem in U.S. society as a whole as well as in the Riverview community and school, how does this shape their views about schooling more generally? According to the cultural-ecological framework, black students' recognition of discrimination should lead to skepticism about whether education will pay off for them.[42] Having shown that members of the black community believe that discrimination would negatively affect them, we now turn to their perceptions regarding the role of education in getting ahead.

STUDENTS' PERCEPTIONS OF OPPORTUNITY AND EDUCATIONAL ORIENTATIONS

Most high school students plan to attend college,[43] and, as it turns out, black students' educational aspirations are actually higher than those held by white students across multiple datasets.[44] The responses of the students we interviewed were consistent with these broader findings.

Black students' educational expectations were basically indistinguishable from white students' aspirations. Of the 42 black students we interviewed, 39 (92.8%) reported planning to go to college. Of the 28 white students we interviewed, 24 (85.7%) reported planning to go to college.[45]

Not only did virtually all of the black students expect to attend college, but most connected this desire to the belief that education would pay off for them in the labor market. When we asked Daryl about his post–high school plans, he said, "definitely go to college; definitely go to college." When asked why he wanted to go to college, he said, "cause the way I think now it is like . . . I know you can't just get no high school diploma and then call it quits. . . . You need to get out of college [graduate] to actually get a nice job." Daryl says his mother talks about college "all the time" and expects him to earn a college degree.

Julius argues that "ultimately, everybody knows that's why we go to college, so we can get a job. . . . It's necessary now to go to college to get ahead." Tammy, who believes that she faces discrimination in her classes and expects to face discrimination after leaving school, still aspires to attend college and perhaps get a job in the medical profession.

While most black students believed that the payoff to college might be limited by their race, they held higher aspirations than white students, who, for the most part, did not think that they would be discriminated against. These students considered enrolling in college after high school as a natural next step, one that ensured them access to comfortable jobs in the future. So, while black students and their parents raised concerns about racial discrimination at the school, they remained invested in educational attainment.

On the survey, students responded to the following question: "How far do you think you'll go in school?" Of all our indicators, this question regarding students' educational expectations was the most powerful predictor of students' grade point averages. We first ran the analysis in a race-only model, without taking socioeconomic status into consideration. The patterns among Riverview students we interviewed were consistent with survey data in Figure 2.2—in the race-only model, black students have lower post-graduate educational expectations than white students. We then ran the model with statistical controls for socioeconomic status. Once these controls were taken into account,[46] black students reported higher educational expectations than did white students.

Black students' educational expectations may emerge from the positive messages they receive about post-secondary schooling from their peers and parents.[47] In our interviews, with students almost all of them reported that they receive positive messages about college from their parents. While many of their parents socialize them to expect discrimination, they also emphasize the importance of education as a tool for overcoming that discrimination. In fact, black students report receiving positive messages about education generally. David says that his parents "just taught me good study habits, and always taught me to hold education on a pedestal." When we asked for more specifics about how they communicated the importance of education, he stated that:

> My parents, when I was young they would read me books every night. They really used to make big deals about accomplishments and all this other stuff and academics. So I think they just set in stone that education was important.

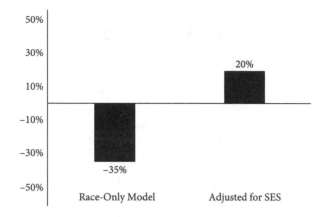

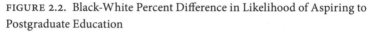

FIGURE 2.2. Black-White Percent Difference in Likelihood of Aspiring to Postgraduate Education

Julius, whose parents are both lawyers, talks about the emphasis his parents place on education and the pressure he sometimes feels from them because of it:

> My parents and I bicker about schools. They really want me to go to a good school. . . . they both went to [a top ten] law school. . . . They're like, "We gave you this opportunity. We're here for you, to provide for you, to give you a stepping stone." Going to college is basically the most important thing to my parents.

Julius admits that he "can barely stand [his] dad right now" because of the pressure he puts on him to excel in school and compete in extracurricular activities in order to be competitive for college:

> He wants us [his children] to be D-1 athletes because we can; but he expects these straight A's. I try to tell him that's not a reality. You can't play sports, and you can't get straight A's in AP's. Next year, the big issue is whether I'm going to play football or not. I'm like, "I've got one last shot to get straight A's." They're like, "Well, you know, blah, blah, blah." I'm like, "Well, you know, I'm not going to be able to play football and do both." He doesn't listen.

Even though many black students at Riverview report expecting to face discrimination when they seek to cash in on their educational investment, they maintain high educational aspirations. In many ways this should not be a surprising finding. While the rewards for educational attainment among African Americans have always been limited by labor market discrimination, high educational aspirations have characterized the black community in every period in US history.[48]

Black students, in fact, often discussed the need to work *harder* in school to overcome the impact of discrimination. As David observed, "I definitely expect the stuff to happen like that. They just say, 'I'm going to be honest with you. It's only going to get harder. We're always here for you and stuff. We've tried to teach you when you were young about good qualities and stuff.' They said I should be fine. I hope I'm fine." Many students echoed this theme of hard work as key to overcoming discrimination. Tammy argues, "Black people, in general just have to work harder than everyone else to get recognized." Keisha suggests, "Black people probably have to work harder to be whatever they want to be."

Echoing what students reported, the black parents we interviewed said they were clear with their children about racial discrimination—both that it still exists and that working hard and investing in education were keys to overcoming it. Regarding discrimination, Hillary stated:

> I think being black is difficult in America. I think that my son will have to try twice as hard as everybody and he'll have to be better educated. He'll have to watch himself everywhere he goes. He'll have to—if he buys a flashy new red car or something and a policeman stops him, I'm sure it will be a racial stop.

Chantal, whose son takes AP and honors classes and who, she notes, is in the top 10 percent of his class, argued:

> Irregardless [*sic*] of . . . how strong we know he is as a student or how capable he is, we know that he's always going to have that thing to deal with—that's why we have always raised him to take that extra step—we've told him he has always got to do more and maybe that is why he is the way he is. So yeah I think it's going to have an impact but I don't think the impact is going to be as strong because I know—if they look at his resume and not know that he's African American, he will be able to get a job with no problem. But of course, once they realize he's African American, they may be shocked and he may have a few challenges. But knowing him and being a competitor and understanding how this works, he would just consider it to be a challenge and something that he knows we all have been dealing with all of our lives and we will continue to.

Parents' messages about the reality of discrimination and the potential of people to overcome these challenges through hard work provided a powerful counternarrative to the discourse about black school failure.[49] As Angel Harris also finds in his analysis of national survey data, Riverview students construct much more complex understandings about the relationships among race, education, and discrimination than the cultural-ecological perspective suggests.[50] Students and parents are able to reconcile the belief that discrimination exists with the conviction that it remains worthwhile to pursue school success and strive for higher education.[51] In sending this dual message to their children that they should expect to face discrimination but that they can overcome that bias in whatever form it takes, black parents are engaging in what psychologists and sociologists call racial socialization practices. Such practices can serve as a buffer against discrimination and enhance students' academic outcomes.[52]

Therefore, while the oppositional culture perspective is accurate about black perceptions that school and societal discrimination are a problem, the link between this perception and students' educational aspirations does not hold.[53] Instead, black students at Riverview and in similar districts seek college and graduate school at higher rates than their white peers. Unlike the oppositional culture perspective would suggest, obtaining more education was seen as an important way to overcome discrimination, and parents and peers were important in reinforcing this message among black students.

RACE AND NEGATIVE PEER PRESSURE

But what about negative peer pressure among black students? The "acting white" argument asserts that (high-achieving) black students face negative peer pressure from other black students who accuse them of "acting white." The original authors of the term, Signithia Fordham and John Ogbu, suggest the resulting fear of ostracism from peers is what leads black students to avoid behaviors associated with academic achievement. In this case, students either disengage from achievement or are forced to find ways to maintain high achievement without being alienated from their peers.

Among the students we interviewed, teasing for high achievement was uncommon. Four of 19 high-achieving black students (21 percent) and four of 20 (20 percent) high-achieving white students reported experiencing some negative peer pressure associated with achievement. In other words, small and nearly equivalent proportions of students from each racial group we interviewed experienced negative peer pressure for achievement.[54] So, while a small number of students argued that achievement-related teasing happened,[55] white students were just as likely to experience it as black students. When we asked Cassie, a high-achieving white student who plays softball, whether other students discourage high achievement, she responded, "I would say that's very true. Um, I'm supposedly the nerd on our [softball] team." Greg, a high-achieving white student, argued that early in his high school career students would accuse him of being a nerd for studying too hard. When asked if he was discouraged from high achievement by his friends, Greg said:

> Oh, yeah. Like, "Oh, yeah, you're a nerd, you know. Like, you read that book." It's like, "No. I had to do it for work." But . . . the older you get, the more that goes away . . . freshman year in high school my friends are all like, "Greg, don't do your homework. You're a nerd." But then this year they're all doin' it.

David, a high-achieving black student who takes honors and AP classes, reports experiencing negative peer pressure "all the time." He claims that it does not affect his achievement because "I think, 'come back and talk to me in 15 or 20 years'" (laughs). He later adds that "I'm used to it; it kind of goes over my head." Dawn, another high-achieving black student, also experienced negative peer pressure that she perceives to result from her academic performance:

> Ever since I've been getting A's, I've been the bookworm. "All Dawn does is read. When do you have fun? It's like her fun is doing homework." Yeah, a lot. I get mocked all the time. . . . In junior high, I noticed it was just people who weren't doing as well, they would like tease me. They'd be like, "Oh, Dawn she's just a genius. She works on a paper three weeks before it's due. I mean, what a bookworm." You know?

Nevertheless, while there is this small subset of black and white students who believe that they are teased for high achievement, the vast majority (80 percent or more) do not. Moreover, students suggest that getting good grades is not in and of itself the cause of students being ridiculed. Instead, they argue that some of the teasing is tied to high achievers' behaviors, such as flaunting their overachieving, isolating themselves from other students, and fitting "nerdy" stereotypes.[56] Paul, a white student with a 3.0 GPA, believes that teasing results from students' behaviors. Talking about a student who gets teased, he says:

> PAUL: He gets teased about it. He's on the baseball team, so he gets heckled a lot, you know, at practice.
>
> INTERVIEWER: Because he gets good grades?
>
> PAUL: No, because everybody gets good grades. It's the way he talks, and how he seems like he's a smart alec. . . . Like stats, he'll like memorize and you know, always talks about them. So nobody wants to hear that. And it's like, "shut up."

In this case, teasing seems to come from other high-achieving students (who are mostly white, given the composition of the Riverview baseball team) because of the "smart-alec" behavior of another high-achieving white student.

Tanya, one of the four high-achieving black students who reported directly experiencing negative peer pressure, argues that "it's never been that bad for me because I talk to everyone." Her comments suggest that students may become a target of negative peer pressure if they isolate themselves from other students.[57] Michelle, a high-achieving white student, makes a similar observation:

> A lot of them [high achievers] are actually the popular people or whatever. A lot of them work hard, or at least they get pretty good grades. The kids that study hard and don't do anything else, they'd start having problems with people. *But that's just because they're introverted anyway* [emphasis added].

According to Michelle, students who are teased or "run into trouble" with peers are those young people who do not find a balance between their academic and social lives. Terrence, a high-achieving black sophomore (3.5 GPA), argues that students might be targets of teasing because they fit stereotypes about nerdy teenagers. As he put it, "If you fit the stereotype . . . glasses, you know, suspenders, and calculator in your hand, yeah."

It seems, therefore, that only a small and nearly equivalent number of black and white Riverview students experience negative peer pressure. Moreover, the negative peer pressure that does exist is not racialized—all

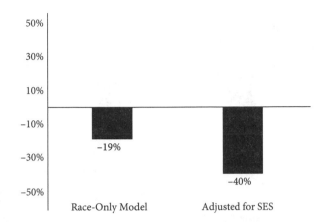

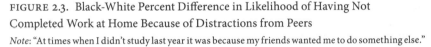

FIGURE 2.3. Black-White Percent Difference in Likelihood of Having Not Completed Work at Home Because of Distractions from Peers

Note: "At times when I didn't study last year it was because my friends wanted me to do something else."

students report being called "nerds" or "bookworms," and black students do not generally report being accused of "acting white."[58]

In the survey, a similar pattern emerged. In fact, across all six indicators we used to measure peer pressure, black students reported less negative peer pressure than whites.[59] One of these indicators (students reporting that they did not study or complete homework because *"My friends wanted me to do something else"*) was associated with students' educational outcomes. However, even when we controlled for students' socioeconomic background, black students were *less likely* than their white peers to be distracted by their friends (see Figure 2.3).

Thus, our data provide little support for the hypothesis that black students experience more negative peer pressure than white students.

RACE AND POSITIVE PEER PRESSURE

While black students in the surveyed districts experienced less negative peer pressure than white students, oppositional culture could help us understand racial differences in outcomes if white students experienced more support among their peers than did black students. We used several indicators from the survey to examine if this was the case. Contrary to what would be expected based on the oppositional culture argument,

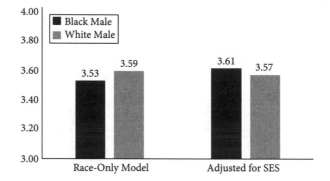

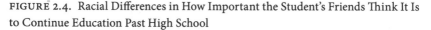

FIGURE 2.4. Racial Differences in How Important the Student's Friends Think It Is to Continue Education Past High School

we found that black students reported receiving *more* support from their friends than did white students. [60] For example, Figure 2.4 illustrates racial differences in how important a student's friends think it is to continue their education past high school, a belief that is positively related to grade point average. We see here again that among students with comparable socioeconomic backgrounds, the slight racial differences that do exist in this positive peer effect favor black students as well.

We also found examples of peers encouraging each other to do better in school in our interviews with black Riverview students. Despite the fact that the oppositional culture framework would predict that low-achieving students should not be bothered much by doing poorly in school, we found that black students with grade point averages below 2.0 were concerned about their academic performance, sought ways to improve their grades, and found support for their academic striving among their friends. Survey results also confirmed this racial difference in positive peer support for struggling students across districts more broadly. In fact, in Riverview, students even reported that those who performed poorly in school sometimes tried to camouflage their low grades from their peers for fear of being teased or ridiculed because of *low* performance.

Karen, a low-achieving black student, argued that she and her friends all wanted to do well in school. She said, "I don't really hang out with people that don't want to do anything after high school. You know? They just want to sit around, then they're not for me. I want to have a family and provide for them." Karen believes that getting good grades in school will pay off for her in the long run, since, presumably, this will give her access to a well-paying job that will allow her to support a family. She adds that "all my friends plan to go to college." Perhaps as a result of these expectations, she reports that her friends are concerned about their grades and try to help each other out academically. "If . . . somebody's not doing too well, we'll talk about how we can help each other out and get each other's grades up." Karen reports that if she and her friends receive low midterm grades, they try to raise them:

> KAREN: Just walk up to your teacher and ask them, you know, "Do you have a range where my grade is," before it gets to the report card point. Before [report cards] come out, you can bring it [your grades] up.
>
> INTERVIEWER: Is that something you do a lot? Do you talk to your teachers before . . .
>
> KAREN: Yeah. Because if something's not right I want to fix it before—'cause all this stuff that's in the grade book, it doesn't—colleges don't see that. They see the final grades. So you want to change that before it gets there.

While Karen's GPA is slightly below a "C" average, she (along with her friends) engages in strategies to improve her grades. The motivation for her efforts comes from her college aspirations and her desire to eventually provide for her family. She also receives support for her academic effort from her friends.

As with Karen, Jarrod reports that the desire to attend college also motivates his peers to seek higher grades. When we asked him to discuss his friends' orientation toward grades, Jarrod replied that he and his friends "told each other that C's are not cutting it no more cause like in eighth grade a C would be like, like the best thing in the world but now we trying to just get A's and B's." When asked why his friends' attitudes were different in high school than in eighth grade, he said:

> 'Cause we didn't know anything about like college. We [weren't] focusing in on that at the point until we got to high school and they started telling us about college and stuff and like they don't accept anything but straight A's and you gotta have 3.6 or 4.0 or all that grade point average. We didn't know anything about that.

Therefore, like Karen, Jarrod and his friends were motivated to strive for higher grades by their desire to attend college. Their college aspirations were a positive force that influenced their academic striving.

Most low-achieving students also reported that they and their friends did not discourage academic achievement. Trevor said that his friends did not respond negatively to students who received higher grades. He mentioned his friend Joshua, who is an honor-roll student:

> TREVOR: My, uh—Joshua—he made honor roll I think. But I'm not sure, I think he made honor roll.
>
> INTERVIEWER: Is there—do people tease Joshua since he's on honor roll?
>
> TREVOR: No. [In a surprised voice]
>
> INTERVIEWER: And the rest of you all aren't?
>
> TREVOR: No.
>
> INTERVIEWER: Okay. Are people proud of him?
>
> TREVOR: No. It would be like "Snap." Like we say something like that. . . . Then we just go on.
>
> INTERVIEWER: Okay. So you're indifferent to him being on the honor roll? You're not proud of him or you're not envious of him?
>
> TREVOR: It's cool. Like, "he did his thing."

In discussing his friend Joshua's performance, Trevor is surprised by the suggestion that his friend would be teased for high achievement. Instead, Joshua is more likely to be given kudos because he "did his thing."

These students' comments are representative of the low-achievers' statements concerning their orientations toward school achievement. The vast majority of students reported that they wanted to perform at higher levels than they currently were and that they received support for these aspirations from their friends. These reports do not suggest that an oppositional orientation toward schooling is prevalent among black adolescents at Riverview. In fact, rather than having low investment in school affirmed, several low-achieving students reported being teased for not doing well. While Trevor reported that his high-achieving friend Joshua received no negative feedback from peers, he also suggested that low achievement sometimes leads to negative sanctions:

> TREVOR: Yeah but everybody else they're doing good … like nobody fails. … Like if somebody fails, we'll laugh. [laughs]
>
> INTERVIEWER: Okay. So you give them a hard time?
>
> TREVOR: Yeah.

Likewise, Rod argued that high achievers do not face negative sanctions "like all that nerd stuff … I don't think people really do that no more … unless you just to yourself or whatever and don't talk to nobody." In fact, he reports that low-achieving students who isolate themselves may also be teased: "They'll probably talk about you more for the F's." Rod went on to argue that students who perform well in a class are often the ones who tease the lower achievers. "Some people get like a 95 on the chemistry quiz, somebody else get like a 63 … the person that got the 95 is the one that's always putting you down. 'You got a 63, you stupid.'" This pattern of teasing for low achievement has also been found by other scholars studying younger African American students.[61] As a result of this teasing, some low achievers try to hide their grades from other students. For example, Rod contends that "if a person gets a low grade, they'll try to hide it. They'll try to hide it as hard as they can."

Shantel discussed similar experiences of teasing for low achievement: "If a teacher asked somebody a question and they didn't know it, well, there can be other kids that talk about them." In fact, black students who struggle at Riverview may be forced to manage their academic challenges through camouflaging low achievement. Contrary to studies that report high achievers having to engage in strategies to hide their academic success,[62] some low-achieving students at Riverview reported hiding their grades because they fear being teased by other students.

RACE AND ACHIEVEMENT-RELATED BEHAVIORS

While black students possess higher educational aspirations and more pro-school attitudes than their white peers, Ogbu argues that the espoused belief in the value of education "is not to be taken at face value. It is often not accompanied by appropriate and necessary effort."[63] He argues, for example, that black students in affluent suburbs suffer from what he refers to as the "low effort syndrome."[64] Others also suggest that the espoused educational aspirations of black students do not necessarily lead to increased academic effort or achievement.

How can black students have more pro-school attitudes than their white peers but perform less well academically? Roslyn Mickelson refers to the disjuncture between black students' high educational aspirations and their comparatively low educational achievement as the attitude-achievement paradox.[65] In an influential study, Mickelson argued that black students' high educational aspirations reflect idealized, abstract beliefs about the role of education in getting ahead. Furthermore, she maintained that these abstract beliefs are distinct from concrete expectations about what will happen for people like themselves, which are more closely linked to actual effort in school.[66] Thus, according to the work of those like Ogbu and Mickelson, perhaps the students at Riverview were saying one thing and doing another—are there racial differences in students' reported academic behaviors?[67]

We used several indicators to examine this relationship, including the number of hours students spent studying each night and how often they really paid attention in class. Our analysis demonstrates that—all things being equal—black students report studying more hours per week, paying more attention in class, and studying more for a typical history final exam than do white students in the same level of classes. Both the number of hours students reported studying and their reported level of paying attention in class had a positive relationship with students' GPAs. When we compared black and white students on hours studying in the race-only model, whites reported studying slightly more. However, in the model where we adjusted for socioeconomic status, this relationship is reversed, with black students reporting studying more (see Figure 2.5).

A similar pattern emerges when we examine the extent to which students report really paying attention in class. As can be seen in Figure 2.6, in the race-only models there is essentially no difference between blacks and whites in reports of "really paying attention" in class. Yet when the model is adjusted for socioeconomic status, we again see a modest but statistically significant difference favoring black students.

These findings still need an explanation. How can black students have higher aspirations and work harder but still not do as well? In a previous analysis of the same dataset, scholar Ron Ferguson provided a potential

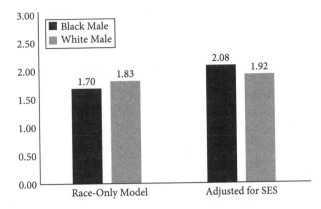

FIGURE 2.5. Racial Differences in Average Hours Spent Studying on Weekdays after School

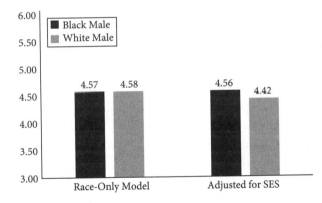

FIGURE 2.6. Racial Differences in Frequency of Really Paying Attention in Class

answer. He showed that even though black students spent the same amount of time on homework, they reported that they were less likely to turn it in. This raised a conundrum. Why would black students who are committed to education and spend time on their homework not turn it in as regularly? As it turned out, these differences in homework completion were accounted for by differences in students' understanding of the material in their classes. Black students understood the class material less well than did their white counterparts, so it probably took black students longer to complete the same amount of homework. As Ferguson writes, "levels of effort among these groups are quite similar, but knowledge, skills, and family backgrounds are not."[68] Ironically, while students spent about the same amount of time on homework, because black students turned in less of it, teachers might assume that they were spending little or no time working on it. Such a pattern could easily contribute to the belief that black students were not committed to education, when social privilege and prior preparation seem to be more likely explanations.

RACE AND AFFECT TOWARD SCHOOL

With regard to educational aspirations, positive and negative peer pressure, and achievement-related behaviors, black students compare favorably to their white counterparts. Students' general disposition toward school is another dimension on which oppositional culture among black students might be found. While there is work that suggests that black students have more pro-school attitudes than whites,[69] we examined an aspect of this issue using our survey data by assessing agreement with the following statement: "I am happy to be at this school." Results suggest that whether looking at race alone or when accounting for socioeconomic background, in both cases black students report slightly lower levels of overall happiness in their particular school environment (see Figure 2.7). While level of happiness was not associated with overall student achievement in our analyses, we also examined two other indicators of affect toward school—how much students "like the books and plays we read in English" and how much they "enjoy doing math problems." Contrary to what would be expected based on the oppositional culture argument, black students

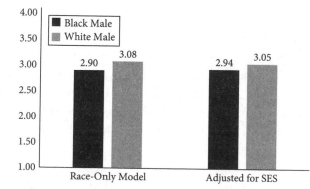

FIGURE 2.7. Racial Differences in Being "Happy to Be at This School"

report enjoying doing mathematics problems at higher levels than their white counterparts. With regard to English activities, there is no significant black/white difference in students' enjoying the books and plays read in English classes.

Again, while these differences in happiness in school are very modest, they are telling. When asked about their individual school, and not school in general, black students express some dissatisfaction. Given that black students don't report negative feelings about specific school activities, it is very likely that black students' lower levels of reported happiness at their schools is likely dissatisfaction with the educational institutions themselves rather than opposition to the actual educative process.

CONCLUSION

So what should we make of the oppositional culture argument as an explanation for the achievement gap at Riverview? The oppositional culture argument suggests that racial differences in school outcomes result from a complex interplay between discrimination at the societal and school levels (school and societal forces) and the responses of minority community members to those forms of discrimination (community forces). One predicted response to this perceived discrimination among black students is the development of oppositional orientations toward educational institutions. Recent research has also suggested that integrated schools like Riverview are places where race-based opposition is particularly likely to emerge.

As this chapter has shown, however, our data do not support the argument that resistance or disengagement on the part of black students is a key component that accounts for racial differences in outcomes. In fact, black parents and students develop a much more complex understanding of the relationship between education and opportunity than the oppositional cultural argument would suggest—seeing education as a tool for challenging discrimination rather than a reason to disinvest from it.

Having examined both our local interview and broader survey data from multiple angles, we find virtually no support for the oppositional culture argument either at Riverview or in other schools around the country that were surveyed. In fact, our data suggest that (all things being equal) black students are in many ways *more* committed to educational achievement and attainment than their white counterparts. Ultimately, at least in the case of Riverview, we find the logic that underlies the oppositional culture argument has it wrong. If anything, instead of perceived discrimination undermining black students' commitment to school, just the opposite occurs: black students are buffered by their pro-achievement orientations in the face of often vast social inequalities.[70] And given recent findings that question the predictive power of these explanations overall,[71] it seems clear that focusing on differences in students' academic orientations in an effort to account for racial disparities in outcomes is, at best, ill-advised.[72] Instead, we feel strongly that there is more to learn about how black and white students experience school differently. In what follows, we take a closer look at these racial differences in school experiences and unpack the meaning they have for members of the Riverview community.

3

The Road to Detention Is Paved with Good Intentions

Race and Discipline at Riverview

All kids do something wrong. Why do the blacks have to be the ones that always have to be disciplined and the white kids are supposed to be understood?

Ms. McDaniel (senior-level administrator)

On any day at Riverview High School, one sees a multiracial mix of students moving seamlessly through the hallways on their way to class. The students wear a wide variety of clothing styles. Some students wear preppy clothing (khaki pants and button-up shirts), while others wear T-shirts and jeans. Some wear baggy clothing associated with hip-hop culture, and others wear all black, in what students refer to as the "goth" style. There are also the identifiable jocks, who wear athletic clothing and letter jackets. The students seem to get along well—there is no palpable tension. One sees groups of students from different racial backgrounds walking together.[1] On the surface, race does not seem to matter much as students move through the hallways to class, to lunch, to the gym. However, in our conversations with all members of the Riverview community, we found that race mattered quite a bit for how seamlessly students moved through the school, both literally and metaphorically. According to members of the Riverview community, the rules that govern the school—written to apply to all—do not operate uniformly.

In the most straightforward sense, school rules are intended to facilitate the broader educational mission—to keep schools safe, to facilitate learning, to ensure that hallways and classrooms are orderly. In practice, the construction and enactment of school rules is much more complicated. This divergence emerges out of what we described in the Introduction as the discrepancy between different aspects of organizational routines—the ostensive aspect (the official and "ideal" of the routine) and the performative aspect (the *actual* practice of the routine in daily life). As scholars of organizational routines point out, one should not assume that the ostensive and performative aspects are identical.[2] The application of consequences to school misbehavior is "less a discrete event than a complex process," influenced by school policy and by the various parties involved (e.g., students, teachers, administrators, parents).[3]

As Ms. McDaniel's quote at the beginning of this chapter captures, this complex process is rife with racial dynamics at every stage, including who is perceived as needing discipline (who gets selected for punishment) and what discipline is judged appropriate to the behavior (how discipline gets processed). Alex Piquero writing about the juvenile justice system and Russell Skiba and colleagues writing about school discipline have talked about these as *differential selection* (institutional practices that might lead minorities to get picked out for wrongdoing more often than their white colleagues, despite similar levels of misbehaving) and *differential processing* (institutional practices that might lead minorities, once singled out for wrongdoing, to receive different sanctions for similar transgressions).[4] While all school community members we interviewed aspired to have the enactment of school discipline be transparent, fair, and in service of learning, almost everyone we spoke to acknowledged that differential selection and processing of students was a reality of life at Riverview, leading black and Latina/o students to be disciplined more often and disciplined differently than white students. Race shaped disciplinary outcomes in ways that school personnel not only did not intend but did not want. As one teacher put it, "So, I would not say that [students] are all treated equally. But I do think, for most of us, we try to treat them the same. And I think for some of us, we have good intentions." He then paused and finished his thought, "But you know what they say about the road [to hell] . . . it's paved with good intentions."

Much of the national conversation about race and school discipline covers the disproportionate suspension and expulsion rates for black and Latina/o students.[5] Recent data released by the U.S. Department of Education's Office of Civil Rights shows, for example, that black students, and black males in particular, are much more likely to be suspended and expelled from school than their peers. Similar to national data, the suspension rates of black and Latina/o students at Riverview are much higher than their overall representation in the school. In 2009 black Riverview students represented more than 70 percent of those suspended in-school and more than 60 percent of those suspended out-of-school, even though their overall representation in the school that year was only about 35 percent.[6] While these patterns are deeply troubling, suspensions and expulsions are not the primary focus of this chapter. Although we view suspensions and expulsions from school as critical for understanding issues of race and school outcomes, most students are never suspended and almost none are expelled. However, all students have daily interactions with teachers, administrators, and other school staff in which their behavior is either regulated or ignored, either approved or sanctioned.[7]

We focus on the school's disciplinary system as it includes all the formal and informal rules and practices regulating movement through school buildings, acceptable dress, when it is and isn't O.K. to talk, what you can or cannot bring to school, and so on. This list includes both the explicit rules encoded in official policy (most reflective of the ostensive aspects of organizational routines)[8] and the thousand "disciplinary moments" that transpire over the course of a school year in a place like Riverview (performative aspects) that are part of the school's culture. These moments communicate to all who is and who is not a full member of the school community.[9] We focus on these day-to-day interactions and show that being white at Riverview provides racial privileges not available to black and Latina/o students.

Some may ask why a focus on disciplinary routines is important to a book primarily focused on academic outcomes. In fact, as we will show, the processes and mechanisms of the disciplinary system tell us important things about the school's overall sociocultural context, what Prudence Carter defines as the "school's norms of academic achievement, its logic for student conduct and presentation of self, its pedagogical content and practices, and its climate of teacher-student, student-student, and other intergroup or intragroup dynamics."[10] All aspects of the school's culture can, as she argues, "reinforce boundaries that adversely impact the academic incorporation of different groups."[11] Disciplinary routines communicate key messages to students about who is and is not a full citizen within the school context. They also have consequences for how students feel about school—do they feel valued, respected, and cared for?[12] More and more we are coming to understand how a sense of belonging can be vital to academic achievement.[13] Disciplinary patterns serve as a barrier to creating such a sense of belonging among students when they contribute to producing what some social psychologists refer to as a "threatening environment"—"settings where people come to suspect that they could be devalued, stigmatized, or discriminated against because of a particular social identity."[14] Riverview community members report patterns that serve as just the kind of "cues" that would raise concerns about identity threat, and potentially negatively affect not only how targeted students feel about the school but also their ability to thrive academically.[15]

Three main patterns emerged regarding the implementation of discipline at Riverview. First, respondents reported lots of evidence of differential selection beginning with a tacit assumption that black and Latina/o students would misbehave and break rules more often than their white counterparts. As a result, when students did break the rules, their behavior was often interpreted differently based on race and ethnicity. As past research has also documented, race and gender influence whether a student's action is seen as silly or transgressive, a minor annoyance or in need of intervention.[16] These variant readings of behavior are consequential, as they result in quite different responses/sanctions. As one 16-year-old junior explained, white students most often receive the benefit of the doubt: "I think, as a white student, I get away with a lot more. I'm not a target of racial profiling." Or, as one teacher observed, school rules were not enforced equally: "They don't set rules and stick to them . . . People have often said it's the black kids . . . they're watched more. I say who is pulled over more by the police. It's like that down here too."

School staff, students, and parents all reported that the disciplinary system was far from a straightforward application of rules. Many inequalities in the larger criminal justice system were echoed in the school ("It's like that down here too"), playing out both in the daily process of "disciplining" students and also in the bureaucratic enactment of the disciplinary system. Discipline was "racialized" not only in terms of the often-discussed pattern of treating black and brown youth as inherently suspect but also in terms of a pattern of treating white students as inherently innocent.[17]

Second, aside from the different pattern of getting selected for punishment (*differential selection*), black and Latina/o students also had different experiences once they were caught up in the disciplinary bureaucracy (*differential processing*). While many of the same underlying ideas/stereotypes shape differential selection and differential processing, the latter is also deeply affected by the different kinds of resources and different ideas about discipline that adolescents and their families bring to the process. For example, a number of respondents described how white parents asserted their children's basic innocence and goodness as a defense against the application of school sanctions when rules had been broken. In contrast, black and Latina/o parents supported their children but were much less likely to try to get them out of trouble. In this way, the disciplinary process seemed to work differently for white students not only because of the way race works structurally (affecting who has access to certain kinds of resources) but also because of the way race works symbolically (affecting how we understand those around us). As one white student put it, "Because when people look at me they probably don't see me as any kind of threat. They don't have as many stereotypes about me as if they were to meet a black person or a Hispanic person." As we will show, race is playing out on multiple levels materially and ideologically—setting the context for disciplinary action by shaping students' (and parents') access to different kinds of resources (economic, social, cultural, and symbolic) and shaping the kinds of cultural belief systems at play in interactions with staff. Some students were much more likely not only to be sanctioned for bad behavior but also to be given more punitive sanctions when they did receive them.

Third, while race mattered, it did not function in isolation. Instead, there was an intermingling of race, class, gender, and cultural style that affected students' interactions with school officials. For example, black and Latina/o students were penalized for exhibiting black cultural styles in terms of clothing and mannerisms while the cultural styles associated with white students were generally rewarded, serving a protective function in potential disciplinary encounters. Likewise, the perception (and reality) of economic resources in families also seemed to play a role in how school officials responded when students violated school rules. Here class status was important, but students' actual and imagined class status was also tied to race in complicated ways. Gender also was important; while black and brown girls and boys all contend with added scrutiny, they do so for different reasons and in different ways. Finally, white students and parents were more likely to exhibit a sense of entitlement when interacting with the school's disciplinary apparatus. White students felt more comfortable breaking rules, and they and their parents negotiated more actively with school officials regarding how their behavior should be treated and defined. For many of them, the rules were not always "the rules."[18]

In its ideal form the Riverview disciplinary system would be a model of transparency and consistency so that everyone knew what the rules were and how they would be enforced (i.e., there would be tight alignment between the ostensive and performative aspects of organizational routines).[19] In practice, we found lots of indeterminacy and unevenness— at least in part mediated by who was and was not understood as needing supervision and monitoring, who was and was not understood as deserving of a second chance, and who was and was not seen to be in need of lessons about obedience and discipline.

SCHOOL RULES

All schools have rules of conduct that dictate how students interact with each other and with teachers and administrators.[20] These rules and regulations, the ostensive aspect of disciplinary routines, typically are written using neutral language, argued to be beneficial to all students, and expected to be applied fairly across groups of students.[21] The following passages from the Riverview student handbook capture the tone as reflected in that manual.

- Students are expected to behave in a responsible and cooperative manner at all times. Appropriate dress and grooming are critical to the maintenance of a safe, educationally conducive school atmosphere and are mainly the responsibility of the student and parent. Maintaining a neat and modest appearance and not wearing clothing that could be deemed offensive to others help promote a comfortable learning environment.
- All students need their current picture ID card to enter or leave the building during the school day.
- Students who . . . leave the room during the period must get a valid pass from the teacher or supervisor. . . . Students without a valid pass . . . face school consequences.

Expectations of students are written to apply to *all* students. They are explained as essential for providing "an educationally conducive environment" and are therefore viewed as important for facilitating student learning. In her book *Bad Boys*, Ann Ferguson discusses the moral authority of rules:

> Conformity to rules is treated by school adults as the essential prior condition for any classroom learning to take place. Furthermore, rules bear the weight of moral authority. Rules governing children are seen as the basis of order, the bedrock of respect on which that order stands. Rules are spoken about as inherently neutral, impartially exercised, and impervious to individual feelings and personal responses.[22]

In part, school rules are perceived as legitimate precisely because they apply equally to all students. Their perceived impartiality and fairness gives them a certain level of legitimacy. As Mr. James, one of the Riverview security guards, argued:

> The [handbook], it's somewhere [shuffling papers to find it and then holding it up], it's right here. . . . This is our guide. It tells us the discipline rules. It tells us the consequences. . . .We don't care if you're white, black, Hispanic, Russian, Asian, Hebrew, Chinese. We're going to follow that book. And that's just where we are. I come into this building. When I come into this building, I don't see colors, I see people. . . . There are no favors. I don't care if your daddy owns [a department store chain] or not. . . . Okay, how much money you got? I don't care if your parent is the booster president or PTSA Chairperson, I don't care.

Here, Mr. James's statements reflect the *official stance* on how school rules work—they reflect agreed-upon rules and regulations that are applied equally to all students. But like organizational routines more generally, behavioral policies have two components: what the rules and regulations state (ostensive aspect), and how these rules are enforced (performative aspect).[23] In fact, as Mr. James admits later in the interview, all students may not be treated exactly the same:

> I don't think the have-nots are always treated the same. I think if your parents can afford lawyers and can talk very loudly, and are

very educated and the like, you might stand a great chance of getting away with something or having something overturned or having it explained away for you or have people that understand it. The have-nots, they're generally—some of them . . . are, you know, they're just lost, and they're seen as rude, disrespectful, impolite . . . And they don't generally get away with it because for the most part, the have-nots' parents are not going to come over here and deal with it.

The "have-nots" here are generally understood along both race and class lines—those who are not among the high-powered, white, upper-middle-class Riverview families. Here Mr. James identifies some of the key ways that he believes a student's background comes into play in disciplinary enforcement. Parents' economic resources help determine if they can afford or would even think to retain a lawyer (which he believes amplifies their voice in the context of the school). Parents' education can help them assist their children in "getting away with something or having something overturned" or reframing the infraction so that it is understood (and recorded) differently. In contrast, the have-nots are less likely to get away with negative behavior because "they're seen as rude, disrespectful, impolite" and their parents are less likely to intervene. This is in part because they have less skill with or time for negotiating with the school as an institution and are more likely to understand discipline as appropriate treatment for undesirable behavior.

Mr. James's observations echo some of what we know about the role of parents' resources in influencing what happens in schools. Previous research shows that college-educated parents with higher incomes are more likely to intervene in the school context, customize their children's school experiences, and feel entitled to make institutions respond to their specific desires.[24] Institutions like schools are also more likely to respond to such parents because of the resources these parents bring to bear on the institution.[25] In this way, social class clearly matters. However, class is not the only dynamic here, and in practice it is hard to disentangle from race. In fact, recent research has shown clearly that race matters above and beyond social class differences in the differential distribution of punishment in schools: "Existing school discipline research suggests that students' SES [Socioeconomic Status] is limited in its explanatory power of the racial discipline gap."[26] And in fact, both in the practical sense and in most people's imagination, race and class are overlapping/conflated.[27] At Riverview, teachers and staff often read class through the lens of race, assuming much more than continental ancestry when they mentally categorize a student as white, black, or Latina/o. Class provides concrete resources, and white folks have more of them, but in "disciplinary moments" whiteness is a resource unto itself.

One can think of schools as a marketplace where people trade various forms of capital in an effort to secure educational advantages for themselves and their children. Unlike our typical understanding of economic marketplaces—where economic and material resources are exchanged for goods and services—the educational marketplace is characterized by economic capital (money and material resources) as well as the exchange of other forms of capital like social relationships and networks (social capital), cultural style (cultural capital), and symbols of competence, innocence, and legitimacy (symbolic capital). These forms of capital are used to access educational advantages, and the possessors of this capital maintain advantaged positions.[28]

Mr. James asserts that parents' economic capital provides access to social relationships with lawyers, which can be leveraged for their children's benefit. Others have shown how middle- and upper-class parents act collectively as opposed to individually to secure benefits for their children in school settings.[29] These relationships become social capital when they provide privileges in the school context. Likewise, parents socialize their children in ways that shape how they interact with and are received in institutions. For instance, schools tend to reward certain cultural styles of interaction, linguistic expression, hairstyles, and clothing.[30] Mr. James argues that have-nots are seen as "rude, disrespectful, and impolite," subjective categories of behavior that have consequences for them in the disciplinary domain. Thus, certain cultural styles (or resources) become cultural capital in the context of schools. Parents and children may also feel more or less entitled to challenge school authority and be more or less skilled in doing so. For instance, the inclination to negotiate with school authorities and the ability to do so effectively is a form of cultural capital in the school setting.[31]

Whiteness itself also serves as a form of symbolic capital.[32] As Paul Connolly wrote in a study of multiethnic schools in Britain:

> Some teachers may be influenced (whether directly or indirectly) by a set of racist beliefs which encourages them to think of white children as being more intelligent and well behaved than black children. In this sense, having white skin represents a form of symbolic capital which brings with it better treatment and more educational opportunities.[33]

Connolly here is capturing the way that race primes certain stereotypes about intelligence and behavior that can translate into, as he puts it, "better treatment and more educational opportunities." Lewis has also talked about the way that race and class get conflated such that economic capital becomes translated into *symbolic capital*.[34] It doesn't matter anymore whether you, in particular, are a white student with wealthy parents when your whiteness becomes the primary signifier that is being acted upon.[35]

Thus, while it was sometimes true that white parents and students were operating with greater resources when negotiating with the school around disciplinary outcomes, it was also true that they often did not have to deploy such resources to benefit from their whiteness. For example, as we will show, when dealing with white students, Riverview personnel often anticipate parental pressure, intervention, or concern. While school staff provided examples of the ways white parents deployed resources on behalf of their children, they also described multiple ways they themselves behaved proactively, *anticipating* that a parent was *likely* to be harassing them if they did not. In these ways, whiteness became a symbolic resource for white students.

While it might seem obvious that some of these resources pay off for students (of course, having wealth helps; of course, knowing the superintendent or principal helps), the ways, in practice, that resources such as relationships, cultural knowledge, and skin color translate into advantages in schools need to be understood as *mechanisms of inequality*. All these moments when schools—through policy or daily practice, intentionally or inadvertently—reward such "non-meritocratic" resources with a lighter sanction for misbehavior, a better course assignment, or more time to answer a question add up to quite different overall experiences and outcomes in school.

DIFFERENTIAL SELECTION FOR DISCIPLINE: RACE AND NEGOTIATING SCHOOL SPACES

White Privilege in the Hallways

One location where the difference in experience stood out was the hallway, where security guards maintained watch. Students repeatedly raised the issue of disparity—what they understood as the constant dance with school "safety" staff that some of them had to do. What most students reported was a vastly different terrain for white students than for black and Latina/o students. As laid out in the "rule book," during class periods, Riverview students had to have a pass if they left class and were in the hallways. However, security guards had discretion regarding how to enforce this rule, and according to many students, black students (particularly males) were most likely to be singled out. Almost all students reported that black students were commonly asked to present hall passes and punished if they did not have them. White students, on the other hand, were questioned rarely. As one white student said, "I've been walking down the hall without a pass and a black guy's been walking down the hall without a pass and the black guy gets stopped and I walk by. That's not fair." Samantha, a white sophomore, identified a similar pattern:

> I think security guards, just like, I think they like point out African Americans a lot more than like white. . . . Like I'll walk down the hall without a pass, and they'll just let you go. But then they'll find someone else and say, "You have to have a Saturday detention." I think it's really uncalled for that they don't stop everyone.

When we asked Tim, a white junior, to tell us who gets in trouble in the school, he said that it was "Almost entirely black kids. It's pretty awful." He believes that this results from the expectation that black students are breaking the rules when *all* students break rules:

> [Black kids] just get singled out. Like I think—I think white kids have been trained more to get away with it. I don't . . . think there's that much of a difference in actual degree of rule breaking but it's more, just you know, white kids, you know, because there's always been an expectation that they're not gonna do it, they learn how to get away with it and not get caught.

For these students, the racial pattern is clear. Black students are more likely to be sanctioned for behaviors that all students engage in. Their overrepresentation in this category of disciplinary infraction has less to do with their overrepresentation as violators of rules and more to do with the heightened scrutiny they face—as outlined above, they are differentially selected for sanction. A number of students recognize this as unequal treatment, saying that it is "not fair" and "awful." They generally agree that black students are "expected" to misbehave and white students are not. There are lessons here for students of both races. Black students understand that they have to be ready for scrutiny, and white students learn, as Timothy put it, that the rules can be bent, they "learn how to get away with it."

Unlike white students who experience the benefit of the doubt, black students like Jen, a Haitian American, must grapple with the consequences of regular heightened scrutiny. When asked about things she would change in the school if she could, she says:

> I don't really like the fact that you have security guards in the [hall-way]. . . some of them they're okay but others it seems like they'll stop you for anything. So I might change that . . . I would be stopped and asked do I have a pass to be walking in the hallway. But if a white person was walking down the hallway . . . they wouldn't get stopped or there's less chances of them getting stopped and asked for a pass.

Again we see a student's perception of the differences in enforcement of school rules. Black students are more carefully monitored than white students, and this heightened visibility inhibits black students' freedom of movement. This issue is important enough to Jen to be one of the primary things she would change about the school if she could.

As we will discuss later, at times in the differential unfolding of discipline, the rules themselves seem to be the problem. In other cases, like this one, the enforcement of the rule is what generates unfair outcomes. In both cases, however, these are matters of school policy and practice—institutional problems; it is not only the school's responsibility to make sure the ostensive aspect of organizational routines, or the rules *as* articulated are fair, but also to ensure that the rules *as practiced* are fair. Importantly, the challenge here is not ill will. As with other staff, the security guards operate with the best of intentions and many see themselves as advocates within the school for minority students. For example, Mr. Young, one of the safety staff, expressed to us that he tells every student he comes into contact with who is going through the disciplinary system, "You have these rights," and then he explains to them that they can appeal any sanctions and tells them how to do it. He argued for creating a student advocacy department that would do for the low-income and students of color all the advocacy work that white and upper-middle-class parents do for their children all the time. "We need to empower these powerless children," said Mr. Young, "and we have an obligation as a public institution to do that. We do not—we should not replicate the inequalities in the criminal justice system in our disciplinary system in this school. . . . It is wrong, and we need to correct it."

This also is not a problem of a white safety staff being especially hard on students of color. As Mr. Michaels, a longtime Riverview teacher, reported when talking about the hallway pass problem, most of the safety staff are black:

> [I was talking about] white kids. In some situations, it's a privilege. I mean the white kid that walks down the hall and the safety officer doesn't ask them for a pass and a black kid walks down the hall, that in all ways looks exactly the same other than race, and the officer asks for a pass. Did that happen because—who knows why that happened? And the safety officer may be black and that happens with adults around here too and over the years I've seen that happen.

Abundant social psychological research on various participants in the criminal justice system has found that all actors, black, white, and other, operate with implicit bias against black "suspects."[36] Social psychologists have shown that even people who express egalitarian beliefs about race often still carry what are called implicit biases or unconscious racism toward African Americans, including widespread belief in blacks' inherent criminality.[37] Two techniques have been used to test these implicit attitudes—rapid priming and implicit association testing.[38] Lincoln Quillian summarizes one of these, the rapid priming test:

> Each respondent's thought process is first "primed" . . . the primes, for instance, could be the words "black" and "white," or images of black or white faces. In implicit prejudice experiments, the prime is flashed too quickly for the respondent to consciously read or recognize the prime. The subject is then asked to perform an evaluation task, such as interpreting the behavior of a race-unspecified target figure acting in an ambiguously threatening way. This procedure produces a consistent result: subjects who have been primed with the black prime tend to view the actions of the race-unspecified target figure as more threatening than subjects primed with the white prime. The implicit stereotype of blacks as hostile and threatening is activated by the implicit prime, affecting judgment of the figure's behavior without conscious awareness that the implicit stereotype has been activated.[39]

As we discussed in the Introduction, race is one of the few primary categories that are cognitively processed "quickly and automatically without the need for conscious thought."[40] This processing makes a wide range of cultural beliefs or racial stereotypes an implicit part of social interactions. These cultural beliefs are widely held because of their relationship to racial structures and hierarchies. As Cecilia Ridgeway writes about in her book *Framed by Gender*, the power and taken-for-grantedness of cultural beliefs depend on our collective daily experience with positional inequalities like substantive racial hierarchies, which provide the "evidence" and justification for such cultural beliefs or stereotypes.[41] Confronting implicit biases, cultural beliefs, and racial stereotypes, then, is not a simple matter of changing minds but a matter, rather, of contending with the full structural and ideological effects of the racialized social system.

The problem, then, is not necessarily how specific school roles are staffed but rather a widespread set of ideas/stereotypes about black criminality and white innocence that shape daily interactions in ways that we are most often not conscious of—who looks suspicious? Who do we expect to be abiding by or breaking the rules? Who do we believe needs to be monitored closely? Nico, a white junior, reports his perception of how stereotypes play out in the way student behavior at Riverview gets read and responded to and in which students get punished:

> Well, it gets back to that old stereotype. If you're a good student and you're rich and if, and if you're white and something comes up like—and you're accused of something, usually they will get away with it because like the stereotype says, "that's not what they do." It's not in their character. But if a black person with some baggy clothes came up there you know, "Bam!" First person you're out.

Similarly, when asked whether some groups of students cause more trouble in the school, black teacher Ms. Jackson responded that there were certainly some groups who were sanctioned more often:

> MS. JACKSON: There are certain groups of kids who are labeled and who tend to get written up more. You know, you can have six white kids in a hallway being loud and teacher will walk by and see that and say, "Move along." Okay? You can have six black children in the hallway being loud and they call security. Okay?
>
> INTERVIEWER: Why do you think there's that discrepancy in terms of security and stuff like that?

MS. JACKSON: I think—well, and not just security, but teachers—I
think it's the perception that people bring with them . . . when
you have people who are brought up to think, or who society
shows them in the movies, TV, da da da, then they come with
that and then that's the perception they bring with them and
that's how they act out on it.

Both Nico and Ms. Jackson discuss the ways that students engaged in similar behavior are reacted to differently partly because of teacher expectations and perceptions. Racial stereotypes shape whether a group of loud
adolescents is understood as a minor nuisance requiring a verbal admo-
nition or as threatening and requiring formal sanction from the safety
department. And while more of the black teachers and staff we spoke to
talked explicitly about these dynamics as things they thought and worried about, many adults observed the differential enforcement of rules, and
all members of the community were seen as being vulnerable to the ways
racial stereotypes can "color" how they view black and white students.

Race and the Dress Code

Similar to the issues related to hall pass rules, members of the Riverview
community also reported that rules about dress code were enforced differently.[42] In this case, black girls' dress was more closely scrutinized than
white girls' dress. The discipline code is very explicit regarding how students should dress:

> Brief and revealing clothing are not appropriate in school.
> Examples include tank or halter tops; garments with spaghetti straps
> or strapless garments; clothing that is "see-through," cut low, or
> exposes one's midriff; or skirts that are shorter than 3-inches above
> the knee.[43]

However, one teacher discussed how race shaped the enforcement of this
policy:

> We had a policy that the girls couldn't have their belly showing.
> All you saw walking in the hall [was] girls with their white bellies
> out. Black girls sent home. They [black girls] were pissed off. [One
> black student] said, "Well, why are you saying something to me. I'm

sitting up in a room with six white girls with their stomach out and you pick me out of the group."

Tiffany, a black junior, had experience with this dress code issue. She says that her teachers "love her" because "I'm the good one in the class. I participate. . . . I'm nice. I'm polite; I do what they ask me to do. I don't act up." She feels that for the most part teachers treat students the same in class around academics; however, she argued that the dress code is not enforced equally for black and white girls:

> TIFFANY: If we go by the dress code, definitely not . . . You know how white people they have like the slim bodies and all that. They can wear the skirts that come like right above the butt cheek. Now, if I were to put on something like that, I'd get sent home immediately. . . . And we're not allowed to wear spaghetti straps. But you see a lot of white girls wearing spaghetti straps, halter tops, tube tops, stuff that we [black girls] would get sent home for.
>
> INTERVIEWER: Do people actually send black kids home for the exact same thing that white girls do? You know what I'm saying? If a white girl and a black girl are both wearing the same thing.
>
> TIFFANY: Um-hmm [affirmative]. . . . Or they give her a t-shirt from the office and make her wear it.

Tiffany argued that a number of her friends had been sent home for the clothes they wore to school and that security guards had disciplined her for her clothing as well:

> That happens to a lot of my friends. I mean, they tried to get me one year but, you know, I wasn't havin' it. I put up a fight. I said, "You know, that's not fair." How come, you know, it's just my luck, a girl [presumably white given the previous statement] just happened to be walking by wearing the skirt . . . It was pretty short. And I said, "Well, what about her? You didn't stop her. Why did you stop me?" So they kinda just let it go.

Here different stereotypes are likely at play—in particular the long history of reading black female bodies as hypersexual while white female bodies are seen as innocent.[44] In both ways, assumptions about white innocence—bodily and metaphorically—yield a payoff as their whiteness buys some students the benefit of the doubt and less scrutiny for both their dress and their behavior in the hallways. In both cases, black and brown students are differentially selected for discipline not because they are breaking the rules more often but because of how race "colors" the way adults read their behavior.

Race in the Classrooms

Students reported similar patterns in their classrooms. As with other areas of the school, teachers have substantial discretion when enforcing classroom rules. Previous research has found that much of the differential selection that transpires in schools, the racial disproportionality seen in student discipline, originates with different patterns in teacher referrals from the classroom, with black students often being referred for more subjective (e.g., perceived defiance) and less serious violations.[45] What we report here is how these patterns develop and how students experience them at Riverview. Students reported that black and Latina/o students' behavior is monitored and regulated more closely in classrooms than the behavior of whites. These differences surfaced in the moments when students moved in and out of the classroom (for example, if they were entering the classroom late or if they asked to leave the classroom) as well as when they violated classroom rules.

For instance, many respondents reported that teachers enforced rules about entering and leaving the classroom differently based on race. Terrence, a 16-year-old black sophomore who takes honors classes, indicated that teachers respond differently depending on whether the students who are late to class are black or white. He cited one example in which a black student was late to class and not admitted, and a white student who also was late was admitted: "The teacher lets the white kid in, but not [the black kid]." He also reported that when students ask to go to the restroom, white students are given more freedom than black students in being allowed to leave the classroom.[46] When talking about students in the classroom, Terrence discussed "the bathroom thing" as if it were something he and his peers complained about regularly: "Like, they say no one can go to the bathroom in the class, but then a black person had asked or a Mexican person had asked and they said no. And then maybe thirty minutes later this white kid asks, and then they let him go." Andre (another black male student) generally feels that students are treated fairly but argues that while "some teachers are fair, some teachers are not." He, too, shares examples of "the bathroom thing":

> My girlfriend, her ... teacher treats this one white girl like ... They talked a lot or something like that. ... since freshman year, but if she wants to go to the bathroom she can go right then and there. And it's like, I guess, her or my friend, like if he wants to go to the bathroom, he can't go.

How and why this unfolds matters less than the fact that it does and the fact that students understand it as a problem. Students like Terrence and Andre believe that race matters when students want to leave the classroom, and their perception of their place in the school is shaped by that belief. We don't think that any teachers consciously, for example, intended to deny black and Latina/o students the freedom to go to the bathroom. Rather, implicit mechanisms may lead teachers who are multitasking and operating in the moment to react to students differently, leading to a different kind of containment or restraint on the movement of black and brown bodies.

Other students reported additional examples of how the enforcement of classroom rules operated differently for different groups of students. Cursing is considered against the rules in all classes. However, students perceived that black students who cursed were sometimes treated differently from white students. As Darin, a biracial (black/white) male sophomore argued:

> They'll be lenient like—like I said earlier, if a kid curses, black kid curses like, [spoken louder and clearer] "God damn I missed the fucking question." A white kid curse like, [spoken softer] "What the fuck?" It's like sometimes the student—I mean the teacher will be like to the black kid, "Watch your mouth!" Or, you know, they'll kick you out. But the white kid, they'll get away with it.

Here, Darin indicates that substance matters less than style—that the race of the speaker mediates how cursing is heard and responded to. Megan, a high-achieving white student, also observed that these rules are enforced differently for black and white students in one of her classes:

> My [first-period] teacher, he tells the class not to swear and gets angry at the black people when they swear. But then there's this white kid

I know, this white kid, he sits next to me, he swears all the time and doesn't get in trouble. And I'm like "what's wrong with that?" But I don't say anything because I'm not going to get involved with this. It's not going to help me because I'm just going to make a fool of myself or just going to stress myself out more.

Megan and other white students receive a pass as they negotiate these classroom contexts. In all of these cases, white students receive the benefit of the doubt. They are allowed to have more autonomy and control over their coming and going, while teachers more actively monitor black and Latina/o students.[47] Mr. Webber, a school administrator who'd been at the school for decades, spoke to this:

> I have to say most of the students who are brought or referred for disciplinary action happen to be black and Latino. Now that does not mean that white students do not get into trouble. People have . . . they are equipped to deal with issues in many different ways and, ah, the fact is I believe that in many situations and this is . . . this is hard to say. I believe that in many situations when teachers deal with students who are breaking the rules, they handle black students and white students and Latino students differently. That in many cases they will in fact talk to the white student and give them *an opportunity to do the right thing*. Whereas with the black student or Latino student they will write them up. "Send them to the dean. Let the dean talk to them." (emphasis added)

These patterns are only exacerbated by the highly racialized tracking system we discuss in greater depth in the next chapter. Several teachers described the consequences of tracking for discipline. As Mr. Webber put it, "See that's the other thing. In an AP class, if a student . . . misbehaves . . . even sometimes downright defiance, they are more likely to get talked to. In a [regular level class] . . . they're more likely to be thrown out." Or, as another white student put it when we asked if the school rules were enforced fairly, "I'm not trying to be racist or anything, but if like a black kid did something they would look at it a lot more than like if a white kid who was really smart and did something." Here this student not only reports that students are treated differently but also associates this different treatment with race and academic achievement.

Interestingly, when Megan discusses witnessing unequal discipline patterns around cursing in the classroom, she takes no action because she does not want to "stress" herself out by addressing this unequal treatment. This sentiment expresses a form of what Tyrone Forman has named *Racial Apathy*, a new form of racial antipathy that is increasing among white youth. Forman defines racial apathy as "indifference toward societal racial and ethnic inequality and lack of engagement with race-related social issues."[48] Like Megan, none of the other white students we interviewed reported intervening in or raising public questions of fairness about the discipline patterns they had witnessed. In contrast to Megan and her peers, black and Latina/o students experience acute frustration about this treatment, report confusion and exasperation as a result of being subjected to it, and also describe experiencing a heightened sense of the importance of their social identities within the school context as a result of it. Jamal expressed some of this frustration when we asked about his impressions of fairness in treatment at the school:

> INTERVIEWER: And do you think that teachers let some kids get away with things that . . .
>
> JAMAL: Oh yeah. (Interviewer: Yeah?) Yeah.
>
> INTERVIEWER: Like in what way?
>
> JAMAL: Just, uh, talking in class and like you'll be talking and then they'll just stop you instead of that person or like—stuff like that. Or they'll get graded higher just cuz.
>
> INTERVIEWER: Right. But like what groups of students usually get—are usually allowed to slide on certain things?
>
> JAMAL: Caucasians, I want to say.

As Jamal puts it, it is hard to make sense out of these experiences—why doing the same things leads to different outcomes.

We have shown that in the hallways and in classrooms, race has implications for students' experiences. As Mr. Michaels (a longtime teacher at the school) talked about, "in some situations, [being white] is a privilege." White students report navigating the hallways freely and not having their intentions questioned, both unearned advantages of whiteness.[49] In this sense, whiteness functions as a kind of silent "benefit of the doubt," a positive estimation of competence, esteem, and honor, or what Mr. Webber described as "an opportunity to do the right thing."[50] With regard to rule breaking, for white students "there's always been an expectation that they're not gonna do it." That expectation of good intentions is part of the unearned privilege that white students enjoy. As Peggy McIntosh writes, it's a part of the "invisible package of unearned assets" enjoyed by whites.[51]

Race is relational (as are other inequalities). For every privileged group there is another group that is penalized. As whiteness leads to racial privileges (unearned assets or credit), blackness or brownness leads to equally unearned racial penalties for individual black or Latina/o students. The flip side of white students' freedom of movement is black and Latina/o students being more actively scrutinized. Such scrutiny can lead them to feel frustration, anxiety, and alienation from the educational environment.[52] It signals to them regularly in small ways that they are not equal citizens within the school.

William Smith and his colleagues discuss how African American students face racial microaggressions on college campuses.[53] These microaggressions are cumulative slights and insults that communicate racial messages, erect racial boundaries, and facilitate racial exclusion. They write:

> As a result of chronic racial microaggressions, many African-Americans perceive their environment as extremely stressful, exhausting, and diminishing to their sense of control, comfort, and meaning while eliciting feelings of loss, ambiguity, strain, frustration, and injustice. When racially oppressed groups are in situations where they experience environmental stressors as mundane events, the ramifications are as much a psychological and emotional burden as they are a physiological response.[54]

Such microaggressions accumulate over time such that victims come to experience what Smith calls "racial battle fatigue," leaving them exhausted and alienated. When members of a community regularly fall victim to these kinds of microaggressions, they often come to feel that the system does not operate fairly. Several recent studies of school discipline find that youth of color and, in particular, black youth perceive school disciplinary systems to be discriminatory. For example, using data from a nationally representative survey of students, Kupchik and Ellis report that African American students perceive less fairness and consistency in the application of schools rules when compared to their white counterparts.[55]

Like the student we quoted at the beginning of this chapter put it, as a white student he is not subjected to "racial profiling." Profiling, as Patricia Hill Collins argues:

> increasingly refers to a seemingly benign set of behaviors grounded in statistical predictions. One places an entire population under surveillance and then identifies possible criminals or threats to society from that population via statistical profiles. This shift toward statistical profiling may appear to be nonracial, yet it gains strength from preexisting forms of so-called racial profiling that long have affected African-Americans in public spaces. . . . One common defense of such profiling is that being stopped more often by police and by security guards . . . is a small price to pay for the greater good of the safety of the larger group. The argument is usually made by members of the larger group. Yet being routinely stopped, searched, and kept under surveillance can be far more odious and ominous if one falls within the parameters of the perceived threat.[56]

While such "inconveniences" may seem small to members of groups who do not routinely face them, they can be perceived as powerful racial slights by those who endure them more frequently. They are also experienced collectively, leading them to be felt far beyond those physically present for any particular incident itself.[57]

Nationally, a growing body of research on racial profiling in the criminal justice system shows that even when blacks and Latina/os are stopped by police and security guards more frequently than whites, they are no more likely to be found engaged in law-breaking.[58] Similarly, the recent data from schools have consistently shown that black students do not engage in more rule breaking than white students do. "Studies using the measures of students' self-reports and school disciplinary records have examined this premise and have generally failed to find evidence of racial differences in student behavior."[59] Black students are disciplined more often, however, and disciplined more often for infractions involving what Vavrus and Cole refer to as violations of "implicit interactional codes."[60] They write, "Our analysis suggests that removing a student from class is a highly contextualized decision based on subtle race and gender relations." Similarly, Skiba and colleagues found that black students were more often referred to the office for subjective offenses such as disrespect or excessive noise, being threatening, or loitering.

This finding is not unlike what Ann Ferguson describes in her book *Bad Boys*. Ferguson studied fifth- and sixth-grade students at Rosa Parks Elementary School and determined that black boys were often disciplined for behaviors that their white classmates also engaged in without sanction. What Ferguson found was that black boys were often singled out for discipline because their actions were interpreted as intentionally defiant or disrespectful. Their behavior was not seen as childlike but was instead "adultified"—interpreted through the lens of adult behavior. Defiant behavior by white students was interpreted differently. When white boys misbehaved, they were more often given the benefit of the doubt. Their defiant or mischievous behavior was more likely to be interpreted as "boys being boys." As a consequence of these distinct interpretations, black boys received harsher punishments than their white counterparts.[61]

Many at Riverview similarly refuted the idea that black students were engaged in more rule breaking than other kids (though they did not have good explanations for why black students were being punished more often). However, when asked about patterns in school rule breaking, a few staff members did suggest that black male students acted out more often than their peers. These staff usually noted that they were not talking about "all" black males, just a few. The infractions they described these young men as engaging in were minor issues of defiance similar to those noted in other studies mentioned earlier. For example, Ms. Cristy, a science teacher, said that black males did get in trouble in her class more often: "I'd have to say that most of the kids that I see that I have those interactions with are African American males. . . . That sucks, but that's the truth . . . they're the ones who are the most angry, and when you talk to them and say, 'Hey, come on, let's get to where you need to go,' they're the ones that blow up at you the most." But, she also said, "It's a real small number . . . a couple of faces that I know I saw last year a lot." Similarly, Mr. Tate, a school administrator, described "a small group of kids" who were generally "a little louder, a little more boisterous. Difficult when confronted." Note that these staff members are not necessarily describing behavior that constitutes rule breaking. What they describe is discomfort with students whom they perceive to be less deferential and somehow more challenging.[62] Whether or not these students are engaged in more *actual* rule breaking than other students, their behavior is noted and understood as qualitatively different. It is also seen as collectively meaningful in a way that individual white students' misbehavior is not. The rule breaking of white students is understood as an individual phenomenon not generalizable to the group, while the "acting out" of a few "boisterous" black males is talked about categorically. One of the long-noted privileges of whiteness is not being asked or expected to represent the group. Moreover, adults such as Ms. Cristy or Mr. Tate generally interpret the behavior they describe in a very narrow context as interpersonal defiance rather than seeing potential connections to broader patterns of differential treatment that can lead to racial battle fatigue.

Race and Cultural Style

While students believed that racial dynamics shaped their treatment in the hallways and classrooms, some elaborated that part of the equation was a dovetailing of race and cultural presentation that led black students to be more actively scrutinized. Maria, a Latina junior, argues, "They'll only stop certain people by the way they look and stuff." For Maria, how people look is linked to the clothes they wear and what those clothes have come to symbolize. When students wear clothes identified with the white middle class, they are more likely to be allowed to move freely. When they wear clothes identified with urban African Americans, they are more likely to be scrutinized by school officials.

Jen, a black student, explains that some students "aren't given a chance from the second that you walk in the door." Many adults, she argues, "judge you by your looks." The students who are singled out and judged negatively for their looks are identified by "the hip-hop look . . . and race." She goes on to say:

> If you've got some cornrows and if you're coming in with some big low clothes on, the teacher's going to be like "here's a trouble-maker". . . when you see a boy walking with some khakis, and like a dress shirt on, you don't think the same thing as when you see a boy walking with some baggy clothes on, even though the boy with khakis can be more of a troublemaker. You just don't think that way.

In other words, Jen and many others perceived that students' clothing primed adults to certain behavioral expectations. "Black" clothing and hairstyles (including baggy pants and cornrows) were penalized at Riverview through increased scrutiny. "White" clothing (including khakis and button-up shirts) was rewarded with additional freedom of movement. Jen also seems to internalize some of these perceptions when she says "you just don't think that way" perhaps including herself as a person who has these perceptions. Like Jen, Colin argues that students are assigned to "good" and "bad" categories based on their cultural presentation. While not agreeing with the assessments made by teachers, Colin argued, "according to teachers . . . if you wear baggy pants or whatever and you have braids, you're bad; like if you have a clean-cut haircut or whatever and you polo or whatever, you're supposedly good."

Blackness itself, and the cultural styles exhibited by some black students, prime school officials to expect or be on alert for "trouble" and can have real consequences for students. For black students, embracing black cultural styles opens students up for greater scrutiny by security officials. L. Janelle Dance described this tendency to "look at black and brown males, not see them, and, then assault or insult them with stereotypes and negative racial icons" as a kind of symbolic violence.[63] The consequences are not merely "symbolic," however, as they can also lead to these students' being punished more for behaviors all students engage in. For black and Latina/o students, this limits the cultural styles they can embrace without penalty and their sense of how free they are to move through the school environment.

By scrutinizing students based on their cultural presentation, school officials set up a hierarchy in the minds of the students regarding what is valued in the school context. White students more easily fit into the cultural styles that the school values. Recall that the "preppy" clothing of middle-class whites, including khakis and dress shirts, signals safety and conformity to school officials. Black and Latina/o students, particularly those students from families that are not middle class, may feel less comfortable embracing these styles. Maria, a working-class Mexican American student, discusses how students' backgrounds can shape their access to the cultural symbols that the school values and their comfort with them:

> Most of the white kids . . . come with Abercrombie and whatever. I don't even know how to pronounce that. There was this one day; I went to the mall with my sister. I walked in that store [Abercrombie & Fitch], I did not feel right. It was all white people around me. I just walked straight out.[64]

For Maria, attempting to embrace "Abercrombie" leaves her feeling out of place. As French theorist Pierre Bourdieu might argue, this is the difference between feeling like a fish in water and a fish out of water.[65] Bourdieu argues that educational environments are infused with (and reward) the cultural styles and dispositions of the middle class. This enhances the comfort that middle-class (and white) students feel in schools and makes their access to institutional rewards easier. For students who are not middle class, access to institutional rewards is more difficult. As we discuss next, others recognize that cultural capital also includes a racial dimension.[66]

When discussing her visit to Abercrombie & Fitch, for example, Maria says, "I did not feel right" and that she "just walked straight out." This is at least in part because of the connotations that the clothing is for white people. "It was all white people around me," she says.[67] Access and comfort with this kind of preppy clothing is tied to social class and racial/ethnic background. For white students, there is more comfort in embracing this cultural style. By embracing this clothing style, school officials simultaneously embrace middle-class whiteness and penalize cultural symbols of blackness and Latino-ness.[68] Students like Maria and Colin must either embrace the cultural styles of the white middle class or be penalized to some extent by embracing the cultural styles most identified with their black and Latina/o peers.

In her book *Keepin' It Real*, sociologist Prudence Carter discusses her research with black and Latina/o high school students in Yonkers, New York, explaining how black and Latina/o students are forced to make choices about the cultural styles they display in schools. She distinguishes between two types of cultural capital that students can exhibit: the dominant capital rooted in the school's middle-class values, and the non-dominant capital that is valued by black and Latina/o peer groups. Schools reward students whose cultural presentation conforms to its own (white middle-class) expectations and devalue the non-dominant version that emerges from black and Latina/o peer groups and communities. She shows how students must negotiate this reality. Some students, those she refers to as the *cultural mainstreamers*, accept the dominant cultural capital of the school and conform to its expectations. A second group of students, the *noncompliant believers*, accept that the route to school success is to embrace the signs and symbols of the dominant culture. However, these students refuse to trade their identification with the culture of their communities in exchange for potential school success. Finally, there are the *cultural straddlers*. These students "bridge the gap" between the other two groups by strategically embracing the cultural styles that benefit them in a given context. In school, they play the game and fit in, accepting the codes of participation in the school setting.

Research by Edward Morris also notes that even those white students who resist school dress codes are read by school personnel as "benign and harmless," while black and Latina/o students wearing the same styles were understood as "purposefully oppositional." Morris argues that white students who reject "preppy" styles can still reap the "latent racial benefits" of their skin color. Says Morris, "Their whiteness still afforded them less concern and monitoring from teachers than that directed at most African American and Latino students."[69] At issue here is not merely the clothes that students are wearing but, of course, what those clothes signify. The cultural styles at play are racialized such that some are protective and serve as cultural resources in the context of school, and others are not. Yet as Morris's work shows, even when white students diverge from the cultural mainstream, they still retain some of the protective functions of whiteness's *symbolic capital.*

DIFFERENTIAL PROCESSING: RACE, CLASS, AND THE ENFORCEMENT OF DISCIPLINE

As discussed earlier, the rules for school behavior are often presented as if they are neutral. This perceived impartiality gives these rules their legitimacy and power.[70] They are stated in neutral terms and understood to be applied to all students regardless of race and social class. Further, they rely on a legal basis for their authority and gain their power from their bureaucratic neutrality.[71] We have already shown patterns of *differential selection* at Riverview, the ways that race shapes how and when students get in trouble. In addition, however, we found that race and class mattered quite a bit for the *processing* of discipline—what severity of sanctions a student received once he/she had entered into the school's disciplinary system. For example, Julius, a high-achieving black student, talks about how race and class are intertwined in the handling of drug violations:

> White kids get caught with pot all the time . . . The school can't be dealing with these folks' parents, because their parents are going to start suing the school. . . . When you get a black kid, and you suspend them for having pot, or you kick them out, what are the parents going to do? They don't have the money, or they don't know the resources. . . . That's why I think it continuously happens.

For Julius, teachers and administrators' perceptions of parents' economic resources and their ability to fight on behalf of their children often pre-empt the enforcement of discipline, with white students most often being the beneficiaries.[72] In these cases it often does not matter whether the individual white student in question has wealthy parents, because whiteness becomes the primary signifier that is being acted upon.[73] When dealing with white students, Riverview personnel assume they are likely to face parental intervention. Thus, many staff report that white parents intervene more often and in particular ways, but they also report how the expectation of that intervention shapes the disciplinary process from the very beginning. Mr. Webber captures this dynamic as he ponders why it is that teachers do not send white students to the office for engaging in the same behaviors for which they refer black students:

> If I hear that so many times from white parents [about their children having bright futures and deserving a break because they are good kids], do teachers not use the same logic? So, could it be that they are reluctant to write up certain things? To call it what it is? Now is there a difference between what a black teacher would do and a white teacher? In some cases there might be. In some other cases . . . I mean, I can't prove it. I do know that something happens with being in the decision-making position, that we also make decisions about people. And so it's not just "the incident." And how I respond to the incident is one thing. How much of that is influenced by *who is doing it* . . . how I respond to behavior. How much of it is influenced by who's doing it? And, for instance, at what point does horseplay change from fun to, ah, inappropriate behavior?

As scholars have discussed, it is in the "moment-by-moment interactions that decisions are made" about discipline.[74] In these moments, status categories shape expectations and perceptions of esteem and competence.[75] These moments when behavior is read either as "horseplay" or "inappropriate behavior" are shaped by subtle, often unconscious processes going on in the heads of very-well-intended people. As this school administrator suggests, in these moments, "who is doing it" matters as much as what is being done or "the incident" itself. We do not believe that whiteness privileges white students in "disciplinary moments" because teachers are acting out of explicit racial favoritism. Rather, whiteness functions as a symbolic resource, above and beyond students' actual economic and cultural resources, because of all the wider cultural meanings race carries with it—and carries with it for all actors.[76]

In fact, a number of those involved in the school's disciplinary bureaucracy acknowledged and lamented the ways that race and class significantly impacted the kinds of sanctions students would eventually face. One example of this pattern observed by multiple school actors is how drug offenses are handled in the school, with black and white students treated differently from one another. Black students, it is argued, are given harsher punishments for similar offenses. Earlier in this chapter, we quote Julius discussing the perception that some parents will use their resources to challenge the school's decisions. Mr. Webber, who is often the first stop for those accused of drug-related offenses, confirms that Julius's conjecture has some basis. He experiences racial differences in the way black parents and white parents interact with school personnel around such offenses:

> I have had parents come in to appeal white students' discipline . . . disciplinary actions. And rarely will they say, "My son didn't do that" or "would not do that" or "My daughter would not." Their issue is, "How do we get it out of the record? Can we not call it that because we don't want it to impact college admissions?" . . . I don't sit down and write down every time, but I'd say I hear it twenty times a year. A student got caught in possession of some marijuana. The parent never said to me, "He didn't have it, he didn't do it." The parent argued that we call it possession, and possession means you have it and you are . . . it's yours to manipulate and to sell, to do what you want to do with. "It was never his. He was just looking at it. It was in his hands. So that possession is not real possession." You know. And they want the possession charge taken out of the record.

This is very similar to what Ms. McDaniel, a principal, called the "entitlement game," whereby parents argue that no matter what their child did or is accused of doing, they are inherently "good kids" who have bright futures ahead of them. Here, Ms. McDaniel describes her long-term frustration watching racial dynamics play out in the review board, where serious disciplinary infractions are brought:

> When white kids come to the board, how their parents approach it is really annoying to me 'cause you've really done something [to get to the review board]. But it's always the entitlement that, "Yes, they did wrong, but it really wasn't that wrong. And they're good kids. And they're in honors classes and can't we just make this alright? And

please don't let them have a record . . ." But, for the blacks kids [white parents say], *"You need to discipline them. You need to make sure that [they're punished]". . .* It just gets on my nerves. All kids do something wrong. But why do the blacks have to be the ones that always have to be disciplined and the white kids are supposed to be understood?

Here, both administrators describe white parents arguing that in their specific child's case, the rules are too punitive and shouldn't be applied. These parents then negotiate with school officials to the benefit of their children in discipline procedures. Here there is a certain level of cultural capital that benefits them in negotiation—the knowledge of legal jargon that they can wield to benefit their children. In marked contrast, Ms. McDaniel described black parents as being much less likely to try to get their children off the hook:

> Black parents . . . 80 . . . 75% of them never even come in to appeal. And that's not to say . . . they shouldn't but, you know what? Their kids did the stuff. We didn't make it up. We didn't make it up. I don't want to say they shouldn't come in and find out about it, but there's nothing to appeal. You did it. You stay home.

None of the administrators we spoke to were sure whether it was because black parents believed that their children should have to suffer the consequences of their behavior, whether they were more likely to regard school decisions as firm and fixed, or whether they just didn't have as many resources (time, knowledge) to intervene. All of them, however, were clear on the patterns they witnessed.

Like their parents, white students also engaged in negotiation around discipline. Here is one example from an interview with a male student:

INTERVIEWER: Have you ever been in trouble?

STUDENT: Nothing serious, no. Int: (starts to speak) [interrupts interviewer] Well, actually I take that back. I was threatened with suspension by several security guards freshman year because, the thing was the school distributed these tiny shorts to the synchronized swimming team, and you know of course the assumption is everybody on the synchronized swimming team is female and so they can wear short shorts and so, um as part of a bet with some of my friends I wore these shorts for a

week and uh—because you know, I mean, I had basically a perfect excuse which was that the school distributes these for the
purpose of wearing so you can't you know, bother people for
wearing them. But I nonetheless got sent to the Dean twice in
one day, and he afterwards just said basically um, "If you wear
them again, then I don't care you know, what you say about
gender equality, it's controversial and so and so we're gonna . . ."

While one might argue that this is not a "serious" or "dangerous" violation
of school rules, it is a clear example of a student knowingly violating school
rules and fully expecting to be able to do so without serious sanction.

When talking about the disciplinary review board, Ms. Rutherford, a
longtime school employee, commented:

They hold review boards, which is a disciplinary action. There
is a whole big committee made up of administrators, counselors,
whatever. And they hold these meetings up here. So I told one of the
administrators one time, I said, "Well, you know what, if you ever
bring a white kid in here you can just walk up and slap the hell out
of me." Because I don't see them. "I don't see you bring white kids to
the review board," which goes back to my saying that these [black]
kids are watched more. So of course they are caught more. They are
referred more. These young white teachers don't know these kids.
They don't understand these kids. I'm not trying to make excuses for
these kids. Some of the stuff they do is not right. But all I am saying
is, "If you will send the black kid in for that, send the white kid in
for that. If you punish a black kid for that, punish the white kid the
same way."

Of course, we have already seen that some white students do come before
the review board. The issue is not just who gets to the review board, but
what happens once kids are there. As Ms. McDaniel discussed extensively,
white parents' elaborate interventions on behalf of their kids are largely
successful in reducing the penalties they face. One of the school safety
staff, Jim, put it this way:

Students who come from low-income families are . . . more
likely to receive the full weight of disciplinary action than a child
who has a father who is a *downtown* lawyer or some—a person who
has connections to the Board. This not only goes—this issue doesn't
only address the accused, it addresses the victims. The child of a

downtown lawyer who comes in to complain that they have been a victim of a crime is more likely to receive—to have his or her case investigated to the fullest. A child from a low-income family who has no resources to draw upon may have their case relegated to the bottom. It may not be pursued. There may be—there may not be—it'll be pursued to a degree, but not to the fullest.

What is powerful is to hear from these different school personnel—deans, principals, school safety staff—that the system they run, the system they oversee and implement, does not operate fairly. They argue that race and class (which are correlated and often conflated in the minds of school personnel) shape how disciplinary infractions are processed. This is not a list of complaints from minority students or parents about perceived mistreatment but reports from those who are in their various roles "in charge." To be sure, some perceived the problem to be larger or more widespread than others did, but almost all agreed that students are differentially processed and sanctioned. Many were annoyed if not dismayed about the ways that they perceived teachers to be differently selecting students for punishment, but they also recognized that the part of the system they typically governed, sanctioning, was also deeply flawed. What left them baffled was what to do about it.

CONCLUSION

Obviously, in contrast to the apparent fairness and neutrality of the rule system, in which all rules are supposed to be applied uniformly to all students, the actual disciplinary process permits substantial discretion, and compelling evidence shows that discretion leads to discrimination. In this case, as illustrated in Figures 3.1 and 3.2, there is a clear divergence between discipline's idealized (or ostensive) aspect and its actual (or performative) aspect.

Importantly, the practice of the disciplinary routine reproduces inequality, while the idealized version (race-neutral rules) appears to justify/legitimize the routine itself. Because the ostensive aspect is presented as the whole—"this is how we do discipline"—there is little room for confronting the different ways in which school personnel enact the rules in practice. As it stands, the Riverview disciplinary routine not only leads to differential selection and processing of students, but in doing so, it imposes

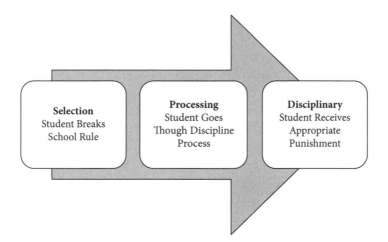

FIGURE 3.1. The Discipline Routine—The Ostensive Aspect

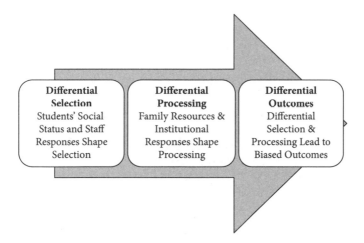

FIGURE 3.2. The Discipline Routine—The Performative Aspect

numerous damaging consequences for school outcomes and for the students themselves as they develop understandings about race and justice.

The *differential selection* and *differential processing* we describe do not emerge because adults at Riverview are mean-spirited; racism today is not the same as in the past. As a number of scholars have recently outlined, older understandings of racism that focused primarily on ill will and faulty racial thinking do not properly diagnose what we are faced with today.[77] Instead, we have a system in which most operate with the best of intentions and an investment in doing the right thing. Yet widespread cultural beliefs and pervasive racial stereotypes about all groups permeate deeply into school buildings, and they shape interactions. Research on the role of status characteristics and implicit bias tells us to expect the kinds of patterns we found. Race works symbolically to shape how we understand each other, whether or not we imagine those we are confronting to be well-meaning and inherently "innocent," whether we imagine that they are highly resourced and thus possibly deserving of careful treatment. Race matters not only in the way it shapes these ideas but also in the way it shapes groups' relationships to institutions, their expectations of treatment, and the resources with which they can enact their expectations. That is, long histories of racial hierarchy mean that there are collective, group-level differences in access to various kinds of resources that matter for school experiences.

In multiple ways, racial meanings become part of how the institution functions such that certain groups get denied full access to rights and privileges. The result is similar to what scholar Nancy Fraser has termed misrecognition:

> To be misrecognized, accordingly is not simply to be thought ill of, looked down upon, or devalued in others' attitudes, beliefs, or representations. It is rather to be denied the status of a full partner in social interaction, as a consequence of institutionalized patterns of cultural value that constitute one as comparatively unworthy of respect or esteem.[78]

The experience for youth of being misrecognized in this way in *school* is a potent one. As we discuss further in the next chapter, disciplinary routines are just one arena in which blackness and Latina/o-ness carry a kind of racial penalty leading to increased surveillance, restricted freedom of movement, and suspicion about intentions.[79] The impact of disciplinary unfairness goes beyond the realm of disciplinary routines, however, as Fraser discusses, conveying clear messages to youth about their status as full partners or members of the community. In contrast, whiteness is a kind of currency (or symbolic capital).[80] It buys white students the benefit of the doubt, the freedom of movement, and the assumption of good intentions and innocence, and it encourages a sense of entitlement. At Riverview and in society more generally, black, Latina/o, and white students occupy distinct status positions.

Our data, along with research by others, suggest there are ways that black and Latina/o students can mitigate the impact of these racial penalties, however. One strategy involves embracing the cultural styles of middle-class whites or at least performing whiteness at key moments. In his book *Whistling Vivaldi*, Claude Steele describes a great example of this when he quotes *New York Times* columnist Brent Staples strategizing about how to navigate his neighborhood without inciting fear:

> I'd been a fool. I'd been walking the streets grinning good-evening at people who were frightened to death of me. I did violence to them by just being. How had I missed this . . . I tried to be innocuous but didn't know how . . . Out of nervousness I began to whistle and discovered I was good at it. My whistle was pure and sweet—and also in tune. On the street at night I whistled popular tunes from the Beatles and Vivaldi's *Four Seasons*. The tension drained from people's bodies when they heard me.[81]

Here, by whistling The Beatles and Vivaldi, Staples signaled whiteness and safety, and distanced himself just enough from negative stereotypes of blackness to walk through the streets less encumbered. Strategies such as this enhance the possibility that black youth or adults will avoid added scrutiny and be granted some of the credits of whiteness. For Riverview teens, comfortably wearing white middle-class clothing styles or carrying themselves in ways that are considered "white" can lead to more freedom and, at times, acceptance in certain contexts. It doesn't provide a "pass" necessarily but can assist in at least complicating the otherwise readily available assumptions, the cultural beliefs primed once they are read as black.[82] This kind of individual-level adjustment to the current realities of race is, in many important ways, however, a lot to ask of black youth who are simultaneously in the throws of adolescence and forming a sense of self. What does it mean to suggest that being seen as "too black" will somehow be deleterious to their treatment in school?

As with long-term findings in the literature on racial socialization, recent work by Angel Harris finds that for black students, a strong racial/ethnic identity, including a sense of closeness to a larger black community and happiness with being black, was positively associated with achievement.[83] He argues, "The only racial attitude that is associated with declines in achievement, educational aspirations, and value attributed to school is regret for being black."[84] Thus, while it might make situational sense for individual black teens to "whistle Vivaldi," the real, larger challenge is how to decouple blackness and brownness from the pernicious stereotypes that follow youth around and lead to their heightened surveillance and punishment.[85] Such individual-level accommodations to racism do not address the larger structural and institutional problem; for schools, the challenge is how to ensure fairness in policies and practices so that all students feel like they are valued and belong.[86]

What, in fact, should a school like Riverview do to address these challenges? One of the major problems here has to do with how rules are implemented—the divergence between the ostensive and performative aspects of organizational routines. If the rules are good rules, they should be uniformly applied—if being in the hall without a pass should lead to detention, if having drugs in school should lead to suspension, if cursing in class should lead to referral, then it should be so for all students. In his book on race and crime, law professor Randall Kennedy advocates for what he calls a "color-blind" approach to policing:

> [I]nstead of placing a racial tax on [minorities], government should, if necessary, increase taxes across the board. . . . [It] should be forced to inconvenience everyone . . . by subjecting all . . . to questioning. The reform I support, in other words, does not entail lessened policing. It only insists that the costs of policing be allocated on a nonracial basis.[87]

So what would it mean to ensure that the "costs" of discipline are "allocated on a nonracial basis?" In this model, all students would be stopped in the hall and asked for verification that they have permission to be there. All students would be referred out of class for infractions of school rules. All students would be suspended for possession of illicit substances. Doing so might well lead to the conclusion that the rules aren't good rules—that they are too punitive, too cumbersome to enforce, or too burdensome on those scrutinized. If that is the case, then the rules themselves should be changed. The problem with the current system is that rules are too often just selectively applied to those students who are deemed more in "need" of punishment, or who do not have the resources to defend themselves or to question the rules. In fact, we believe that if rules were enforced in the universal or "nonracial" fashion Kennedy advocates, without exception or discretion, it might quickly lead to demands for the rules themselves to change rather than just demands for exceptions to the rules in the case of "my good, well-meaning (white) child." In this case—a change in the rules—the interventions of highly resourced parents would pay off for all children, rather than just for their own children.

An alternative example more in line with the conclusion that the "rules aren't good rules" or that the current system of rules and punishment is part of the problem is a growing movement to change punishment in its current form. Many schools and districts in the United States and globally are beginning to explore the possibility of a whole new way of managing questions of discipline in school. Signaling a major paradigm shift, this involves moving to a focus on restorative justice—turning away from a focus on blame and punishment, to a focus on repairing the harm that violations to collective norms do to relationships and communities.[88] These kinds of developments can be challenging to implement, but such ideas are worth pursuing, for the consequences of the highly racialized disciplinary system as currently practiced at Riverview and elsewhere are too high.

4

"It's Like Two High Schools"

Race, Tracking, and Performance Expectations

So we have great diversity at this school, but it's like two ships traveling in parallel lines—they don't ever really cross.

Ms. Hicks (school counselor)

As Ms. Hicks observes, Riverview is a diverse school. It has been officially desegregated for decades. However, as she also describes, it is far from a model of integration. Once black, Latina/o, and white students pass through Riverview's entrance, they mostly pass by each other on the way to different classrooms. As is true of many high schools across the country, Riverview's academic hierarchy is highly racialized; classrooms are internally segregated, with high-level courses dominated by white students and "basic" classes filled predominantly by black and Latina/o students.[1] In fact, of the many possible measures of "racial achievement gaps" at Riverview, racialized tracking is often the most glaring—it is the physical manifestation of what is otherwise often represented only in abstract statistics. When we spoke to Jim, a school safety officer who'd grown up in Riverview, he described the situation this way:

We instituted integration and it started in 1967, okay, when I was bused to [elementary school] as a white boy.

Now, we've hardly gone anywhere since 1967 because we just reproduce segregation inside the school.

In some ways, the racialized academic hierarchy, what some scholars refer
to as "second-generation segregation," at Riverview is not new. As Jim
suggests, such hierarchies have existed here and elsewhere for as long as
the schools themselves have been desegregated.[2] The question remains,
however, how is it that a school like Riverview, with its expressed commitment to diversity and equity, can have what feels like "old-fashioned"
racial hierarchies embedded within them despite the elimination of formal mechanisms of segregation decades ago?[3] Such hierarchies are not a
manifestation of group-level differences in ability or intelligence. While
once popular, the idea that there are genetic group-level differences in
intelligence has been thoroughly debunked.[4] Even beyond this, however,
as psychologists are increasingly pointing out, the heavy focus on cognition in trying to understand educational outcomes is largely misplaced.
As Aronson and Steele discuss, academic competence "is not just something inside a person's head . . . [but] is quite literally the product of real or
imagined interactions with others."[5] For example, as they argue, whether
you feel respected, welcomed, and/or treated well not only shapes social
relations but also influences motivation, performance, and learning.
Intelligence is less stable and more fragile than we typically acknowledge,
and a host of contextual factors influence whether any of us are able to
realize our potential.[6]

Further, "culture"—a typical substitute for "genetics" in discussions
of school outcomes—is also a dubious explanation for "racially stratified
academic hierarchies."[7] As we discussed previously (see Chapter 2), we
find little if any evidence that an oppositional culture on the part of black
students explains these patterns. In fact, if anything, black students are
more pro-school than white students. So what are the "new" racial dynamics generating these "old" patterns? Important to addressing this puzzle
are the general findings in the social science literature of the past several
decades on race relations and racial inequality. That is, social scientists
have documented that the way that race works, and the forms that racial
prejudice or animus takes, have changed. Race does not necessarily matter
less than it did in the past. It just matters *differently*. In studies of racial segregation, scholars find that, while legalized segregation of schooling ended

more than 50 years ago, many schools and districts in the United States remain highly segregated.[8]

While school segregation is still too prevalent, the political challenges associated with it are fundamentally different than in the past because the processes that lead to such segregation are different. No longer the result of formalized and explicit rules, school segregation is now perpetuated through housing segregation, the way that school boundaries are drawn, and parental choices about school enrollment. Building on recent work by scholars such as Karolyn Tyson, Roslyn Mickelson, L'Heureux Lewis-McCoy, and Carla O'Connor and colleagues, we seek to similarly interrogate the school-based mechanisms that contribute to second-generation segregation within schools like Riverview.

To be sure, Riverview High School is not solely responsible for the racialized hierarchies therein. Students arrive at Riverview with some skill differences.[9] Academic differentiation begins in the elementary schools, and some of the school dynamics that can generate academic skill hierarchies begin then. But these skill gaps get exacerbated at the high school level. Moreover, clearly there are class differences among families, and family background matters for school outcomes. Past research, however, shows that black-white achievement gaps are not explained entirely by family background, and that even those resources that black families have do not pay off in the same way in school as they do for white families.[10] Growing evidence shows that something happens in schools to negatively affect black achievement. As O'Connor, Hill, and Robinson put it, "The fact that blacks evidence greater receptivity to school effects but nevertheless lose ground over their schooling careers should prompt us to conclude that it is the failure of schools to 'add value' that places black students at academic risk."[11]

Thus, while acknowledging that schools are only part of the equation, we examine the important role school organizational practices and policies can and do play in contributing to uneven outcomes. In many ways, the fact that course-taking at Riverview is racialized should be no surprise. Research by a number of sociologists of education has consistently documented racialized tracking within supposedly integrated high schools.[12] We build on this past work by exploring further the mechanisms that produce these patterns and how those in the school make sense of them. How does race get embedded in school structures? What role do racial dynamics play in generating stratified academic hierarchies? How do teachers, staff, and students make sense of race and of the racial hierarchies within which they are embedded, and how does this sense-making shape school personnel's practices? The stakes here are high and reach beyond the school grounds—racialized tracking is only one example of how seemingly "old-fashioned" racial hierarchies persist today, long after the original mechanisms that produced them have disappeared. When we ask what it is about the way that race works that leads Riverview to produce racialized academic hierarchies—how it is that such hierarchies are not a source of daily outrage—we are concerned not only with school dynamics but also with racial dynamics writ large. A better understanding of racial dynamics will help us to better understand schools, and a better understanding of school dynamics can also help us to understand racial dynamics in general.

As we discussed in the Introduction, schools are embedded within a larger structure and culture that sets some of the parameters for what is possible within them, including shaping the nature of interactions and experiences. For example, white and middle-class families who have more resources are able to deploy those to provide advantages for their children within schools (even "integrated" schools), securing them a better overall experience and increasing their access to additional educational resources.[13] This is one way that racial inequality becomes embedded in organizational structures and processes. Similarly, racial ideologies and understandings shape school interactions and practices. For example, we find that Riverview students, teachers, administrators, and parents discuss an environment in which black (and Latina/o) students are seen as less capable than their white peers. We know from abundant past research that race shapes beliefs about intelligence and competence.[14] Research further shows that these kinds of status beliefs about race are a part of interpersonal interactions. We argue that these beliefs emerge from the general perceptions that people hold but also from the way that race and achievement are understood and framed locally.

Moreover, school hierarchies (embodied in tracking) reinforce stereotypes and status beliefs because people conflate tracks with race. Racialized tracks become the kind of positional inequalities that seem to affirm status beliefs. Or, as Lawrence Bobo and colleagues put it, they "provide the kernel of truth needed to basically breathe new life into old stereotypes."[15] Local explanations for differences in achievement often go back to something wrong culturally with the students (and their families) as opposed to something wrong with the institutions. In this way, tracking strengthens the status beliefs—it is an institutional mechanism through which status beliefs get reinforced. As Karolyn Tyson argues, if ideas about race are linked to achievement in schools, it is school structures like racialized tracking that produce such links.[16] In what follows, we argue that important work in social psychology concerned with the relationship among social structures, institutional practices, and intergroup understandings can provide new insight into how these dynamics unfold in schools and, in particular, help us make sense of the persistence of racialized academic hierarchies in a context like Riverview.

ACKNOWLEDGING AND NOT ACKNOWLEDGING THAT RACE MATTERS

When we spoke to adults at Riverview, we heard over and over again from teachers, staff, and administrators that racial issues remained at the school, but all these personnel also sought to make sure we understood that, as school administrator Ms. McDaniel said, "It's racist . . . it is inadvertent, though." Longtime white Riverview teacher Don Michaels put it this way:

> African American parents are especially aware of the fact that they need to be vigilant and that they need to come over and make sure that their students are being treated right. Because sometimes they aren't, and I hate to say it, but it's still true now. And I'm not saying in a sense that people are purposely doing something because of race, but institutional racism is there. I mean it just is. And I don't think anybody can deny that.

These community members discussed Riverview as a highly racialized educational terrain, but one in which adults operated with good intentions. What does the "inadvertent" or "institutional" racism Ms. McDaniel and Mr. Michaels discuss look like?

We use the terms *institutional* and *everyday* discrimination to describe the dynamics we witnessed because they best characterize the negative impact that even "inadvertent" racism can and does have, and because they highlight the particular ways that race currently works. By *institutional discrimination*, we mean such things as highly racialized school practices and structures (e.g., tracking) and the way school practices reward the social and cultural resources that students bring to school (e.g., cultural capital, social networks).[17] This kind of discrimination includes "decisions and processes that may not themselves have any explicit racial content but that have the consequence of producing or reinforcing racial disadvantage."[18] As Devah Pager and Heather Shepherd put it, this frame of institutional discrimination "encourages us to consider how opportunities may be allocated on the basis of race in the absence of direct prejudice or willful bias."[19] *Everyday discrimination* includes all the ways that race-based status beliefs and racial stereotypes shape interactions and expectations (often in ways that we are not even aware of)—"the subtle, pervasive discriminatory acts experienced by members of stigmatized groups on a daily basis."[20]

In trying to understand dynamics at Riverview, for the most part we did not find evidence of explicit racism or intentional favoritism. What we found instead was an expressed philosophy to close the achievement gap and an almost universally espoused commitment to equity but in a situation where almost everything about achievement in the schools is racialized—how school community members understand themselves and each other, how they interact with one another, how decisions are made about which students belong in which classes. Both formal and informal school practices and structures (including tracking, school discipline, and the many daily exchanges among students, parents, and school personnel) are in multiple and complex ways shaped by racial dynamics.

Differences abound not only with regard to achievement outcomes but also with regard to the actual organization of classrooms and spaces. Ms. Hicks, the African American counselor quoted at the beginning of the chapter, described the school this way:

> It's really diverse. Unfortunately, I don't think kids really have the opportunity to take advantage of that diversity, because when you look at the basic-level classes, you're going to walk in and 70 percent of those kids are going to be black. When you look at the honors classes, 70 percent of those kids are going to be white. So we have great diversity at this school, but it's like two ships traveling in parallel lines—they don't ever really cross. All the black kids play football; the white kids play soccer . . . If you look at the cheerleading squad, I think there are two white girls on the cheerleading squad. If you look at the volleyball team, it's almost all white. It's like two high schools. The white kids have found their niche, and it's not the same place as the black kids'.

Or as a longtime Riverview teacher put it:

> As much as it seems like we're together, we're integrated, we're not integrated. We're diverse, but we're not integrated. We just go to school here together.

Here two different Riverview staff members describe a context of formal integration and informal segregation, "two ships traveling in parallel lines" that rarely cross. Ironically, in trying to capture the extent of separation, the counselor actually underestimates the extent of the racialization of tracks. White students make up 48 percent of the student population but nearly 90 percent of the advanced placement classes and 80 percent of honors classes (see Figure 4.1). As we will discuss further, these stark realities are obvious to all. For newcomers, the situation can be shocking—how does a community that expresses an explicit commitment to diversity and equity tolerate such patterns? How does the de facto segregation become so taken-for-granted that adults and children can go to school every day without outrage or surprise?

While we are discussing institutional and everyday dynamics analytically as if they are distinct, in practice they overlap. To illustrate both forms and how they intersect, we provide an example from parental involvement at the school. There are clear aggregate racial differences in the resources that black and white and Latina/o Riverview families can draw on. While there are a number of middle-class minority families in the community,

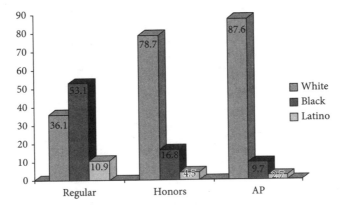

FIGURE 4.1. Percentage of Riverview Students across Tracks in All Subjects by Race

their resources aren't the same as those of white middle-class families, and there are fewer minority middle-class households.[21]

Race, Class, and Symbolic Capital

Riverview is a largely middle-class community with a median household income of nearly $70,000.[22] However, black and Latina/o families earn less than white families on average (see Table 4.1). While whites make up 69 percent of the city's population, they make up more than 93 percent of the residents living in the census tracts containing the top 20 percent of income earners.[23] These patterns highlight the extent to which the community is segregated across race and class lines. One common measure of segregation is the dissimilarity index, which examines how evenly dispersed different racial groups are across a city's neighborhoods (0 indicates complete integration, and 100 equals complete segregation). The Latina/o-white dissimilarity index is 48.6 and the black-white dissimilarity index is 68.1, meaning that in order for the population to be equally distributed across Riverview's neighborhoods, substantial numbers of each racial group would need to be relocated.[24]

Again, as this table makes clear, Riverview is a largely middle-class community. Median family incomes for all groups are above national averages, and poverty rates are well below national averages.[25] However, as is also true nationally, white families, on average, have far more resources

TABLE 4.1. Key Demographic Characteristics of the Riverview Community

	Median family income (2011 dollars)	Family living in owner-occupied housing (%)	Individuals below poverty line in 2010 (%)
White (non-Hispanic or Latino)	$81,000	58	8
Black (non-Hispanic or Latino)	$50,000	44	16
Hispanic or Latino	$46,000	37	19
Asian/Pacific Islander	$46,000	24	23
Native American	n/a	n/a	n/a

Source: U.S. Census Bureau, American Fact Finder. All numbers are rounded off to prevent easy identification of Riverview.

than do black and Latina/o families. These resources are not merely financial but translate into other advantages, such that white families tend to have more educational resources (computers, books, etc.), more flexibility in time to spend dealing with children's education (either monitoring homework or coming to school to intervene), and more cultural and social resources (ability to advocate successfully for a child in trouble, knowledge about how to provide best chances for college admissions, friends with influence at the school).

However, while it is true that white families have more resources, it is also true that in the daily functioning of the school they do not always have to actively deploy them to gain advantage. As we discussed in the last chapter, race and class often get conflated such that school personnel tend to assume that most white students come from middle- or upper-middle-class families and that most black and Latina/o students do not. These kinds of assumptions often operate at subconscious levels and involve presumptions about more than socioeconomic status, including presumptions about such things as likely family investment in education and student academic trajectory.

We first got a sense of these dynamics talking to Ms. Morgan, an African American teacher in the English Department, one day after a workshop at the school. She stopped one of us and said she had been thinking throughout the discussion about how she tends to worry more, to more closely monitor white students in her class. As she put it, it was not that she cared more about them or wanted them to excel more than her other students (if anything, the opposite was true), but that she "knew" that their parents were likely to be upset if they did not do well. As she put it, she was realizing that much of the time parents did not need to come in or say anything, *just the idea that they might was powerful.* Thus, if a white student was not doing well, she followed up, lest she hear about it from their parents later. In this way school personnel often read and then act on the most available and visible marker: racial phenotype. Skin color becomes a signifier for a host of other indicators, and whiteness becomes symbolic capital for white students. Parallel to the pattern we described with regard to disciplinary issues in the last chapter, as busy Riverview personnel move through their day and make decisions about academic concerns, they are not only responding to actual parental interventions but also often acting in anticipation of likely or imagined probable parental pressure or concern. Like Ms. Morgan, many other Riverview staff describe themselves acting proactively, often in advance of any immediate parent request. As you'll see further from the examples below, none of the actions taken by school personnel are explicitly racial in nature. And even more important for understanding how institutional discrimination works, the point we are highlighting here is that the resources white families have access to (including whiteness itself) pay off in many subtle ways in large part because of how the school responds to them. That is, not only do we need to pay attention to the fact that white families on aggregate have more resources to deploy, but we also need to attend to how the school's interactional practices, rules, and structures treat whiteness as a symbolic resource and make it possible for racial resources to pay off to the advantage of white students.

Ms. Hicks, a counselor, talked about how this often works:

> It's hard, because I would love to say, "Yes, they're all treated the same." But I think the reality is they're not. The squeaky wheel gets the oil. So if you're a parent, and you come, and you say, "My child got a C. You need to help me figure it out." And I know that you're going to call me every day, I'm going to go to that teacher and say, "You know what? What's going on? Tell me what's happening." After I find out what's happening, I'm going to get back to that parent. I'm going to advocate for that kid. Whereas, if you are a kid and your parents are not going to call me every day or hasn't called me, we have 286 kids on our caseload, it could take me a month to realize that you have two or three C's.

As Ms. Hicks describes, her caseload is such that it is difficult to closely manage, much less keep track of, hundreds of students' needs. However, when parents make requests, or have made them in the past, or if she *recognizes* a parent as one who is likely to call every day, then she becomes an advocate. Above, she discusses both *actual* calls and *likely* calls, both actual and anticipated "squeakiness." Teacher Don Michaels also spoke to this issue of "squeaky wheel" parents:

> It goes back to that issue about which parents are gonna play an active role, and the squeaky wheel and so on. And I know just from conversations with teachers there are some teachers that will simply say "you know this kid really didn't deserve the C- but I knew that if I gave him a D + I was going to get a lot of grief from the parent," and the tradition has tended to be that it's more likely to be a white parent than it's going to be the black parent.

Bill, a member of the school's safety department, talked about similar dynamics with regard to management of school infractions:

> You know, sometimes I see minority students that may be having a problem or get into situations, and sometime the school almost can sense that a parent won't get involved; and the process is kind of slower. When there's a student and they know the parent is gonna get involved, it tends to be a different process and the speed of the assistance kind of (laughs) speeds up.

Bill describes fellow staff "sensing" that a parent will or won't get involved and thus acting accordingly—with more or less perceived pressure to move quickly.

As these examples illustrate, school personnel do tend to describe different aggregate involvement patterns between white and minority families. But they also describe how those experiences generalize to cases where parents do not even get involved because they do not need to. Moreover, what they consistently describe are the ways in which such actual or anticipated parental intervention *pays off* with quite different outcomes for the students. This differential treatment is a matter of school practice and thus policy—even if implicitly so.

Here the performative aspects of organizational routines are highly consequential and in stark contrast to the school's formal or ostensive aspect. As Mr. Webber, one of the associate principals who has been worried about such school practices for some time, put it:

> The school has a responsibility to advocate for those kids who do not have advocates and to also try and prepare those kids who come unprepared ... We live in a society where not every parent can give the kind of time and attention that we would want to see them give. We certainly can't fault them for it ... We still have a responsibility for kids to do the best we can for them ... I mean, that's why equity is so important. A level playing field. To provide the best teachers, to provide the best experiences. Our graduation requirements are not graduation requirements for those who come to us best prepared to do school and with home support. They're graduation requirements for everybody ... because it's right and because it's good, and I think so much of what we have to do has to come out of that framework.

What these numerous examples from different school community members begin to capture are the many small ways that racial dynamics contribute to different school outcomes. As part of school structures, policies, practices, and everyday interactions, these dynamics involve not only real, material racial inequalities but also the status beliefs that are a part of daily life.

INSTITUTIONAL DISCRIMINATION, SYMBOLIC CAPITAL, AND PERFORMANCE EXPECTATIONS

To help understand the dynamics of institutional and everyday discrimination and how the two types intersect, we turn to some theory from social psychology. This work is useful for framing not only how race became so consequential, but particularly for thinking about these dynamics in places like schools where almost everyone has good intentions, expresses support for diversity, and wants all students to do well.

In recent decades, social psychologists have put extensive energy into trying to understand how social identities and status characteristics like race or gender organize social relations. The first relevant theory comes from the work of Cecilia Ridgeway and her colleagues on *expectation states theory*.[26] In many ways, expectation states theory echoes the notion of symbolic capital that we discussed earlier. Like the abundant work in psychology on implicit bias,[27] expectation states theory suggests that status characteristics like race influence everyday interaction because these characteristics shape "performance expectations." The theory suggests that we read someone's race, gender, or other status characteristic and anticipate whether she will make more or less valuable contributions than others because of her status. Repeated experiments have shown actors consistently defer to those with high status, giving them more chances to participate.[28] The beliefs that fuel performance expectations are based on widely held ideas, like stereotypes, in the culture, associating greater social worthiness and competence with certain categories or status characteristics (e.g., whites). Most of their effects happen outside conscious thought—people are not literally weighing characteristics ("Okay, he is white and male and therefore should get extra time to speak"). Thus, it isn't thoughtful and deliberate privileging, but an implicit and unconscious process. Latina mom Adriana spoke of these kinds of dynamics in our interview with her:

INTERVIEWER: So you think that white, African American, and
Latino children are treated the same in Riverview schools?

ADRIANA: I think expectations for kids of color are different.

INTERVIEWER: What do you mean by different?

ADRIANA: I think expectations are less. I think you have to prove
yourself. I think you have probably most white kids coming
into school, and the assumption is they're going to be a particular kind of kid and they can learn in a particular way. It's a positive assumption. I think that there's not necessarily a positive
assumption for most kids of color. And I think those kids have
a burden to sort of prove that they can do as well.

As this mother describes, the differences in expectations go both ways,
with "positive assumptions" for white kids and a burden for kids of color
to "prove that they can do well." Like most parents we interviewed, she was
not implying that a vigorously racist staff was deliberately treating kids
differently, but rather, that subtle expectation differences lead to quite different contexts of engagement for students.

In fact, *expectations states theory* is a theory of *behavior*, not thought,
and thus helps us see how processes can occur broadly and not just among
those with strong conscious prejudices—it is not about whether you are
individually sexist or racist but about the fact that whites, for example,
are generally believed to be more competent than people of color. This
assumption makes race a salient status characteristic in mixed settings
and therefore impacts performance expectations formed by everyone in
the setting, including nonracist whites and confident people of color.[29]

Performance expectations also tend to shape behavior in self-fulfilling
ways, as the greater performance expectations are for people, the more
chances they get to perform, the more likely they are to speak up, the more
likely their contributions are going to be positively evaluated and affirmed.
Additionally important for understanding Riverview is that when socially
valued rewards like track placement or school awards are distributed
unequally, these reward differences can reinforce performance expectations. By creating differential expectations of performance or outcomes,
the unequal rewards appear to be "deserved." For example, those in high
tracks are thought to be enrolled in them because they are smarter and
deserve to be there.

Obviously, how the people involved in interactions behave matters, and when an actor is consistently assertive and engaging in high-status behavior, it can lead others to have different performance expectations. But this works only in limited ways. Low-status groups often report that they have to perform at *higher* levels to be judged as *equally* competent (or as the old saying goes, "work twice as hard to be considered half as good").[30] This is because when a low-status actor performs well, their performance is scrutinized since it is inconsistent with expectations for them. Thus, not only are lower status members given fewer opportunities to participate, but when they do, their performances are evaluated by stricter standards, which makes it more difficult for their performances to be judged competent and harder for them to achieve high status in groups.[31] It is also true, as the earlier quotes illustrate, that when members of high-status groups do not perform well, the fact generates surprise, concern, and the need for possible intervention. The power of these dynamics, sometimes called *expectancy effects*, lies not in the momentary beliefs, brief student-teacher interactions, and single outcomes, but in the *"cumulative consequences of entrenched beliefs about ability over the course of a school career"* (emphasis added).[32]

The many daily exchanges between teachers and students (e.g., the amount of time allotted to answer a question, the kinds of feedback given) communicate to students whether they are expected to succeed. Talking about these dynamics at Riverview, one administrator stated, "I don't care how small it is. You know, from the teacher who says, 'You won't be able to do that.' To the counselor who says, 'Oh, you can't go to college.' There's little things all along that are discouraging." Claude Steele has discussed some of these dynamics as "cues" in his writing on *stereotype threat*.[33]

In Claude Steele and colleagues' research on stereotype threat, they show that the negative stereotypes associated with status identities affect performance for all groups when they are operating in a domain in which the stereotype is relevant (e.g., the elderly with memory tasks, girls with math tests, etc.). To quote Steele, stereotype threat involves the "threat of being viewed through the lens of a negative stereotype, or the fear of doing something (e.g., performing badly on a standardized test) that would inadvertently confirm that stereotype."[34] Multiple experimental situations confirmed that when stereotype threat arises, testers perform worse than predicted on standardized tests. The effect for performance is both to dampen black students' outcomes and to lift white students' outcomes.[35]

Importantly, research shows that such effects are not a result of some internalized dynamic that we carry around with us or are predisposed to, but are responsive to the context and contextual "cues" therein (e.g., like racialized tracking) that convey whether the negative stereotype about our group might be at play in a particular place.

These theories, *expectation states theory* (EST) and *stereotype threat*, essentially capture how the cultural beliefs and collective understandings of race (i.e., racial ideology) that we have discussed impact behavior and evaluation at the micro or meso level and reproduce status hierarchies. For example, EST suggests that rather than seeing differential treatment as contradictory or unusual, we should expect to find it in a context like Riverview. EST predicts different performance expectations in classrooms, study groups, and so on, and suggests some of the mechanisms at work that allow racially disparate patterns to emerge.

RACIALIZED TRACKING

In fact, as we saw from Figure 4.1, tracking at the school is highly stratified by race. White students are heavily overrepresented in honors and AP courses, while black and Latina/o students are heavily overrepresented in low-track courses.[36] However, not only is the distribution of students in tracks highly racialized, but the tracks themselves have become racialized. Thus, the local discourse is not just that some kinds of kids tend to be in certain classes but that those classrooms have become racialized spaces.

Julius, an upper-middle-class, high-achieving black student, described the school this way: "The fact is that Riverview is two schools in one. There is the honors white school, and then there's the other school." Similarly, Richard, a high-achieving white student, speculated, "I mean, if you look at the numbers, I'm betting there are more white kids that are in the honors classes, and more black kids that are in minority classes." As these quotes from Riverview juniors show, the tracks themselves have become identified as *belonging* to different racial groups. They are not just high and low tracks but "honors white" and "minority classes." Over time, community members come to generalize the fact that white students are more often in high tracks to those being white tracks, tracks where white students belong and deserve to be. Black and Latina/o students' overrepresentation in basic and remedial classes translates into those being "minority" spaces. These status hierarchies get translated into performance expectations in multiple ways.[37]

When we spoke to Maurice Webber, he said, with a shake of his head, "I think that sometimes the expectations [for black and Latina/o students] are lower." These expectations get communicated to students in lots of subtle ways. A white teacher described a peer's recent behavior thusly: "There was a teacher who had a minority student come into their honors class, and, you know, he was your stereotypical baggy jeans, big shirt, hat turned sideways, you know, and she said to him, 'You know, I think you belong in my next period, you're too early' and assumed that he was a general student. And he's like, 'No, no my schedule says I belong here.'" Here she describes how, in implicit ways, "black," and particularly the "wrong" performance of blackness (baggy jeans, big shirt, hat turned sideways), signals "not-honors" to adults in the school. The teacher's resulting reaction to question the student's presence in her honors class also signals to him key information about how he is perceived.

Both teachers and students reported these kinds of interactions between race and performance expectations. In his interview, Julius, the high-achieving African American student, reported his struggle with getting into high-track courses:

> My freshman teacher didn't like me. She didn't recommend me for U.S. History AP. My mom had to spend a couple of hours on the phone getting me into the class. Even though I'm a kid who takes extremely hard classes and gets good grades, they just don't let you in. They make it very, very difficult for you to take the classes you want.

Daryl, an African American sophomore, offered, "They [teachers] don't expect much from black males." And many of the staff of color concurred. As Ms. Tyson, a school secretary, put it, "Well, if you are a student of color, could be an African American student or Latino, there are assumptions that you don't care about school, that you . . . you don't have the capability of being successful in school. And so those are negative messages that they have to deal with, ah, every day." One high-achieving black student talked about the strategy she uses to try to preempt low-performance expectations:

> NIA: The first week of that class, I basically let my teacher know how I am. I get to know my teacher. I just prove myself to the teacher the first week. Like I don't even allow him or her to judge me by

my cover. Right away I let them know this is how I am. Like, "I'm not how you think I would be."

INTERVIEWER: So you're, in a sense, sort of preempting that so before they can. . .

NIA: Right. So before. . .

INTERVIEWER: Make a judgment that you. . .

NIA: Yeah. Before they can make any type of judgment of me being a certain way or, you know, because of that in their mind, they want to treat me a certain way. I don't even allow for that to get to that stage. I just right away tell them like, "I do my homework, I work hard, I'm very happy, and this and this and this. You don't have to worry about me."

Nia makes it clear that she does not want teachers to "judge [her] by her cover"; she is deeply familiar with the reality that much of the experimental research on performance expectations documents—that her race or "cover" will lead many to expect less of her—and she strategically communicates to her teachers that no matter what they think about and expect of black students generally, they should expect a lot from her.

It was not only African American students and staff who observed these dynamics. A number of white students reported perceptions among school officials that white students were smarter and better behaved. Gabe, a white junior, reported:

> I'm white, so I'm expected to be smarter. Usually, when someone sees me, they always think I'm smarter than most people . . . I think that usually the perception is . . . that black people are dumber than white people, and Hispanics are not as smart as everyone else . . . So if you have a really smart black person, that's when you see the most, "That's weird." In one of my classes, there's one black kid in the entire class; there's zero Hispanics. It's all just white people. And that's, it's weird.

As he puts it, Riverview community members experience dissonance when exposed to "a really smart black person" because the pairing does not mesh with expectations in a context in which there are large numbers of black students in the school and almost none in advanced classes. The racially stratified academic hierarchy seems to confirm widespread stereotypes about intelligence and makes seeing a smart black person "weird." Gabe registers the strangeness of the whole situation, however, when he acknowledges that the whiteness of his advanced classes is, in fact, also "weird." Leah, a white student, spoke about these widespread racial stereotypes also, putting it this way:

> I definitely think that there are stereotypes that go along with all races . . . and whites are not excluded . . . So I feel like people see me, I'm like a middle-class white girl. You know, so . . . I feel like people expect . . . me to be a certain way. They expect me to be respectful and quiet and intelligent and stuff like that.

For Leah, being white meant that people held high expectations for her in the classroom *because* she was white. People expect a "middle-class white girl" to be "respectful and intelligent." White students like Leah, particularly girls, reported receiving the benefit of the doubt across school contexts, inside and outside of the classroom.

Students also reported these dynamics in their interactions with other students. Maria, a Latina sophomore, stated, "Well, there's been times where I've been in classes with white kids, and I tried my best at times. When I do, the white girls, they're always going in their own little clique, and look at the Mexicans as if we were dumb or something. It just makes us feel bad." Students reported that their classmates engaged in subtle practices that communicated that they felt that black and Latina/o students were less capable academically. David, a high-achieving black junior, put it this way:

> I just think that kids aren't used to seeing a successful . . . black male student. Whenever I do something that's . . . just like normal. They're like, "Whoa." . . . A lot of times racism is indirect. They won't come out directly and say, "Whoa. You're black. Black males aren't supposed to do that." There's like undertones and stuff that you can kind of pick up.

Other students also suggested that there were ways that classmates made other students feel ostracized. One student, Juanita, a high-achieving Latina junior, discussed how one African American student was treated as an outsider in her ninth-grade biology class:

> When I was a freshman, I was in my biology class . . . there were a couple of us who were Hispanic, and then there was this one African

American girl . . . I, at least, always felt that a bunch of the kids in my class weren't so accepting of her, because it was like she was intruding on "us," our otherwise perfect biology class. I never liked that. . . . It was like, "Why is she in the honors class?" The vibe some people give off.

Experienced as the kind of racial microaggressions discussed in the previous chapter, these exchanges are exactly the kinds of identity threat cues that signal to students that negative racial stereotypes about their group are at play. This echoes previous research by Karolyn Tyson and others that similarly has found that black students in high-track classes experience lots of subtle and not-so-subtle resistance to their presence from white peers.[38]

These kinds of cues can come not only from interpersonal interactions but also from institutional arrangements. Not only do black and Latina/o students feel the brunt of the kinds of interactions Maria, Ms. Tyson, and Daryl describe, but the ever-present fact of racialized tracking links race with achievement in a manner with which they have to contend.[39] Citing an example of racialized tracking's effect, Joan Cristy, a special education teacher at the school, explains how the experience of being in a special education class is qualitatively different for different groups:

MS. CRISTY: If a new kid comes in the class and they're any other . . . race [than black, kids will say], "You don't belong here. This is the black class." . . . And [the new students] hang outside in the hallways until after the bell. And it's not because they're trying to be a jerk and push the limits, it's because they don't want to be identified.

INTERVIEWER: They don't want people to know they're coming in this room?

MS. CRISTY: Um hum (affirmative). And I don't think it's just because of Special Ed, I also think it has to do with race and just, like, see we're all put in a box. And that's because they're not fortunate to be in a lot of classes where they're all mixed. They don't see that just because of the *nature of things*. But they kind of [understand the class as] "it's black and we're dumb." So something has been taught, something has gone to them through their educational experience, which is just so painful. You know? And yet—then on the other side, you know, the Latino kids or the white kids who also are in Special Ed, they have the same thing and it's just

> simply because they know they're in different classes. "I'm differ-
> ent." *They just happen to associate it with their individuality.*

We have added emphasis here to two points. One is Ms. Cristy's comment that the fact that these students are never in classes where "they're
all mixed" is "because of the nature of things." It is certainly not the
nature of things but rather the *structure of things*—how classes are organized—that generates these patterns. Moreover, whereas she observes
that for black students placement in special education becomes evidence
of their collective lack of ability, for other students, as she put it, "they
just happen to associate it with their individuality." In the case of the
white students, this echoes the general pattern where white students are
understood (by others and themselves) as individuals with specific idio-
syncratic experiences.

PERFORMANCE EXPECTATIONS, TRACKING, AND BLACK PARENTS

The patterns reported by students and staff were echoed in our conversations with black parents. For example, many black parents were cognizant
of and concerned about low expectations for their children. They talked
about these low expectations as a burden they needed to contend with in
supporting their children's education. When we asked Barbara about what
caused racial differences in school outcomes, she argued:

> I think expectations are jaded. And I think they sometimes
> judge people by very superficial things. Just because you don't
> speak the King's English doesn't mean you're not intelligent.
> Sometimes a child may be speaking a certain kind of way, and
> they just make assumptions about [how] well they can do or
> where they belong.

In addition to believing that teachers had low expectations for their children, some black parents also talked about teachers' lower expectations
of *them*. For instance, Pamela argued that among teachers, "the expectation is that a lot of students, mainly students of color, just don't have the
parents that care." Parents recognized that these lower expectations had

multiple effects, for instance, making it less likely that their children would get placed in high-level courses and making it more difficult for them to intervene on their children's behalf.

Several black parents discussed advocating to get their children into honors and AP classes. While high school course-placement decisions were made based on a combination of teacher recommendations, students' grades, and test scores, parents could also override the school's decisions. As we discuss in detail in the next chapter, white parents exercised this right frequently and generally experienced very little resistance (and even encouragement) from school staff members. In contrast, many black parents who sought to exercise this same right experienced resistance from school staff. They characterized their communications with the school staff using words like "conflict," "fight," and "resistance." In some ways, this resistance seemed to reinforce the perception of upper-level classrooms as "white" spaces and communicated to parents that staff members doubted their children's ability to handle these rigorous classes.

When Robin's son was in eighth grade, he "was getting B's, almost A's" in algebra, so she contacted his teacher about the possibility of her son enrolling in honors classes in ninth grade at Riverview High School:

> I had a conversation with his eighth-grade math teacher about him being in honors level classes; that was toward the end of the year in the spring. For some reason, the teacher just turned on me after that, after I started asking about him being in honors-level classes. He seemed supportive; but then, a month later, he started failing my son. My son was doing excellent. . . . the eighth-grade math teacher sabotaged him . . . and gave him a D or an F, at the end of the year. . . . so when his papers came to Riverview, the recommendation didn't match. So the math chair called and explained that she thought he should repeat algebra in high school. I had to fight for that. It was a big mess.

While Robin was an active parent and intervened in the course-placement process, she reports that she was not fully aware that parents had the *final say* in their children's course placements. She learned about parents' ability to override the school's decision "after I had been fighting with the high school. After freshman year, I strongly demanded that he be in an honors-level English class." So while parents have the ability to override placements, this was not communicated to Robin until after her child's freshman year was over.

When we asked another parent, Barbara, about how students were placed in certain classes, she said, "I know that they generally make decisions . . . for honors, you can, a lot of parents don't know this, but you can take honors if you want to. You don't have to be recommended for honors." Even with this knowledge, she discusses conflicts that she has had with teachers over her daughter's placements:

> I had an argument with the teacher when my child was a freshman because she'd taken the exam that they take, the standardized exam. She doesn't do very well on standardized tests. She didn't do very well. I wanted her in the honors track in humanities. The teacher said, "Well, she did this and that on the test." I said, "Yes, but her middle school teachers highly recommended her for the honors humanities track. These are teachers who've known her through the years. You're going to tell me on the basis of one test that she shouldn't be on the humanities honors track?" I said, "Well, if you won't let her in, then I'm going to the principal, because I happen to know that if I think she should go in there, she can go in there." And so she did. She's an excellent student. But, despite the fact that they had strong recommendations from her middle school teachers, they were going to tell me just based on this one entrance test. I was not standing for it. I'm sure a lot of parents would have.

Other parents reported facing similar conflicts with the school. Pamela, who is a teacher in one of Riverview's elementary schools, argued that black students often needed advocates to get them into higher-level classes. While discussing her daughter's placement process when she entered the high school, Pamela talked about getting support from her eighth-grade teacher:

> When my child was in eighth-grade, she was a student at the school that I'm teaching at. Her language arts teacher collected a portfolio of work for all the students. They make placements of the students in their eighth grade year by a test and also teacher recommendation. The teacher recommended that my child be put in a mixed-honors class. . . . But if you have someone that's fighting for you to be put in the mixed-honors classes, then you have the opportunity to move up into mostly honors classes. But you have to get the push to be first in the mixed-honors to be able to have the opportunity to go up to honors.

While Pamela discusses getting support from this teacher, the teacher still had to fight with the high school department chair to get her daughter in the mixed-level language arts class. "I know that the department chair is who her language arts teacher had to go to fight for her to be in the mixed-honors class. She had to go fight with the department chair." She added that African American students face more challenges getting into higher-level classes:

> If you're a high achieving African American student that doesn't do well on tests, you need someone when you're first going into the high school to put in a good word for you, to say, "This student doesn't need to be in these [basic] courses. This student needs to be challenged with the students that are in the honors courses because they're able to do that same kind of work."

In both Barbara and Pamela's cases, they had the support of middle-school teachers and prior academic performance on their side, but a teacher and the department chair resisted placing their children in honors courses. This in a system in which parents are supposed to have the final say and decisions are not supposed to rely on test scores alone. As we discuss in the next chapter, rarely did white parents we interviewed report this level of resistance regarding course enrollment changes. This represents an added burden faced by black parents to get something that is more easily available to white parents.

To be sure, not all black parents reported resistance. Some were able to intervene and gain access to honors classes when their children had originally been placed in regular-level classes. For instance, Davina discussed a smooth process of getting the schools to change her daughter's course placement:

> My daughter, she on her standardized tests . . . she did not do very well. And she was an honors student throughout her time at junior high. And then I had to, I decided that she needs to be placed in certain classes at certain levels, because I know she could do well because she has always done well. So I called the school and asked her to be placed, in certain classes at certain levels, because . . . And she was placed in those classes. And the general classes she was placed in, she was bored in them you know, but the other classes she did fine. She did well. So I was glad that you know at RHS, at least you could call to say you know that. "I know my child did not [do] so well on those standardized tests, but I know she can do better and if she's

placed in these classes at a higher level, I know she will perform."
And that was done. And I'm happy I was able to do that.

However, while Davina and a few other black parents experienced smooth placement processes, this was not typical.

While getting into upper-level classes could be a challenge in and of itself, parents were also concerned with racial dynamics in those classes and how their children dealt with racial isolation once they got there. Shana talked about her son's experience in his AP classes when he attended Riverview:

> With the AP classes . . . he took European History AP, there were three African American students and two of them were bi-racial. He was the total African male. And there were three classes offered. There were three European History classes and they had an activity called the salon, where the students had to dress up as 18th-century figures and then present maybe, "I like Beethoven and this is what I did" or whatever, and there were no African American students. And as they move up through the levels at the high school, like in my son's honors English class, there are three African Americans out of 26 kids. In each of the classes he has at the honors level, it may be him and one other child. And that seems to be the norm at the high school.

Shana argued that the racial composition of the classes made her son feel isolated to the extent that he wanted to leave the honors class:

> So last year, my son asked why, if all the other black kids don't have to take the honors classes, why is he required to take them when the work was more vigorous and he could just really take regular classes and be fine and be with the other kids that were African American. And I explained to him about why it's important to take honors classes. How that will help him with his future, and that you can't always worry about what the peers do because there will come a point where the peers will be left behind and you must move forward.

Like Shana, Robin described her son as experiencing these classes as white-dominated spaces in which they were not fully integrated:

> I feel that [he's] a black child in a white world with no help, no support, no leadership, he feels kind of alone. He feels good when he's with his friends, you know, doing whatever the friends do. But then when he goes to his honors classes, he's the minority. That is one of

the biggest problems with Riverview High School. In an honors-level class . . . You're still a minority. You're a minority in the country; now you're a minority in your educational system.

Robin worried about the real educational and psychosocial implications for her child. These experiences had the potential to impact his academic performance and his emotional well-being. As we have discussed previously, racialized tracking can reinforce lower expectations for black students, trigger stereotype threat, and lead to them experience racial microaggressions based on interactions with classmates and teachers as well as the structure of the classes themselves. Despite the many challenges black parents had in getting their kids into upper-level classes and their concerns about their children's experiences once they got there, there were lots of reasons why those who had the knowledge and capital to do so still pursued such classes.

TRACKING'S CONSEQUENCES

Not only does track placement have consequences for *students' sense of self,* track placements also have consequences for the *curricula they receive,* and for their treatment more generally. For example, when Mr. Webber was telling us of his concern about how race shaped expectations, he struggled for a moment to convey exactly what he meant and why he was so worried, but then went on to say:

> I have walked too often into lower-level classes that are predominantly black or Latino . . . and found the activities that are going on, the instructional activity, to be less than or a lower quality than I would find in some other classrooms. It is more likely in a [lower level] that is predominantly black and Latino that if students finish, they will be finished a few minutes before the bell at the end of the period and standing at the door, whereas in the predominantly white honors classrooms, teaching goes up to the bell. You know, bell to bell teaching. It's that kind of thing. It's that kind of thing. The requirement for assignments may be different and the question is, why?

Lower expectations for black and Latina/o students not only means they are more often in lower-level classes but that those classes collectively provide a less rigorous educational experience. Abundant research over the last 30 years has found that the achievement differences between those in high and low tracks grows over time no matter where students begin in terms of test scores.[40] Those placed in low tracks learn less/show lesser gains over time than similarly situated high-track students. The benefits to high-track students seem to be not the grouping itself, but the enhanced curriculum, special resources, and supports. Everyone, regardless of prior achievement, benefits from the placement.

Like findings elsewhere, evidence from a number of sources at Riverview suggests that lower-track classes offer lower-quality educational opportunities with less experienced teachers and less challenging instruction. African American history teacher Vesta Paul put it this way:

> You give that new teacher three classes of the lowest-achieving students outside of special ed in the school, and you call that setting the students up for success? That's not right. The students that are at the lowest level, at the bottom of the gap, they need the best teachers in school.[41]

We got numerous casual comments from community members about the widely acknowledged fact that the upper-level courses provide a stronger educational experience. White Riverview parent Janet stated, "Well, and everybody told us if she didn't take the honors classes she would be bored silly ... This is what they say is that the teaching quality is not as good amongst the teachers who don't teach honors." In a slightly different vein, another white parent responded to a question about racial inequities in the school by raising questions about lower-track classes:

INTERVIEWER: Do you think that white, African American, and Hispanic students are treated the same in the Riverview schools?

MARGARET: You know, I don't know. I don't know about kids in sort of the ... quote, unquote "basic" classes. I don't know how that's perceived. I mean my sense is that, um, it's a different school for those kids, but I don't know if it's the color of their skin or if it's sort of the ... the track that they're on academically.

Here Margaret indicates that because race and track are so deeply intertwined at Riverview, it is hard to know if the problem with "basic" classes is the "color" of most of the students in them or the "track" itself.

Teachers also reported these patterns. Mike Sellers, a white social studies teacher, put it this way:

> I think there's some structural issues just flat out with . . . tracking. . . . whether people admit it or not, it is a destructive force in some kids' lives. In particular, minority kids . . . Some of these classes that are at the lower level aren't taught at the level which would allow kids to do college work in three years or whatever. So there's a huge thing. What are we doing with our (sighs) our so called "basic-ability" students? Are we, you know, expecting enough of those kids too, so that they can meet the challenges that they're going to get [in college] or whatever? . . . I think there's too much of a disconnect in expectations.

Mr. Sellers bemoans the fact that tracking leaves some students underprepared for the next stage of their academic journey. Mr. Webber raises similar issues:

> Academically, the rigor in the classroom is often determined by the level, which . . . Okay. My belief is that a "regular" class should be as challenging for a "regular" student as an AP class ought to be for an AP student. Being in level two ought to still be college credit . . . because we want everyone to go to college. The way our vision statement runs, our mission statement, even a "remedial" student is college bound. . . . maybe at a different pace, different rate, but still college bound. Every class ought to be challenging, every class ought to force students to learn and to grow. But not every class does. And, yes, it's true. The experience students have is often determined by the track.

As he points out, what often takes place in classrooms (what we might think of as the performative aspects of organizational routines) is in direct conflict with the school's explicit commitment to provide students with a college-preparatory curriculum (the ostensive aspect of organizational routines). The official story, the ostensive aspects of the organizational routines of tracking, still presents it as a race-neutral process with race-neutral consequences. It is purported to objectively place those of different aptitude, skill, and commitment into the appropriate tracks and then to provide those in different tracks with a curriculum that addresses their needs. Institutionally, the ostensive aspect buttresses the imagined fairness of the process. This legitimizes the process of placement and encourages both those in high and low tracks to feel like they are where they deserve to be even as the actual performance of the tracking routines (both in placement and implementation) is far from race neutral.

Do these track placements just reflect an unfortunate but "real" difference in students' academic potential or commitment? Interestingly, a recent experiment by a relatively new teacher in the school confronted this issue directly. As with all subjects, there are major differences in students' mathematics course taking, which begins early on in their educational careers. During fourth grade, students are tested in mathematics. Based on a combination of those tests and teachers' recommendations, each student is then placed on one of two different "tracks," one that leads to higher-level mathematics in high school (e.g., calculus by twelfth grade) and one that does not. By fifth grade, the vast majority of students placed in the upper-level mathematics sequence are white. By eighth grade, most of these students have taken Algebra I, a critical milestone for students who want to reach high-level mathematics in high school. Historically, by the time students reached the twelfth grade, very few African American and Latina/o students were in upper-level mathematics courses.

After joining Riverview and being surprised about the racial demographics in AP math, Mr. Bettencourt, a white longtime public school teacher, decided to try to remedy this situation by starting a new program. Realizing that most African American and Latina/o students in the high school were never going to have an opportunity to take advanced or AP math courses unless their coursework was accelerated, this teacher issued an invitation to students doing well in Algebra I to spend four hours a day with him for six weeks in the summer to take geometry so they could essentially catch up to those who had been tracked into the accelerated program years before. Over three-quarters of the invited students accepted. Within a few years, he had dramatically increased the number of African American and Latina/o students taking calculus at the high school. While not systematic in its design, this experiment demonstrates that structural arrangements in the school were serving to narrow options for some students—students who are capable of succeeding in advanced courses that they have not historically been channeled into.[42]

As described by those we spoke to, the kinds of institutional processes that lead to tracking include multiple discretionary steps where more subtle processes are at work (e.g., processes related to teachers' expectations of students). Literature on occupational inequality shows that in places where discretion is possible, discrimination is likely.[43] As Mr. Bettencourt stated with regard to tracking in mathematics:

> You know that in Riverview, probably the impetus behind that isn't racist, but it plays out because of how race plays out in Riverview and dovetails with class and etc., etc., that, you know, not that many of the minority kids are already a year ahead. Some are, an appreciable number are, but percentage wise, not that many.

A great deal of recent research has shown the multitude of ways that racial stereotypes are a part of everyday school life, negatively affecting students of color.[44] In the implementation of programs such as the math-tracking practice in the district, even school personnel with the best intentions might well be hindering minority achievement without doing so deliberately.

Consequences of Racialized Tracking for Racial Attitudes and Understandings

The structure of tracking in schools like Riverview is troubling for a number of reasons, both academic and nonacademic. As we have already indicated, there was lots of evidence at Riverview that tracking conveyed complicated messages to those on the bottom and at the top about race and ability. Ms. McDaniel, a top-level school administrator who was soon to retire, spoke about it this way:

> I think kids just don't realize that they can do things. They just kind of accept that role. You know, it's like, "I'm really not a good athlete, so I don't want to go out and do this in gym." You know, everybody is not Michael Jordan, but you can still contribute to a team ... I don't even know if they really think about it too much anymore ... But I think they just kind of accept it. ... This is kind of a crass statement, [but they must wonder] ... "How did everybody white get to be really smart?" And it's another piece ... chipping away ... that's kind of the little insult. "Why am I not with them? We were always together." So. You know. ... I know that they think about it, but I think another piece of it is we just really don't talk enough about it. You know, *it just happens.*

What Ms. McDaniel captures is the conundrum of institutional discrimination—this kind of chipping away in which there are no clear perpetrators—things *just happen*, but happen in a way that consistently benefits some more than others. Over time, students can come to, as she put it, "accept that role." When we spoke to Elaine Peters, a senior white district administrator, about why there were not more black and Latina/o students in high-level classes, she said:

> Well, one, it's historical. [They think] "I don't belong here." But too, it is recruitment. Yeah, I think in a situation, as much as I can imagine what it would be like to be an African American kid in this high school, I wouldn't see—unless I'm being pushed by home or pushed by a teacher and home to do so, or a group of friends, which is possible—I wouldn't see that as where I needed to end up. But if I'm even an average, strong white student, my kids, my friends are gonna be there. I mean it's gonna kind of sweep me along. So we have to orchestrate the recruitment. You belong here . . .

Here, Ms. Peters describes racialized tracking as a kind of institutional inertia. It conveys not only, "this is the way it is" but "this is the way it should be"—communicating to students where they belong and sweeping them along. As Karolyn Tyson found in her research on North Carolina schools, students internalize institutional messages about who is and who isn't smart, and that information shapes their own sense of which courses they belong in. "Students' deliberations center in large part on their assessments of where they belong: that is, where they believe they will be most comfortable both academically and socially . . . The new laissez-faire system of tracking operates to produce outcomes not unlike the older, more formal system."[45]

Don Michaels discusses what some of the long-term consequences of low institutional and interpersonal expectations can be:

> We have so many kids that are very capable but, for whatever reason, have never been pushed to their limits, and it's really hard when I get them as juniors and [getting choked up] excuse me, I didn't realize this was gonna catch me like that but I haven't thought about it in a long time. It's really hard when you get them as juniors to try to do damage control there, and oftentimes that's just what it is—damage control—because they've lost faith in themselves, they don't trust the system, and it's really hard to get them to realize what they're capable of doing in their lives.

All of three of these school staff describe a process which builds over time, "chipping away," and all express the need for explicit action in opposition to even begin to affect change—direct conversation, orchestrated recruitment, engaged damage control. But as we discuss shortly, such direct action faces a number of barriers.

Importantly, tracking not only conveys multiple messages to students about what they are capable of but also conveys messages about "race" in general. As we will discuss more in the next chapter, several parents spoke to us about how the racialization of tracking shapes students' ideas about race:

> MRS. FOSTER: I have been unpleasantly made aware of how my children speak . . . along racial lines after they're at the high school. I mean they're much more, ah, I don't want to say prejudiced, but you know, [they're] much more willing to group people into groups, which was not the case at the parochial school . . . in comments like, "The basic classes are mostly African American and Hispanic kids" and "All they do is fool around and they're not interested in their education." You know, I mean blanket kind of statements like that which are . . . you know, is that true? Could be . . . I think because race and socioeconomic level is so often linked in the United States that perhaps that's the way they see it.
>
> INTERVIEWER: Do you intervene when they say stuff like that?
>
> MRS. FOSTER: Yeah, but, you know, I don't think I'm making an impression because their experience is different than what I'm telling them.

As Mrs. Fosters implies, abstract sentiments about racial equality often ring hollow in the context of experiential data that suggest otherwise. Jim, a white longtime member of the school safety staff, spoke of tracking and its effects on how students understand each other the minute we asked about "achievement gaps" at the school:

> JIM: I believe that too many white people in this building harbor negative conceptions of the ability, of the intellectual abilities of African American and Latino students. And some of these

perceptions are unconscious. They're low expectations. I believe that tracking is the single most damaging—damaging policy that we could have if we are interested in closing the minority achievement gap.

INTERVIEWER: Why is tracking so bad?

JIM: Tracking reproduces segregation that is at large in society. We are separating—what you wind up with are classes that are thoroughly as segregated by so-called ability as they are, as they would be, if you segregated them by race. And you are teaching children that they are different from each other. You are teaching one group that they are better than another. You're teaching the other group that they are inferior to the other. You're teaching them that they're strangers, that they are not brothers and sisters. You are teaching them that they cannot coexist as brothers and sisters. You are teaching them that they are not members of the same human race.

Jim worries that, as economist William Darity put it recently, the exclusion of black students from high-level courses "makes race-thinking become racist-thinking ... [constructing] an equation between being black and being an inferior student, particularly in white students' minds."[46]

CONCLUSION

In our research, we find that institutional and interpersonal/everyday discrimination are persistent factors in school outcomes. Often "apparently" nonracial and well intentioned, these practices contribute to different school experiences and, we argue, cumulatively translate into different outcomes for black, white, and Latina/o students. It is not just single episodes of discrimination but the accumulation of these in the institutional and interpersonal domains that likely have negative consequences for black and Latina/o students. As Rebecca Blank and her colleagues argue, discriminatory practices accumulate over time, so measures that focus on episodic experiences of discrimination "*may provide very limited information on the effect of dynamic, cumulative discrimination*" (emphasis in original).[47] For example, they argue:

Discrimination in elementary school may negatively affect outcomes in secondary school and diminish opportunities to attend college. Even single instances of discrimination at a key decision point can have long-term cumulative effects. For example, discriminatory behavior in teacher evaluations of racially disadvantaged students in early elementary school may increase the probability of future discrimination in class assignments or tracking in middle school.[48]

The effects of differential performance expectations may seem in each instance to be small (e.g., assumptions that students are in the wrong classroom, resistance to black parent's intervention efforts, lowered expectations for students in regular-level classes), but as previous work on expectancy effects shows, these expectations shape teachers' moment-by-moment interactions with kids—the amount of time they give a child to answer a question, the amount of help they provide with thinking through challenging problems, whether or not they provide specific feedback, and how much approval and encouragement they express. There are a thousand small, almost invisible ways teachers convey to children whether they expect them to succeed and they accumulate over time.[49] As we have seen, these expectations also shape interactions with parents and how teachers respond to them when they raise concerns.

In a comprehensive review of the teacher expectations literature, Ron Ferguson argues that "teachers' perceptions, expectations, and behaviors probably do help sustain, and perhaps even expand, the black-white test score gap. The magnitude of the effect is uncertain, but it may be quite substantial if effects accumulate from kindergarten through high school."[50] As we have argued, however, this discrimination is not just individual but also institutional, including the very structure of tracking and the daily ways that differential performance expectations help produce racialized hierarchies by reinforcing ideas about which groups are intellectually able and which groups are not. It is therefore the combined everyday and institutional discrimination that provides advantages and disadvantages to students. Here we see a complex set of interactions between meaning and structure such that institutional discrimination interacts with already available racial ideologies to both produce and then justify racial patterns in educational outcomes.

Discussing these dynamics in schools, however, remains difficult because often when words such as *discrimination* are used, school personnel feel defensive. Frank conversations about race are hard, and abundant research shows that those working in schools often avoid confronting such issues directly.[51] The issue, however, is not whether school staff are racist, or any more racist than anyone raised in our society today, but whether school practices equalize or exacerbate racial inequalities. Clearly, schools could be doing a much better job at monitoring how even apparently "nonracial" practices differentially reward children. The problem is not that racial stereotypes and status beliefs are a part of school life—why would we expect them not to be? But if schools want to challenge the many ways that status beliefs, racial stereotypes, and other forms of implicit discrimination penetrate deeply into the classroom, it is important to begin with the fact that they currently do. With color-blind ideologies dominating many school discussions about race, incorporating this truth into the dialogue is especially challenging. As Ridgeway argues in her discussion of performance expectations, while the consequences of status beliefs are inevitable, it is possible to reduce their effects in generating inequality if we acknowledge they exist and attempt to expose the inequitable processes they prime. Similarly, forewarning students about the existence of stereotype threat can help diminish its impact.[52] Current school structures, however, make confronting the performance expectations and stereotype threat even harder because they affirm ideas that need to be challenged. For example, as Lauren Resnick writes regarding the identification of students as gifted and nongifted and the assignment of instructional tasks based on those designations:

> [This] system is a self-sustaining one in which hidden assumptions are continually reinforced by the inevitable results of practices that are based on those assumptions ... Children who have not been taught a demanding, challenging, thinking curriculum do not do well on tests of reasoning or problem solving, confirming our original suspicions that they do not have the talent for that kind of thinking.[53]

Widely held status beliefs persist in part because of the way they get affirmed in these kinds of structural arrangements: "They are supported in people's everyday experience by positional inequalities" between racial groups. The very taken-for-grantedness of cultural beliefs that makes them so powerful in fact depends on daily experience with positional inequalities like racialized tracking to provide the evidence and justification.[54]

With regard to racism, prejudice, and negative racial attitudes, structures like tracking do the important work of generating the circumstances and forms of inequality that sustain particular notions of race.

Therefore, the costs of educational tracking and performance expectations are not limited to the loss of educational potential. They are also found in the ways in which students may come to meet lower expectations and believe that low levels of performance are all they are capable of. Scholars have raised serious questions about tracking for a long time. Jeannie Oakes outlines many of those concerns here:

> Everywhere we turn, we see the likelihood of in-school barriers to upward mobility for capable poor and minority students. The measures of talent seem clearly to work against them, resulting in their disproportionate placement in groups identified as slow. Their achievement seems to be further inhibited by the type of knowledge they are exposed to and the quality of learning opportunities they are afforded. Further, the social and psychological dimensions of classrooms for those at the bottom of the schooling hierarchy impose more constraints on students. [Experiences in low-track classes] appear not only to restrict their chances of learning but also to socialize students in such a way that they are prepared to stay at the bottom levels of institutions, not only as teenagers in schools but in adult life as well.[55]

So it is not just the immediate denial of opportunity that matters, it is the long-term implications of these practices as well. Schools are creating inequality and also reinforcing ideas about who deserves and does not deserve the best educational opportunities.

As with the previous chapter on discipline, one of the troubling findings here is just how much of what transpires at the school seems contrary to what the school and its staff intend. Many at the school and many of those seemingly "in charge" were, in our conversations, cognizant of potential problems and thoughtful about how race mattered. One high-level district assistant superintendent spoke to us as if she had just recently read the latest research on performance expectations and stereotype threat:

> But race does confound the experience of school for kids of color—well at least in part. The way I explain this to faculty is that we live in a racist society, it is more likely that our kids of color grow up in a world where they're hearing messages that they aren't so smart

and that particularly, actually it's by about fifth grade let alone as high school students, they've really given up on this notion of effort and school: Those who would do well in school are the kids who were smart, and those who don't do well in school are the kids who are not so smart. And that combination of believing that it's just about your innate ability, along with a racist society that says this innate ability has not been evenly handed out … that just permeates the water we drink and the air we breathe and the movies we watch and the TV shows. And so we have to, I think, begin to really unpack that ourselves as adults; first of all be conscious of the way in which that gets into our own heads and allows us to accept less from kids. And then help them begin to understand this kind of oppression that goes on because it is everywhere, even though it's wrong and it's not even accurate.

So why is there not more change afoot at Riverview? How does such inequality continue, largely unchallenged, when so many people see it as a problem and state that they are committed to fixing it? We take this up in the next chapter. In particular, we examine the actions of white parents who, we argue, play a pivotal role in the perpetuation of racial inequalities in Riverview.

5

Opportunity Hoarding

Creating and Maintaining Racial Advantage

> *What the best and wisest parent wants for his own child, that must the community want for all of its children. Any other ideal for our schools is narrow and unlovely; acted upon, it destroys our democracy.*
>
> John Dewey[1]

> *What does (or does not) go on in the minds of "nice" white people which allows them to ignore the terrible effects of racism and, to the extent that these effects are recognized at all, to deny that they bear any responsibility for their perpetuation?*
>
> Sandra Bartky[2]

> *What happened to all the dumb white kids?*
>
> Principal McDaniel, Riverview

One of the pivotal conundrums raised in the last several chapters centers on why, given the clear clash between the school's expressed values and the deep racial inequities therein, Riverview has not made more aggressive attempts to change. Many staff, including those at the highest levels of the administration, recognize the problems in the way things are currently organized. They have sincere and good intentions and seem genuinely dissatisfied with at least some of the patterns in current practices and outcomes. Yet, as we discuss shortly, their attempts at reform often seem anemic at best. When we dug deeper into this puzzle, much of the answer seemed to revolve around a group of people not often discussed in conversations about racial achievement gaps—white parents.

Efforts to address the black/white achievement gap often focus on some version of the question "What's going on with the black kids?" However, the gap inherently involves a relationship between racial groups, and, as we've tried to highlight throughout this book, racial dynamics often provide advantages to whites as much as they disadvantage blacks and/or Latina/os. For example, white students benefit from the performance expectations we discussed in the last chapter as much as black and brown students are harmed by them. As white sophomore Gabe stated, "I'm white, so I'm expected, I guess, to be smarter." Policies and practices like tracking often lead to benefits for white students in that their greater access to certain kinds of resources (material, social, cultural, symbolic) get turned into capital in the context of school and translates into access to higher quality educational experiences.

As we saw in the previous chapter, the tracking structure at Riverview contains clear racial hierarchies. Not only are there "racial achievement gaps" in test scores, but the school's actual physical organization is like the racialized tracking observed by Karolyn Tyson, or what Carla O'Connor and colleagues have called a "racially stratified academic hierarchy."[3] In this chapter, we explore the role of white parents in the construction of such hierarchies.

Herein we tackle two questions. The first is captured in Principal McDaniel's quote from the opening of this chapter, "What happened to all the dumb white kids?" While the question may seem crass, at the time she was speculating that black students themselves must wonder what happened to all the white kids they used to be in class with in elementary and middle school. Are *all* the white kids really smarter? They didn't use to be. Thus, rather than asking the often posed, "Why are so many black and Latina/o students in low-track classes?," we instead seek to understand why so many white students are in high-track classes.

The second and related question for us is how do the mostly liberal white families who choose to live in Riverview and send their children to Riverview High School understand the racial realities of which they are a part? To put it in Sandra Bartky's words, "*What does (or does not) go on in the minds of 'nice' white people"* when they try to make sense of Riverview's racial achievement gaps?

In fact, we experienced several hiccups when we first tried to map out the answer to this last question. As we will outline, the perspectives of Riverview's white parents are not simple or entirely straightforward; they involve competing interests and complicated trade-offs. What we found highlights the many contradictory sets of demands/wishes/priorities that white middle-class parents are working with. We heard from many community members, including white middle-class parents and many Riverview staff, that white parents often choose to live in Riverview because they want their children to be educated in a diverse community. However, those same parents expressed concern about protecting educational quality for their children, and for them this often meant defending a system that reproduces internal segregation in the school (and thus meant their children were not actually in diverse classrooms). They conveyed (at best) deep ambivalence and (at worst) outright hostility toward changing the rules and practices that, for the most part, benefit their children and disadvantage others.[4] Thus, they play a key role in the perpetuation of a set of structures and practices that benefit their children and harm others.

COMMITTED TO DIVERSITY?

As stated above, one reason many white parents gave for choosing to live in Riverview and sending their children to Riverview High School was its racial and economic diversity. The school's mission statement itself emphasizes diversity and equity as key values, and members of the community pride themselves on the racial, cultural, and economic diversity found in the city. Mr. James, a school safety officer, highlighted the diversity when we asked him how he would describe Riverview students:

> Diverse—ethnically, socially, academically, spiritually. I mean, just diverse. And I think that's what makes this place so wonderful. And we find a way in this building to celebrate that diversity. . . . We're hoping that our students will learn and will do better at respecting that diversity. You know, realizing that just because we're not culturally the same doesn't make [one person] better than the other.

Joe and Mindy, parents of a Riverview student,[5] discussed their move to Riverview and explained that diversity was one of the key attractions:

> JOE: [The diversity] was a real plus when we were deciding to come here. I still think it is a plus despite all the issues and problems that there are. Just because I think it tells you more about life in the world.
>
> INTERVIEWER: Oh so you moved here for the schools?
>
> MINDY: Yeah because we almost bought a house in [another suburb], but we're just like, "Ugh, can't do it!" [laughs].
>
> INTERVIEWER: What about it?
>
> MINDY: It's just all white bread, all wealthy, no exposure, it's just everybody is privileged and entitled, it's like, "Um, no."
>
> INTERVIEWER: So you moved to Riverview partly because of the diversity in the schools?
>
> MINDY: Yeah. I love that. Yeah.

Most of the parents we spoke to echoed these sentiments. As one put it, "I think there's a real value to being in a diverse school. I really do." They had made a deliberate choice selecting to live in and send their children to school in Riverview rather than a number of other less diverse options nearby.

Parents are right that Riverview High School is diverse. However, that "diverse" student body does not translate into a truly integrated school. As Ms. Watson, a Riverview teacher, stated, "We're diverse, but we're not integrated. We just go to school here together." In terms of racialized tracking structures, Riverview students from different racial groups lead largely separate lives in school. As we saw in the previous chapter, when it comes to courses, race and educational level overlap substantially. In basic-level classes, the majority of students are black and Latina/o, while in honors and advanced placement (AP) classes, the majority are white. As in most U.S. schools, tracking has become a taken-for-granted practice at Riverview, even as it re-segregates students inside the school. Listening to these parents talk about the value of diversity raised the question of whether they realized that the school was largely re-segregated internally. Did they care? What were their understandings about and orientations to the tracking system within the school?

COURSE PLACEMENT: PUSHING HONORS

Initially, we explored with parents what classes their children were in and how they felt about them. As noted in the previous chapter, Riverview's classes are divided into three levels—basic, honors, and advanced placement (AP). When white parents explained their children's course enrollment, for the most part they described an uncomplicated, almost automatic placement in upper-level classes (honors and AP). These parents conveyed a sense of inevitability, as if they took for granted that their children would end up in these classes. One parent stated, "He's in ... everything's honors. And he'll do, I think, three AP classes as a junior." Timothy (a white middle-class father) said his daughter "takes honors classes when they are available. And ... they're probably all honors at this point." In fact, one of the first things that struck us in our interviews with white parents was not just that so many of them said their children were enrolled in high-track classes,[6] but their felt sense that their children *belonged* in these high-track classes. For the most part they expressed a sense that this was the right and appropriate place for their children. For many, this was conveyed in their explanation that placement in a high track was practically automatic.

For example, one parent, Joe, described his daughter's placement as almost natural, if not inevitable: "She was placing into and getting recommended for the honors, and we were both honor students when we were kids, so we thought, 'Yeah, of course.'" In this case, their daughter was not so sure she wanted to be in honors. "When she started out in the fall, she was in all honors. And she was very overwhelmed by it all, and wanted to drop back. And we just kind of said, 'You stick with it,' you know."[7]

Like Joe's daughter, Deborah's son was in all honors classes, and even when he wanted out of honors French, he was encouraged to stay. "Let's see," said his mother, "He was in all honors. He had all A's except he did get a C in French but we think, you know, he tried at one point ... to get put back in regular French. And his teacher said, 'Why don't you try to stick it out?'" In this case, not only did the parents encourage him to stay in the honors class, the teacher did as well. Even when white adolescents themselves are reticent or feeling uncomfortable in higher-level courses, the adults in their lives consistently pushed for them to remain there.

This was true not only of pushing them to stay but also of pushing them to move up. Judith, for example, felt that people at the school had tried to push her daughter, who takes honors classes, into the AP track. As she stated, "People have consistently tried to push my daughter into higher tracks, and instead of doing that she's taken honors classes and resisted the higher track in math." While her daughter did not take the highest-level AP course, she was still enrolled in honors rather than the basic level. Similarly, an English teacher encouraged Lisa's daughter to take a class for honors credit:

> In freshman year Jessica . . . was in a mixed-level [English] class that started out at the basic level because that was the recommendation. And her teacher said, "You can do honors. You're smart. You know, you might have to work a little harder, but you should be an honors student." And, she pushed her, motivated her, and I think Jessica got a B + in the honors level in her class.

As a parent, Lisa had accepted a mixed-level placement for her daughter (who was taking the course for basic credit). However, the teacher pushed her to take the course for honors credit.

Even when parents discussed a practically automatic process of placement into honors or AP classes, they still were able to explain how the bureaucracy of placement worked. As Elise describes, she understood generally how course assignments unfolded and knew that parents could intervene if they wanted to. She had never involved herself, however, because, as she explained, until now the system had worked for her:

> I have a general sense [about how Riverview decides which level of class a child takes]. I believe it's mostly teacher recommendations coming in from eighth grade . . . There's a test I'm pretty sure. And although I've been told by other parents that if you don't agree with the placement you're given, the counselors are very receptive and open in talking to you . . . The placement seemed fine, and so I never had to do that . . . it's worked for me.

While the system had thus far worked smoothly for these parents, placing their children where they wanted them, this wasn't true for all.

Although most white parents talked about their children being automatically tracked into honors or AP classes, some of their children initially received basic-level assignments. When this happened, with just a few exceptions, those parents worked actively to get their children into the "proper" placement: upper-level classes.[8] While grades, test scores, and teacher recommendations were supposed to be the main determinants, parents themselves were able to influence the final decisions. The Riverview Course Selection Guide states that students may be assigned to classes by the department chairs based on several criteria, including test scores in specific subjects, grades, completion of prerequisites, and teachers' recommendations. Parents may seek an alternative course enrollment if students meet the prerequisites for the class. However, this reassignment must be done with the approval of the department chair. The reason for permitting the parent override, according to school officials, was to create more access to the upper level for students from underrepresented groups or who presented special circumstances that merited additional consideration.

In some cases, a student is assigned to honors classes for most subjects and a parent intervenes, against school advice, to have his or her child placed in honors in the other subjects where the child was initially assigned to basic classes:

> INTERVIEWER: Were they put [in honors] automatically, or did you have some say in that process?
>
> PARENT: Well, you do have a say. Uh, all of Kelly's were automatic from recommendations from eighth grade. I guess the whole process that ... they utilize test scores, they utilize eighth-grade teachers' recommendations, etc. It's where they make all these decisions. In my son's case, Math was honors. English was honors. For some reason, they put him in Biology basic and that's the only one I fought. And the head of the Science department was awesome. And I spent quite a while talking, and her feeling was that his Reading scores weren't high enough and she was concerned he would struggle. And I said, "Well, I'd be more concerned if his Math scores were low and his Reading scores weren't low." They were just not to the standard she felt an incoming freshman with all the other honors classes [should have] ... I said, "I've been here before. Let's see what he does."

This parent's experience with the head of the Science Department was reflective of how most white parents talked about intervening in course placement decisions. As she said, "They were very flexible. Because I'm articulate enough to be able to say, 'Here, you know, let's look at all the facts, it's la di da di da.' And they go, 'Oh, okay.'" She perceived that her own ability to be, as she put it, "articulate" with school officials was an asset in getting the course assignment that she wanted for her child.[9]

In a more complicated case, Noreen's son Anthony was not enrolled in any honors classes out of eighth grade. As she explained, he didn't have the test scores for an honors placement but "he made it clear to his counselor that he didn't want to be in the [basic] classes. And they gave him like six weeks to kinda show that he would be able to handle it, and he did that." Noreen explained that they called the school and said, "Well, you know, he really wants to be in honors. We want him in honors." In Noreen's case, she and her son were able to get the school to respond to the placement that they wanted.

Janet tells a similar story. Her daughter's history teacher did not recommend her for the AP course, but the school enrolled her in the class anyway. Likewise, Jackie reported that her daughter Shannon's teacher thought she should not take the honors chemistry-physics sequence because "[The teacher] thought it might be a little bit too much for her." They enrolled her anyway, and while she was not doing well in chemistry, Jackie explained that this was because of the teacher. "She's struggling a little in Chemistry but this is the teacher who doesn't teach. So I'm finding when . . . when Shannon does well, it's because she has good teachers. And when she struggles, it's because she doesn't . . . My personal feeling is it's not her fault when she's not getting the material."

Some parents were mildly critical of the course placement process. Margaret, for example, explained that course assignments could be a bit haphazard, with recommendations varying quite a bit depending on the teacher:

> My impression is that it's a little bit up to each teacher . . . in terms of their recommendation for the following year. So I don't know what the cutoffs are. I know kids who have, um, been recommended . . . for AP classes and gotten like a "B-" in the class. And I know other kids in the same class who've gotten a "B+" and not been recommended.

But she didn't worry about it too much. For the most part, teachers had recommended her son for honors, and when they did not, she and her husband had gone ahead and done what they thought was best:

> He started Japanese instead of French when he got to high school. And they had placed him in basic Japanese, which I thought was ridiculous even though . . . I mean, I think we just signed him up

for honors and that made sense. I mean he would have been recommended for French honors had he gone there. So that made no sense. So I think that was the only one that we just decided on ourselves.

Similarly, Lisa explained that when she was unhappy with her daughter Jessica's placement, she just called the school: "I contacted the teacher, talked about this interaction with the Special Ed teacher who is kind of my primary contact, and then I went to the department chair. And the issue was resolved immediately." While all of these parents had to intervene to ensure that their children were enrolled in honors and AP classes, for the most part, they did not experience resistance from the school; their requests were processed smoothly. They got what they wanted with minimal interaction with school officials. They also expressed no hesitation about being entitled to and capable of challenging the decisions of school officials and advocating for what they wanted even against the wishes and recommendations of school personnel.[10]

In one respect, this is how the process is supposed to work—it makes sense that if a parent thinks the school has underestimated a child's skills he or she should be able to appeal a placement. However, a number of teachers and administrators raised questions and concerns—while a combination of grades, test scores, teachers' recommendations, and parents' input were all supposed to be considered in placement decisions, many teachers and administrators felt frustrated with how the parental part of this process had been unfolding in recent years. According to teachers, race (and class) played a role in who pushed for and got access to upper-level classes and who did not. At issue here was not just that so many white families were pushing their children into classes that did not seem to be the best fit for their abilities, but that their doing so was exacerbating already troubling racial patterns. Even more, school personnel raised concerns about *why* so many white students were pushing to get access to high-track classes in the first place.

In our conversation, Valerie Ross, a black teacher in the Math Department who has worked at Riverview for a number of years, talked about the historical changes she had witnessed in how students were distributed across the various course levels. During her time at the school, she had seen pressure from the community lead to an evolution in the tracking system:

> When I first got to the high school and for years afterward, the high school was a bell curve. There were very few lower-level, low-achieving kids, very few high [achieving,] and the majority was in

the academic middle, which really is where it's supposed to be. And now, it's just the opposite. We find tons at the low end. We've got tons at the high end, and the academic middle is this very small piece. Somewhere along the line the community, which is very involved in academics, decided that in the academic middle of the high school there were "behavior problems." And because the school allows the parents to make the final decision as to what level the kids are in, we have a lot of kids in honors who shouldn't be there. Good kids. Nice kids, and they do their homework every day but they shouldn't be in the honors track.

As Ms. Ross sees it, "the community" has driven the transformation in how students are distributed across educational tracks. She went on to add that the pressures have come mostly from a particular segment of the community—middle-class white parents from the city's "south side."

What Ms. Ross and many others (including parents) report is that white parents are more likely to intervene about course placement any time their child is not automatically tracked into honors or AP. She feels strongly that this pattern has negative consequences:

> I truly think that they [school policy makers] have created a monster, and a monster which supports the academic achievement gap by allowing the parents to have the final say. That regardless academically, what is good for your child, it's not academically sound. . . . What happens is, a lot of times they put their kids in the honors classes, they don't do well, or as well as they want. They're getting C's. And then they're paying, the ones who can, pay big bucks for tutors to teach the kids the whole time. For what?

Other teachers discussed similar patterns of parental influence. Mr. Keyser, a white English teacher, argued, "I think we have some very vocal and very interested parents. I think the majority of those tend to be the wealthier, well-educated people that know how to manipulate systems." Celeste Tompkins, a black home economics teacher, described white parents always working to maximize kids' experiences, saying they "want everything for their children yesterday" and basically work the system to this end. "They're able to discern that 'yeah, you know, I've got an average student, but what can I do to help my student be more successful?'" Often, parents seek honors because they believe it provides the best context for their child's success and because, as we will discuss more in the next section, they know it provides the best education at Riverview.

While it would be hard to criticize parents for advocating for their children, this "working the system" takes a lot of energy from the school personnel working within it. Staff report that meeting these demands takes time and attention away from the needs of other students. For example, black school social worker Mr. Morris talked about all the energy it takes to manage the demands of top students and parents:

> Although we want to serve everyone, sometimes the efforts and the energy . . . towards straight-A students . . . which is great, which is . . . they're tax paying and great people . . . but, you can only take so many calls, make so many appointments, answer so many e-mails. We want to hear more from other parents, but we realize that if they increase their volume and then we've got everything in-between, we'll never get anything done.

As Mr. Morris explains, school personnel do not do as much outreach as they would like because they simply do not have enough time in the day to handle the requests they already receive. Giving inordinate attention to "straight-A students" was not what they wanted to be doing, but "you can only take so many calls."

Principal McDaniel talked about the strong sense of entitlement among white middle-class parents and the struggle about whether to meet their demands or expend the energy resisting them. As an example, she talked about the trend of white kids in honors who are getting "A's" wanting to undergo Special Education testing so they can get a learning disability label and receive extended time for taking standardized tests.[11] As she put it, "We have to fight about it, and then we eventually give in." As Principal McDaniel begrudgingly suggested, responding to this external pressure sometimes leads teachers and administrators (herself included) to make decisions that go against their best instincts and benefit some students over others.

PERCEPTIONS OF QUALITY ACROSS TRACKS

As we noted in the previous chapter, parents explained they wanted their children in the upper-level classes because they believed those courses were better (as is true of high-track classes nationally). They believed that high-level tracks had greater resources and provided a better education (including better teachers with more experience). Some white parents asserted that if their children were not assigned to honors and AP classes, they would leave the school. Noreen, for example, argued that upper-level classes were the only option for her children:

> You know, I think it's an excellent high school. You know, especially for kids who are in, you know, the honors program, you know, and AP classes . . . With our daughter who's now entering in the fall . . . [after a debate about whether to send her to Riverview or private school] we told her that, you know, "if you, you know, can't get into [honors] and, you know, you can't make, you know, attain the grades, then you're . . . you're out of [Riverview]."

Noreen was just one of many who expressed a belief in the superiority of high-track classes. Following are a few examples of the ways parents talked about the school and the differences between the tracks:

> JANET (white middle-class mother): I think that as an honors student, I think the school certainly is set up to benefit her. And I don't know . . . I really don't feel that I can speak to what kind of resources are being invested in other kids. Um, but I think, for her . . . I'm certainly not dissatisfied . . . I'm certainly satisfied with the level of classes that she's being offered, what's available to her, I think . . . she's got an excellent education going.
>
> DEBORAH (white middle-class mother): The system works . . . right. The system works good if . . . you're on top of things . . . this is what I've always heard about Riverview is that if you're on the honors track it's an excellent school . . . I mean Riverview is one of the best schools. I think if you are in an honors-level track at Riverview High School, I think you do very well. I can't speak to the other levels.
>
> DONNA (white middle-class mother): [Our daughter], she's a very good student. She carries a lot of honors classes. And I feel that on her level, for her, that the school is gonna have a lot to offer her. And she does get paid attention to by her teachers . . . [Interviewer: The system works for her?] The system works for her.

As these parents talked about course levels, it was clear that they viewed honors and AP classes as the best in the school. When they compared them (reputationally) to the lower-level classes, they judged honors and AP to be superior, even when they had little direct experience with the basic-level classes.

The Riverview Course Guide states that students at all course levels receive "rigorous course work that prepares them for college and career." This official document suggests that all students, regardless of course level, will be pushed to do challenging work. The principal's overview at the beginning of the course guide suggests that all students will take a "strong program with challenging courses." While this was the official statement about the course levels, most staff we interviewed agreed with the white parents. As we outlined in the previous chapter, lots of staff raised questions about the level of actual rigor and challenge in "regular" classes. Mr. Webber suggested that while the official documents said that all classes should prepare students for college, some basic-level classes did not:

> Academically, the rigor in the classroom is often determined by the level . . . Every class ought to be challenging, every class ought to force students to learn and to grow. But not every class does. And, yes, it's true. The experience that students have is often determined by the track.

Mr. Webber worried about the contradiction between the stated rigor of the courses and students' experience once they were in those classes. Even students who had experienced both upper- and lower-level classes felt that the basic classes were not very challenging. As one black female Riverview junior put it:

> When I moved down from my honors to my basic, I didn't know how far back I was actually going. I just kind of got frustrated. 'Cause it was so easy. Like you find yourself doing bad because it's so easy, you just don't try. . . . And it's boring and it's frustrating. And in this school, it's kind of backwards because the really good teachers are the honors and AP teachers and the bad teachers are the regulars. And it seems like it should be opposite.[12]

As the research literature has shown to be true nationally, Riverview community members consistently described the honors and AP classes there as offering a higher overall quality of educational experience than lower-track classes.[13] In many ways for these families, within the context of this large school, enrolling primarily in honors and AP courses served as a form of quality control ensuring they would have access to the best teachers and resources.

DIVERSITY IN THE CONTEXT OF
RACIALIZED TRACKING

White parents valued Riverview's diversity. They also were invested in and assertive about their children's placement in upper-level classes. However, the very tracking system they supported was a key institutional mechanism that undermined true integration and equity inside the school. One might assume that these seeming contradictions emerge because parents just aren't aware of the racial patterns in course placement. How often do parents of high schoolers actually visit classrooms during school hours? However, that seemed not to be the case. In fact, between public discussion (in local press and at the school) about racial achievement gaps in the district and reports from their own children, almost all the parents brought up the racial imbalance in the school's different tracks during our interviews with them. Furthermore, many not only mentioned the racial dimensions of tracking at the school in the abstract but referred to their children's lack of interaction with black and Latina/o students and understood that it was a result of the classes they took.

For example, as one father put it: "It's not like I'm roaming the hallways during school hours, but I suspect that most of the honors classes are mostly white or Asian kids. And those are the classes that he's in . . . you know, he's not a sports guy, so um, and he just has never had a whole lot of interest in it. So he's not on any athletic teams. There's, I think there's a decent number of Hispanic and African American kids in the band. But I still bet it's not proportionate to population or anything." As he explained, racialized tracking is amplified by differences in extracurricular activities, making it so that some students have almost no contact with students of other racial groups.

Another father, Timothy, explained to us, Their honors and AP classes . . . there were not many kids who were Hispanic or African American in those classes. And from what I understand, there's a high percentage of African American and Hispanic kids at the high school. So they're not represented in the high . . . the upper classes—the honors and AP classes. Similarly, Jackie discussed this racial imbalance: "When you think of the statistics, most of the remedial kids are from the lower-income, um, black families. Most of the high-achieving kids and honors kids are the white kids."

When Deborah spoke to us about what she values about the school—its diversity—she also reflected that her son does not get to take full advantage of the diversity because of his courses:

> I think, um, you know, he has the opportunity to be . . . to come into contact with, um, kids from different cultures, different backgrounds, and that is a positive thing. Now he tells me also that he—in his honors classes—there's not as much diversity . . . So that, I think, shapes his experience, too.

Michael and his wife, Karen, discussed the effect these kinds of patterns had on the racial composition of their kids' social networks. Michael argued that they were "pretty mixed in terms of girls and boys . . . I don't know that they have any black kids that they hang out with that I'm aware of." Karen identified some black friends but then argued, "They're in swimming, which is mostly white with a few exceptions, and then their class is the honors class, which is mostly white." She went on to add, "It's probably a good thing that they do have the elective classes where they are meeting kids from the general school population where it's not all just this little honors class." These parents were clearly aware of the effects of the tracking system at the school as they articulated the various ways that their children's interactions with black and Latina/o students at Riverview were circumscribed.

Over the course of our interviews with them, most white parents talked through these seemingly contradictory positions. They let us know how important it was to them that their children attend a diverse school (diversity provided one clear motivation for sending them to Riverview). They also articulated a strong desire for their children to be enrolled in higher-track classes (which they understood to be educationally superior). They expressed an awareness of both the racial patterns in track placement and the disparity in the quality of education offered at the different levels. Yet despite the seemingly obvious tensions between their valuing the principle of diversity and the lack of it in their children's classes, few parents expressed any interest in changing the current system.[14] One parent put it this way:

> What would I change? There are people who would change the leveling system. I would not. I would not. I would attempt to figure

out a way to make the boundaries, well, see, they've tried that though, they'll do mixed honors. I don't know what I'm trying to say there. So I'm gonna sound stupid. Cause again . . . with that much diversity. What do you do? Truly. And I know there are parents who are great proponents of just "no leveling," but sorry, I don't want my kid to sit in a class of 30 and have it be a waste of their time. I just don't, you know. I've been there. I was not um, I don't know what I would change to be honest. I've been, overall, really truly, overall, it's a pretty good institution. But . . . my children are all at the honors level.

Here, an otherwise articulate parent stumbles trying to talk about what to do regarding "the leveling system." She is not interested in getting rid of it, perceiving that doing so would negatively impact her kids. They are "at the honors level" and for them things are working well. The fact that this system does not work well for *other* kids is left unaddressed. This parent also captures the tension for white parents between wanting their children to be in a diverse school and also wanting to ensure that they have the best educational experience. The current system of racialized tracking almost guarantees that these desires will be in direct contradiction with each other. Thus far, most parents seem ready to sacrifice an integrated experience for an advantaged one.

We are deeply sympathetic to the struggle of parents trying to ensure that their children receive a good education and recognize that there are major structural challenges in the ways schools and school systems are organized. Yet these parents are not just passive recipients of an unjust system. According to many staff members, white parents have actively opposed and even undermined attempts to rethink the current tracking structure, and they continue to campaign against such change.

INSTITUTIONALIZING AND MAINTAINING WHITE PRIVILEGE

Long before we began this research, school leaders at Riverview had identified the racial patterns in their student outcomes and recognized these achievement gaps as a major problem to be addressed. School leaders also understood that racialized tracking played an important role on multiple levels. For example, it was clear to most people we interviewed that upper-level classes in the school were better, and that there was a racial imbalance in these courses; current school structures were exacerbating the very achievement gaps they were hoping to close. However, addressing such inequalities was difficult, in part because of the active role played by white parents in maintaining the status quo. Many teachers and administrators talked about powerful parents—white and middle-class parents—who knew how to "work the system" to get what they wanted from the school. Mr. Morris, for instance, commented that trying to do something about the achievement gap "will be met with opposition" from white parents because "folks who are benefitting from the gap really don't want the attention to be put on the gap because they want their kid to have the perfect education. These parents start planning and optimizing for kids in second grade, like it's war, preparing for battle."

School personnel described the pressure they felt from middle-class white parents not to change anything about the tracking system or any of the related practices that currently created and/or reinforced white students' advantages. One such advantage—grade weights—was embedded within the tracking system itself. While the higher quality of teaching in upper-level classes was a clear advantage to being in them, students in these classes also benefited through a bump in their grade point averages (GPAs). Students enrolled in honors and AP classes receive weighted grades. Those taking classes for honors credit receive an additional half point on their GPA in each class they take. For example, a student who takes a class for honors credit and receives a B, which is typically a 3.0 on a 4.0 scale, would instead get 3.5 points toward his or her overall GPA. If students take AP classes and take an AP exam, their grades are weighted one whole GPA point. In this case, a student who earns an A in an AP class and takes an AP exam as well earns 5 GPA points. As a result of this policy, students' GPAs can become inflated. When school officials talked about the "achievement gap," the distribution of grades for black and white students was a key issue. On average, white students had much higher GPAs than black students. During 2003—2004, 83 percent of white students had grades in the A–B range and 47 percent were in the A–A minus range. For black students, 49 percent were in the A–B range and only 17 percent were in the A–A minus range. Mr. Michaels talked about being surprised early in his career about the distribution of grades and coming to realize the substantial consequences the weighted grading system has:

> I remember talking with Mr. Webber when minority student achievement first became a real focus in the '90s. He was showing the

> distribution of grades based on race, and the thing that shocked me was not so much the grades of the minority students because that, there was a wide range. What shocked me was the grades of the white students. There were a number of kids that were getting A's and B's that I really don't think are operating at what I consider an A or a B level. Now how do you explain that, I don't know. But part of the achievement gap in my opinion is that the white grades are higher and that's gonna be exacerbated by the fact that with the weighted grade system . . . and then what that does to the grade point . . .

Mr. Michaels remarks here about being "shocked" by the "grades of the white students." Operating with a basic understanding that white students are not inherently "smarter," teachers like Mr. Michaels wondered why their grades were so much higher. Similar to the question Principal McDaniel posed ("Where are all the dumb white kids?"), his reaction speaks to a kind of dissonance triggered for those who recognize that the wide range of skills and abilities within all groups is not reflected in the achievement distributions.

Despite their awareness of weighted grades' stratifying effects, administrators argued that doing away with them was, at best, an extremely challenging proposition; the resistance from powerful parents would be too much for the school to overcome. Ms. Foster, for example, argued that "some changes [would be] just too much for the district to take," stating that she would "love to [do] away with the weighted grades . . . but I think people would just die." Weighted grades provide an important advantage not only within the school for class rankings but also in the college application process, as most selective universities use the weighted GPA in the admissions process.

Other school personnel argued that in addition to formal weighting of grades, there was a more informal advantage playing out for white students—grade inflation. White history teacher Mr. Michaels discussed how he believed that external pressures led to grade inflation through informal mechanisms:

> The other thing if I had to pinpoint, and I think that's a big one and it's one of those elephants that I'm not sure we've addressed, and that's a real touchy one, too, to bring that whole issue up, but the whole issue of grade inflation with white students . . . [Interviewer asks about grade inflation and whether teachers ever feel subtle pressure from parents.] Oh, it has to. I mean how much does it play out?

I don't know, but absolutely that's gotta be a factor, and it goes back to that issue about which parents are gonna play an active role, and the *squeaky wheel,* and so on.

Mr. Witten, another white teacher in the Social Studies Department, also discussed how students' grades were inflated based on perceived pressure from parents:

> I think there are a set of expectations of higher end ... that everybody is going to go to Harvard or Yale ... or Stanford or wherever, and it's an incredibly competitive environment today. I think there's a level of grade inflation that there was a time when a C meant you were doing good, average work. Now if you give a kid a C, it's a crime.

Other teachers and administrators agreed that instructors in upper-level classes were likely to inflate students' grades because of pressure from parents, pressure that was not perceived from parents of basic-level students. According to these teachers and administrators, the most active parents (and those who were able to exert the most pressure) received advantages for their children. While the school's policies emphasized fair treatment for all students, these school personnel argued that there were some advantages for the more active, mostly white, middle-class parents of students in upper-level classes. While parents' actions clearly help produce such advantages, the school still has a key responsibility here, as it is the school's practices (even if inadvertent or unintentional) that allow those parents' behaviors to translate into advantages for their children.

In fact, almost all the administrators we interviewed spoke at length about the pressure they felt from white and middle-class families to stay the current course. These families resisted proposed reforms they saw as potentially threatening their children's educational experience in any way. Elaine Peters, one of the district's high-level administrators, discussed the challenges faced in trying to make changes. In this case, an effort to create uniform content standards had led to hundreds of meetings over the course of the school year, many to reassure those she called "high-end parents" that the change wouldn't negatively affect their children:

> I counted them at one point. [I attended] over 200 meetings with parents of kids ... to talk about the standards and the fact that we needed common standards for all kids, not different standards for

different kids, and to reassure people that our high-end kids were not gonna [lose out] ... this was not about dummying down the curriculum.

Principal McDaniel echoed this idea that the haves are always there, fighting for what they need. She describes a sense of anxiety among this part of the community about addressing racial achievement gaps, lest the changes negatively affect their own children's experiences:

> White parents are a little more okay with [the fact of] minority students' [under-] achievement because I think [they are] very fearful that [addressing it] would mean all the resources and everything would go toward kids who weren't achieving ... And take away from "my kid." But I think they see that they're not mutually exclusive. We are not getting as much eye rolling and "Oh my god" because parents see that their kids' programs are not impacted. "We still have APs."

While the school continually tried to reassure the parents that efforts to improve the experience and achievement of minority students would not negatively affect those who are currently on top of the achievement gap, some were skeptical. Believing that there were not enough resources to do everything well, these parents of "high-end" students seek to ensure that their children continue to get the best of what Riverview has to offer. As Ms. McDaniel explains, the efforts by concerned parents to protect their kids from being negatively affected by attempts to address minority achievement had shaped the school's endeavors to narrow the achievement gap. At the time we spoke to her, few of the school's efforts to address the achievement gap had targeted the overall structure of the school, which played an important role in reproducing racial inequality. Instead, to assure those whose children were in the high tracks that their schooling experience won't be affected, they had largely layered supplemental programs onto the existing structure.

Evelyn Macgruder, a parent and former school board member, talked extensively about the resistance to change among white middle-class families she had witnessed. She explained that these parents did not want change that might jeopardize what worked for them. Rather than fundamental restructuring, the school introduced programs like Achievement Via Individual Determination (AVID), a nationally recognized program that focuses on students who are moderate achievers to help prepare them for four-year colleges. At Riverview, the program targeted black and Latina/o students and emphasized developing study and organizational skills (i.e., note taking) and enrolling in challenging honors and AP courses.

Riverview was also a member of a national network focused on reducing the racial achievement gap through research, interventions, periodic meetings among school teams, and an annual conference. These conferences involved student representatives from the participating districts in facilitated discussions about how to address the achievement gap. Two other programs targeted at reducing this gap included a collaborative enrichment program with a local university designed to increase the number of students of color who participated in upper-level high school mathematics, and the summer program discussed earlier designed to accelerate students through the high school math sequence.

As mentioned earlier, these efforts did not change the core structure of the high school. Instead, they were attempts to help more students of color gain access to upper-level courses. Each intervention produced some positive results. However, these successes turned out to be a mixed blessing. Several teachers discussed how programs like those discussed earlier, which were created in part to close the gap and address minority students' needs, eventually became populated by white students.[15] Heather Grant, a white science teacher, pointed out that one program, created to help students who were at the border between regular and honors be successful in honors, a program started with minority students in mind, was now mostly white. Talking about this and other similar efforts, Lynn Lessing, a black counselor, said there were lots of risks in trying to address the achievement gap because of resistance by white parents. In creating programs for minority kids, she pointed out, "As soon as we find out that they're working, white parents are going to want their kids in those programs, too. We're going to have to say, 'No, these are just for kids of color because we are trying to close the gap.'" She felt quite cynical about whether anyone in the administration, including the superintendent, would be willing to say that, for fear of losing his or her job.

In addition to these efforts to provide more access within the current tracking structure, some interventions were launched to modestly change the tracking system itself. In conjunction with district leadership, some teachers and departments pushed for moderate detracking. According to teachers and administrators, parents of students in the upper-level classes found ways to thwart even those efforts. School and district leaders carefully considered each of these efforts because powerful actors on the school board and in the community needed to be convinced that the changes would maintain the high level of rigor for high-achieving students. According to school personnel, once parents of upper-level students (mostly middle-class and white) became skeptical that the school's efforts to reform tracking would be in their children's best interest, they used multiple strategies to undermine those interventions.

Various school staff used the term "white flight" to describe one set of strategies parents deployed to challenge or undermine reforms to the tracking system. One typical form of white flight was a threat from parents to pull their children from Riverview public schools and enroll them elsewhere (e.g., as when Noreen told her daughter that she would take her out of Riverview if she could not stay in the honors track). Many teachers and administrators mentioned this form of white flight as a constant subtle and not-so-subtle threat in the air. However, a lot of families had moved to Riverview for the schools, and given the high property taxes they paid for this access, there was some incentive for parents to stay in the Riverview public school system.

Another form of "white flight" that teachers spoke of was internal to the school. Rather than leaving the system, it involved the trend we discussed earlier of moving children out of regular classes and into higher-level classes. When some curricular departments tried to make that less of an option, they discovered yet another new form of the internal "white flight." This newer tactic emerged in response to the History Department's effort to detrack sophomore social studies. The department revamped the curricula to create an area studies focus for all the sophomore classes, with the idea that every class would be mixed ability (basic and honors mixed together) and students would select classes based on interest rather than level. History teacher Mr. Michaels described what happened next:

> The whole idea of having classes across the board reflecting the mix of the school—one issue which I don't think gets talked much about is white flight, for lack of a better term. When the U.S. History team classes were created, I think there was a movement of some white kids into American Studies because that was perceived as a safe place to be for whatever reason, and in some cases I'm not sure they're even conscious of it.

Mr. Michaels interpreted these white students' movements as an effort to avoid students of color. "Safety" and "mostly white" became synonymous. Mr. Fell, another history teacher, was more explicit in tying these enrollment patterns to race:

> And my feeling—I've expressed outrage over this issue several times. I think the community is using it—using our regional classes as a form to try to re track themselves. We're trying to detrack, and I don't really care what anybody's opinion is about whether tracking's good or not. It does trouble me though when people try to segregate by race . . . So I guess every year I'll get a couple of honors kids walk into my African class and it's half honors, half [basic], and they'll say, "Oh, I'm sorry, is this Africa Honors?" And I'll say, "Yep, this is it, mixed ability," and then they'll go home and tell mom and dad that there's actually some [basic] kids there, and in my opinion many Riverview parents translate [basic] as black and honors as white and I'll . . . have phone calls from parents saying, "You know I didn't know my child was gonna be in a class with those 'basic kids,'" which to me clearly means "those black people."

Rather than engaging in a traditional process of white flight by enrolling in a different school, Fell argues the parents stay in the school and engage in selective enrollment patterns that serve a similar purpose. White parents move their children into "regional" classes like Russian and Middle Eastern History, which enrolled fewer black students. As he put it when we asked him to explain the dynamics involved:

> Now I'm getting back to my original point, how they can still segregate. Many of my honors kids that I had as freshmen had parents who strong-armed them, white kids, into studying like, Russian history. And they said, "Well, Mommy, I have no interest in Russian history, I wanna study Africa." They say, "You're taking Russian." Or, "Mommy, I have no interest in Middle East" . . . "You're taking Middle East." And those classes have become largely white honors, Russian and Middle East.

While parents couched their decision making as being about the instructional quality of the levels and worked hard to make sure that their children were in the highest levels, most teachers and administrators we talked to also noticed racial dynamics in the course-selection decision making. While all felt like it was at least partially influencing parents' decision making, some felt race was a primary part of the decision-making process. For instance, Ms. Watson, a black parent, argued that students and parents work the system not so much in search of academic quality but instead to avoid classes with black students (or because they conflate the two):

> MS. WATSON: Students know how to work the system. They don't want to be in the classroom, or even the parent, who doesn't want their student to be in the class with a lot of us, and the student has asked to leave the class. Now you think how in the world can that be. . .? It's not fair, it's not something that's said, but it's said.
>
> INTERVIEWER: But you said, there's a "lot of us," but what do you mean by that? [laughs].
>
> MS. WATSON: [whispers] black folk. [laughs]
>
> INTERVIEWER: [laughs] black folk, OK.

Ms. Watson argues that, even if they don't say so out loud, race is at play in white parents' and students' course selections. While there is really no evidence that this processe of course selection has a direct effect on student outcomes, it does reflect a way in which racial dynamics reinforce internal school segregation.

As math teacher Mr. Bettencourt argued in discussing math tracks in the previous chapter, many understood that complicated racial dynamics were a part of how tracks ended up so segregated. Yet they also believed that no one was operating with "explicit racism" in the traditional sense. And, of course, there is no part of the process that is explicitly designed to penalize any racial group, as Mr. Bettencourt put it: "the impetus behind [tracking] probably isn't racist." But the reality remains that white students have greater access to the higher-level courses and less exposure to black and Latina/o students.

As the school engaged in more efforts to create mixed-level classes and to open up the honors level to more students of color, another form of white flight that teachers and administrators perceived was more middle-class white parents and students enrolling in AP classes. White district administrator Elaine Peters explained:

> There are also kids who just opt out of that detracking, they take U.S. AP. So one of the things we have done I think is—I'm not

sure if it's good or bad, but it coopts some of that concern because kids who are really high flyers, there's an elite something for them in every discipline that they can shoot for. They have not been under-attended to.

School administrators felt regular pressure to make sure that the "high-flying" students were taken care of. Thus, even in the midst of initial efforts toward detracking, the interests of high-achieving students were ever-present. This process contributed to the expansion of the AP level, leading to what Ms. Ross described earlier as the new hourglass distribution of students. As one staff member stated during a conversation, "AP is the new honors."

LEGITIMIZING HIERARCHY

The white parents we interviewed held seemingly contradictory views. They valued diversity and equity in principle but embraced a tracking system that was inequitable and undermined diversity in their children's school.[16] These parents knew about differences in opportunities and outcomes across racial lines but resisted attempts to change the tracking system, even marginally. When we started our research, members of the Riverview district had been actively talking about issues of race and school outcomes for more than a decade. They had hosted workshops and professional development days on the subjects of race and achievement, implemented special programs, engaged members of the community in dialogue about race and school outcomes, and included reducing the achievement gap as a stated goal in official school documents. Moreover, members of the community stated that they believed in integration and the positive outcomes associated with it. So how does deep belief in the virtues of integration coexist with these stark disparities in students' opportunities and outcomes? How do people who believe in racial equality come to accept such stark racial disparities?

An important but rarely asked question in the achievement gap literature is how people in privileged positions understand and justify their positions in racialized achievement hierarchies. How do people come to believe that they've earned their advantages and that others have earned their disadvantages? In her book *Divided Classes*, Ellen Brantlinger shows how middle-class whites negotiate and justify their advantages in schools. She argues that members of the white middle class:

> are inclined to attribute stratified school structures and outcomes to the essentially superior traits of higher social classes and the natural result of fair competition in meritocratic schools and job markets. Furthermore, they insist that for life to become more equitable, the poor must become more like themselves.[17]

Similarly, Amy Stuart Wells and Irene Serna, studying detracking, examine the resistance of parents whose children typically enjoy a privileged status within a hierarchical system. They describe the many ways white parents justify their advantaged status as they explain their resistance to change. The parents they study, like those in Riverview, want diversity and value democracy but still pursue special treatment and the best classes for their children. A key part of how parents are able to manage the contradictions in these positions, they argue, is through having available a set of narratives that naturalize their status and justify their opposition to reform. White parents allude to the "family backgrounds" of those in lower-status tracks.[18] They believe the system is fair and organized around merit and ability and that those who have advantages have them because they have earned them. They then deploy a coded kind of cultural racism to explain that their resistance to detracking is not about race at all—they challenge detracking reforms not because they oppose "racially mixed classes" but because they want their children in classes where students are "equally motivated," and have the same "family values."

In our interviews we found that Riverview parents' thinking echoes the findings of these others scholars. When asked why tracks and school achievement are racially unequal, many of the white parents first did the verbal version of shrugging. They weren't really sure, but most eventually offered explanations that focused on family and parental causes, social class, and parents' cultural values and moral character. For example, most of Riverview's white middle-class residents believe that educational inequality results from the deficiencies of black families rather than from the institutional practices of the school or their own everyday practices as white parents. For better or worse, they believe black students' families were falling short in multiple ways. Karen, for example, said, "Well,

I feel . . . from what I can tell, the, those children and probably those families, who are African American, have lower expectations than the typical average white family." Noreen also suggested that issues with black families were at the root of the achievement gap:

> Unfortunately . . . I really think you have to look at the parents and the home life . . . You know? Because I think it has . . . a lot to do with background. You know, unfortunately, and that often falls along, you know, racial lines.

Like those in Brantlinger's and Wells and Serna's studies, the middle-class whites in Riverview draw on many of the central storylines of the dominant racial ideology of the post–civil rights era, *color-blind racism*. These storylines are, as Bonilla-Silva explains, *"the racially based frameworks used by actors to explain and justify . . . the racial status quo."*[19] As outlined by Forman and Lewis, the central tenets of color-blind racism include the following assertions:

> That (1) most people do not even notice race anymore; (2) racial parity has for the most part been achieved; (3) any persistent patterns of racial inequality are the result of individual and/or group-level shortcomings rather than structural ones; (4) most people do not care about racial differences; and (5) therefore, there is no need for institutional remedies such as affirmative action to redress persistent racialized outcomes.[20]

As a number of authors have recently chronicled, when explaining why racial inequality in socioeconomic standing persists, whites often deploy some version of tenet #3 from above, what some call "cultural racism"—a new take on the "culture of poverty" theories that became popular in the 1960s. This use of the language of cultural difference (or deficiency) when talking about racial matters can even, as Bonilla-Silva discusses, appear compassionate. Whether said derisively or gently, however, the ideological impact either way is to suggest that it is racial minorities who need to change for inequality to change.

Riverview parents deployed many of these common color-blind frames when trying to talk about racial achievement gaps, suggesting that they weren't sure it was really about *race* per se but about culture, or family background, or social class. While some parents like Karen and Noreen talked about race specifically (even if indirectly), many, as in this example from Margaret, talked around social class:

> I don't think that it has anything to do with the color of anyone's skin. I think it has to do with, um ... A lot of it is what kids get at home in terms of support. I think, um, I saw it when my kids were little. That ... that there were certain parents who were ... were available and around to help them with their homework and other parents ... who are just overwhelmed and busy. I think that most of it is economics.

Margaret suggests that a lack of home support possibly related to "economics" is the problem. Parents from lower-income backgrounds perhaps are not available much or are tired. Deborah, another middle-class white parent, used similar language, focusing on the role of class and values:

> I don't think education is ... supported at home. And I don't think it's an African-American thing as much as it's a low-income thing. So, if you separate out, you know, the low-income kids, I think that ... that, you know, it's not necessarily a two-parent household and it's not ... education is not stressed and there's a lot of parents are very busy making a living and can't pay attention. And, um, so I think it ... a lot of it has to do with what's going on at home. And not being supported academically.

Like Deborah, Sheldon, the father of a white Riverview sophomore, argued that social class and educational values are connected. "The African American students that do well are generally the ones whose parents are professionals. Otherwise, they don't." Implicit here is that "professional" black families had more of what Darity refers to as the cultural "right stuff" and are more like middle-class whites.[21]

Some parents argued more directly that race really was not an issue. For example, Sam Jensen, another father, used his own experience to maintain that the problem was really about *poverty* and not about race. "Part of my job involves doing stuff in Appalachia, okay? And there you have plenty of poverty as well. And you have plenty of kids that are living in single-parent households, no academic history. No real understanding of the value of education, and they're white. And it's the same situation." The challenge, however, is that Riverview is not Appalachia, and while it is certainly true that African American students at Riverview had fewer resources generally than white families, the poverty rate is relatively low. The complicated conflation of race and class in popular culture means that even in a context where many blacks are middle class and most are at least solidly working class, there is an assumption of widespread poverty. In this way, the argument that the problem is not "African American values" but "poor people's values" is not as "race-neutral" as it otherwise might appear.

Riverview is clearly a liberal community, and parents clearly are correctly uncomfortable with suggesting there is something wrong with black families in some collective way. However, even in their downplaying of the significance of race in "racial achievement gaps," implicit racial logic is a part of the connections they are making among racial achievement gaps, social class, and parents' educational values. These parents simultaneously avoid race-specific talk and shift the discussion to ground on which they seem more comfortable. As researchers who study racial discourse have shown, white people often avoid race talk, choosing not to use race words in order to avoid appearing racially insensitive or racist.[22] As Deborah argues, "I don't think it's an African American thing as much as an income thing," suggesting that class and not race is driving the gap.

The other major effect of explaining outcomes in terms of family is to suggest that it is not the practices of the schools that lead to different outcomes but differences in parents' values and commitment to education. For example, Riverview parent Lisa suggests that there is too much "race" talk going on and that really fixing Riverview's problems will involve shifting cultural attitudes:

> I think it would be nice if that was maybe ... If race was de-emphasized and the emphasis was on parental involvement, coming to school, um ... those are the problems. It's not because somebody's black, white, Hispanic. It's more of a cultural attitude towards education and school. And I'd like to see the emphasis put on that. For example, what's the correlation between attendance and achievement? You know? We don't hear about that. We hear there's a racial gap but. . . . I think in some respects the emphasis on race does a disservice to everybody 'cause it's not talking about what's really important.

So for many white middle-class people, the racial achievement gap was about differences in income level, family cultural values, and different investments in education. As Pamela Perry found in her research in California, white youth and parents often shift the blame for inequality off of themselves and "onto the 'victims'", particularly African Americans and their families.[23]

Some parents talked less about family and instead spoke about black peer culture, citing some version of the oppositional culture hypothesis to explain what was going on. For example, Deborah suggested that black students' peer groups were not as committed to education because it was not seen as "cool" by their peers:

> From what I experience with my second son and some of his friends, it's not cool to do well at school and there's that attitude among some kids. And I don't know if, you know, that's an athlete thing or . . . or, uh, you know, what that is.

Timothy suggested multiple possible explanations for the gap but felt that negative peer pressure was among the most "viable":

> Kids are growing up in families that were discriminated against and, uh, are lower income, lower, um, schooling . . . less schooling, and so that gets perpetuated. As I understand it also for, uh, particularly African American kids, there's peer pressure to not do well. At least this is what the media plays up. So I think there must be some of that going on that perpetuates an older . . . or much older problem.

As we addressed in Chapter 2, even though Timothy is right that the "media plays up" this hypothesis, there is little truth to it being a significant cause of differential achievement outcomes.

Interestingly, Timothy was one of the few parents who talked about possible institutional or structural origins of achievement gaps. Timothy argued that there may also be subtle school-based processes that influence racial patterns in course enrollment:

> My guess is that there's some legitimate reasons in terms of class . . . school records . . . academic records that keep these kids . . . the minority kids out of honors and AP classes. But that there may also be some steering going on, some assumptions being made that so-and-so can't succeed in an upper-level class. I would think that that's probably going on.

Another parent, Sascha, discussed how middle-class white parents them-selves might engage in practices that discourage African American parent involvement (particularly among low-income blacks):

> For example, PTA meetings at [Central Elementary], Sara was eight. And I'm attending one in a home that must be a million dollars in a very upper-middle-class white environment. ... And I said at the PTA meeting ... 47 percent of our school population is African American and if we are looking to bring them into the community, truly, do you really feel that these young mothers, who are unedu-cated, are gonna be comfortable coming and sitting in this meet-ing? Or I know, "Let's hold the meeting at the [Central] Community Center," you should have heard the hush. [Laughs] You know, let's put it in an environment where these people can walk, where they can bring their children ... Do you see what I'm saying?

While a few parents like Timothy and Sascha discussed roles that school practices or even themselves as middle-class whites played in perpetuating racial inequality, most focused on moral and cultural deficits in African American families as more important. This pattern fits with a general shift away from beliefs in inherent racial inferiority toward cultural and moral justifications for racial stratification, which are echoed in abundant survey research findings.[24] Survey research demonstrates that as whites' explana-tions for racial inequality have focused less on inherent ability, more focus has been placed on cultural/moral deficiencies of African Americans. As Larry Bobo and his colleagues have shown, a large percentage of whites in the contemporary United States believe that they work harder and are more intelligent than blacks and that racial inequality is tied to blacks' lack of motivation.[25]

Also, importantly, generic questions to parents about racial achieve-ment gaps almost always lead to answers focused specifically on black families. For all the white parents we spoke with, conversations about "minority student achievement" meant "black student achievement" and Latina/os were almost never referenced. While Latina/os are a small but growing part of the community, blackness seems to persist as the central referent for whites when it comes to thinking about racial dynamics in Riverview.

While white parents themselves deployed various kinds of color-blind racist language in trying to explain racialized tracking and achievement gaps at Riverview, they also expressed concern about how the situation at Riverview itself might be negatively shaping their children's racial attitudes. They recognized that their children were developing race-based interpretations of their black peers' abilities, in part because of racialized tracking. As Tyson argues in *Integration Interrupted*, they are right to be concerned, as the structural arrangements of racialized tracking can link ideas of race to achievement for all students within the school.

As we discussed in the previous chapter, students often understood and talked about the tracks in racial terms. As Richard, a white sophomore, argues, "I mean if you look at the numbers, I'm betting there are more white kids that are in the honors classes, and more black kids that are in minority classes." Without a structural frame for understanding the stark racialized reality of these educational hierarchies, the tracks become "facts" awaiting an explanation. As Noreen put it, her kids respond to her entreaties not to think in "group" terms with the "evidence" of their Riverview "reality":

> I want my kids, in their gut, to feel that it's wrong to make a judgment call based on color … but as my own kids will tell ya, "Mom, you know, that's nice, we get what you're saying to us, but the reality is, this is what it is. They don't talk intelligently."

We heard similar language from upper-level students when they talked about students in the basic-level courses. Among upper-level students, there was a perception that students in lower-level classes were not there because of a skills difference but because of a values difference—they did not care about school. Caitlin, a high-achieving white sophomore who takes upper-level classes, stated this very directly in an interview: "Most people," she argued, "assume that the non-honors [students] don't try at all." Another student, Richard, focused on the implications of students' home lives in accounting for racial outcome differences: "It's nurture; it's how they're raised." This was true even of a few high-achieving black students. For example, Tammy suggested that the students she hangs out with, all high-achieving black students, "kind of share the same ideas … we don't want to be like the norm for black people in school." When asked what this norm was, she stated that "they tend to not do well." Even though she has never been in a "regular class," Tammy suggests that those classes are filled with people "who don't really care. They're just going to school to go to school."

Marie is a white swimmer and water polo player. She carries a 3.2 GPA and plans to go to college. She takes honors classes and mixed-level classes in which honors and basic-level students participate. Interestingly, she doesn't describe herself as an overachiever. "[I am] an okay student ... I usually keep a B or an A average. And then sometimes, I'll slip down to a C in a class, but probably nothing much worse than that." However, she is clear that the problem for real low-achievers is their lack of commitment. "People that don't want to work hard in school, they're not going to get anywhere in life."

These ideas about students taking lower-level class (or earning lower grades) connect to what is often referred to as the *achievement ideology*—the belief that schools are places that reward merit and that the way to reach high levels of achievement is by making the commitment to education.[26] What we see here is students who have been successful and see themselves as good students, distinguishing themselves from students who are not performing as well. In doing so, they are drawing boundaries between themselves and these other "less-committed" students. There are students like themselves who care about school, and there are other students without the same level of dedication. In this construction, school outcomes are the result of the level of effort and commitment that students put forward; other factors are largely not considered. As other scholars have observed, students seem to suggest that lower achievers should be more like them and their friends—more committed to education.[27]

As we examined the narratives of students in the upper-level classes, along with the accounts of their parents, we found that they gave moral, cultural, and socioeconomic explanations for differences in students' positions within the achievement hierarchy. They argued that low-income and black families did not give their children a sufficient sense of the importance of education. Without that insight, they maintained, the students lacked the motivation to work hard enough to be successful. They also argued that parents were not instilling a proper work ethic in their children and that these factors led to differences in outcomes.

While some parents suggested that teachers' expectations played a role in students' achievement levels, institutional practices were largely absent from parents' explanations. There was an implicit (and sometimes explicit) contrast drawn between the students and families at the bottom of the achievement hierarchy and those, like themselves, at the top. Unlike their assessments of black students and families, higher-achieving students and their parents argued that they, themselves, and those like them had strong educational values, worked hard, and earned their positions in the hierarchy. By emphasizing these moral, cultural, and socioeconomic boundaries, parents and students avoided racial explanations for differences in outcomes and instead focused on more "acceptable" explanations.

By not using racial language, but employing arguments that attach cultural meanings to race and class categories, people continue to justify racial privileges and reinforce racial stratification. White respondents can, to quote Bonilla-Silva, "talk nasty about minorities without sounding racist." Middle-class whites then justify their privileged position and simultaneously account for the failings of others. Learning to justify privilege is an important skill for the middle class, and schools are an important place where this skill is cultivated.[28] Significantly, such reasoning also justifies doing very little to intervene on the evident inequalities.

The point here is that inequality is built not only through structural arrangements and institutional practices but also through micro-level interactions. How do members of the white middle and upper class rationalize their positions in status hierarchies? They engage in ideological work, including the marking of symbolic boundaries between deserving and undeserving social actors,[29] or people "above" and "below" others.[30] A key mechanism is the creation of *symbolic boundaries* using ideas drawn from a larger social milieu. Lamont and Molnar argue that "symbolic boundaries are conceptual distinctions made by social actors to categorize objects, people, practices, and even time and space."[31] They add that these boundaries are "an essential medium through which people acquire status and monopolize resources,"[32] or, as Charles Tilly argues, that allow them to "hoard opportunities." Just as Weber highlighted the centrality of status groups in social inclusion and exclusion and in monopolizing valued market positions, work on symbolic boundaries emphasizes the link between ideas about social groups and their differential access to valuable resources.

Symbolic boundaries are related to *social boundaries*, which "are objectified forms of social differences manifested in unequal access to and unequal distribution of resources . . . and social opportunities."[33] Symbolic boundaries do important ideological work because they "are often used to enforce, maintain, normalize, or rationalize social boundaries." Therefore, we can think about racialized tracking as a social boundary that is in part "enforced, maintained, normalized, and rationalized" by symbolic boundaries established as people in Riverview make sense of students' positions within these race (and class) hierarchies.

REPRODUCING RACIAL ADVANTAGE IN RIVERVIEW

It is clear that white parents are actively engaged in shaping their children's school experiences. At least one consequence of their cumulative behavior, we argue, is to reproduce their racial advantage. Of course, most white parents don't feel personally responsible for other students' educational outcomes. They see themselves as personally and organizationally advocating for their own kids. Some do not even need to do much advocating on behalf of their kids—as one of them put it, "the system just works." The fact is, though, that the current organizational practices are benefiting white students, and most white parents seem to be aware of this. They actively work the system on behalf of their own kids, passively accept the status quo as it benefits them, and/or resist changing school practices. They also largely explain unequal outcomes as the responsibility of those on the bottom.

One might describe white parents' general orientation to these racially stratified academic hierarchies as a form of what Tyrone Forman has called *racial apathy*. Forman argues that racial apathy is a modern form of prejudice or racial animus. "Rather than an active and explicit dislike of racial minorities," he says, racial apathy "refers to lack of feeling or indifference toward societal racial and ethnic inequality and lack of engagement with race-related social issues."[34] At Riverview, racial apathy includes not only a general disengagement from the racial inequalities at the school and a lack of any sense of responsibility to do anything about them but also a process of *delegitimization*. As Forman explains, this is the process whereby certain groups are categorized into "negative social categories so as to exclude them from social acceptability."[35] In fact, many Riverview parents express some sympathy about what they perceive to be the hardships that some black families face. In the most generous reading, they believe those hardships mean that black families have less energy, time, or resources for their children's education and that, as a consequence, black children are behind educationally. In the less generous reading, they believe that these parents and their children are not as invested in education as they themselves are. In either case, they believe achievement gaps aren't necessarily a school problem because they arise from different family practices, something for which schools (and they) cannot be expected to be held accountable. White parents then feel little responsibility themselves for how racial inequalities play out in their children's school. The few black children in honors classes are evidence that blacks who want to achieve can achieve (and those blacks sometimes draw on similar narratives as whites when distinguishing themselves from same-race peers who are lower achieving).

As Mary Jackman points out, the nature of stratifying processes today contributes to this kind of apathy or disengagement. Such processes are more diffuse than they once were.[36] In this way they are easier to disengage or distance oneself from:

> What is often overlooked is that the collective and institutionalized character of the expropriation renders it particularly invisible to its beneficiaries. When a relationship is regularized and institutionalized, it is simply a case of "c'est la vie." Personal acts of aggression are not required to claim one's due as a member of the advantaged group; benefits simply fall into one's lap. There is thus no need for deep, personal insight into how things work, nor is there any feeling of personal accountability or guilt for the expropriated benefits one enjoys. Indeed, it is remarkably easy to view one's benefits as the natural outcome of individual endeavor and to overlook the dreary fact that those benefits have been delivered at someone's expense.[37]

But the evidence from Riverview is that while parts of the hierarchies are institutionalized and invisible, other parts are visible, actively constructed, and defended. To understand this, we cannot disconnect the present either from the larger social context or from the larger historical context. In particular, placing these racially stratified academic hierarchies in the context of this history forces us perhaps to think differently about what we are seeing—as just another version of the same thing that has been true for quite a long time with perhaps a new set of legitimizing narratives. The part of that historical thread we zero in on here is the key role white actors play and have always played in reproducing their own racial advantage.

As we have discussed throughout this book, a variety of mechanisms starting early in their lives put most whites, on average, on different educational trajectories from most blacks, on average. Reflecting neither inherent talent nor cultural values, the skills gaps that can result are often represented as being an outcome of collective deficiencies rather than differential opportunities.[38] As philosopher Elizabeth Anderson puts it, "Ideologies of inherent group difference misrepresent the effect of group inequality as its cause."[39] The resulting segregation at schools like Riverview has multiple other consequences. Not only are the higher-track classes better, thus increasing any already existing skills gaps, but the consequences for intergroup relations and perceptions are also not good.[40] As we already know from work on race relations and integration, bringing racial groups together can reduce prejudice when those groups have equal status. However, when groups have unequal status, stereotypes can be reinforced rather than diminished.[41]

While clearly not a monolith, white parents are racial actors whose actions work cumulatively to protect the advantages their kids receive from the way the schooling is currently organized. Their behavior may only rarely be obviously "racial" in the ways that, for instance, historically aggressive opposition to busing was, but whites are still fully participating in the racial hierarchy and work to ensure their children's privileged status.[42] Their advocacy—pushing their children into high-track classes and resisting efforts to detrack—seems in part to stem from what group position theory describes as the way dominant groups can develop "a sense of proprietary claim over certain rights, statuses, and resources."[43] For many of these families, honors and AP is where their children belong. The fact that they advocate to protect the current tracking system that their children benefit from should in some ways then be no surprise. As originally articulated by Blumer and more recently elaborated upon by Lawrence Bobo and Mia Tuan, group position theory recognizes that group-based interests flow from the institutionalization of a racially stratified social order. As Bonilla-Silva points out in his theory of racialized social systems—racism is not just about ideas but interests.[44]

Recently, several scholars have built upon Charles Tilly's notion of *opportunity hoarding* to describe some of these dynamics.[45] Diverging somewhat from Tilly's original more narrow definition, these scholars define opportunity hoarding as the process through which dominant groups who have control over some good (e.g., education) regulate its circulation, thus preventing out-groups from having full access to it.[46] With regard to school systems, Elizabeth Anderson writes, "U.S. whites have long hoarded opportunities by establishing school systems that provide no, or an inferior, education to blacks, Latinos and Native Americans."[47] At Riverview, such educational opportunities were intertwined with educational tracking, the organizational routine we focus on in this chapter. Opportunity hoarding involves not only efforts to control access to the good in question but also the development of legitimating narratives that explain and justify limiting access. As Anderson describes:

> A group that has acquired control over an important good favors its members in granting access to it. Favoring in-group members does not entail any kind of prejudice toward or stigmatizing representations of out-groups. A group may be merely indifferent toward out-groups—or even like them, but favor their own group more. However prejudice and stigma arise from ethnocentric opportunity hoarding and exploitation through at least two routes. First, advantaged groups may cultivate prejudice and stigma to reinforce group boundaries and motivate in-group members to keep their distance from out-groups. Second, when ethnocentric conduct generates systematic categorical inequalities, dominant groups create stigmatizing stories about marginalized and subordinated groups to explain and rationalize their disadvantage—mainly by attributing their disadvantage to deficiencies of talent, virtue, or culture intrinsic to the group.[48]

DiTomaso, in her book *The American Non-Dilemma: Racial Inequality without Racism*, in fact argues vigorously that this dynamic of in-group favoritism is *the* linchpin of racial inequality today. "I argue that it is the acts of favoritism that whites show to each other (through opportunity hoarding and the exchange of social capital) that contribute most to continued racial inequality."[49] While DiTomaso is writing primarily about how white favoritism works in the labor market, the parallels here are important. Her respondents, like ours, are not as focused on directly blocking racial minorities as they are focused on securing advantage for their own. As she highlights, whites do not have to "engage in negative actions toward racial minorities in order to enjoy the privileges of being white."

However, white middle-class parents are not just advocating for their own children. They are also advocating for the maintenance of the structures of inequality that facilitate their advantage. This resembles the behavior Pamela Walters found in her study of white responses to broad school-policy movements (e.g., vouchers and funding equalization). Walters shows that whites basically worked to "delay, dilute, or stop" policies that they perceived would undermine their competitive edge.[50] In her definition of opportunity hoarding, she argues that "behavior that reserves for one's own children the best possible educational opportunities," has an "inevitable flip side of which is excluding others from those same good opportunities."[51]

One could question whether what we observed should really be considered opportunity *hoarding* if technically everyone could have access to high-track classes (the good in question). However, part of the desirability of high-track classes is their exclusivity. In our conversations with white parents, one of the attractions of these courses is that they provide a measure of quality control within a large system. They know that in a school of Riverview's size and scope, not all teachers will be high quality, but they also know that the best teachers will be assigned to high-track classes. They believe these classes are filled with the most talented and educationally invested students and they don't want their children's educational experience contaminated with or diluted by "basic" students who are, in their minds, less focused and less skilled. And their interest is not entirely "race-netural." As Wells and Serna discuss in their study of parents' resistance to detracking efforts, these parents assign students to deserving and undeserving categories:

> While the symbols used by politically powerful people to express their resistance to detracking differed from one site to the next, race consistently played a central, if not explicit, role. Although local elites rarely expressed their dissatisfaction with detracking reform in overtly racial terms, their resistance was couched in more subtle expressions of the politics of culture that have clear racial implications. For example, they said they liked the concept of a racially mixed school, as long as the African American or Latino students acted like white, middle-class children, and their parents were involved in the school and bought into the American Dream.[52]

Not that black and Latina/o parents don't want their kids to get ahead or have advantages. Racial minority and white families generally have the same hopes and dreams for their children, but as Tom Shapiro argues in his book *The Hidden Cost of Being African American*, they have different "capacity to follow through on their hopes and deliver opportunity."[53] Whites collectively have far more access to what Shapiro has called "transformative assets," or unearned, inherited assets that enable families to succeed "economically and socially beyond where their won achievements, jobs, and earnings would place them."[54] Importantly, while Shapiro documented these resource differences and the key role they played in different family outcomes, when he talked to families about their accomplishments, they spoke about their own merits and effort. Even as they regularly deployed them to their advantage, white families did not recognize these transformative assets as consequential. Instead, they believed that their successes were based solely on hard work in pursuit of the American Dream. One white respondent, Briggette Barry, acknowledged that she had received "fifty or sixty thousand dollars. . . . maybe \$5,000 a year"[55] from her parents during her marriage. However, when asked how the family had obtained their assets, she argued that "we worked our butts off for what we have."[56] So despite acknowledging substantial financial support from her parents, Briggette Barry is convinced that she and her husband obtained their position in the social hierarchy through hard work alone. She legitimizes her position as the result of working hard in a meritocratic system. This was a common pattern among the middle-class whites interviewed by Shapiro. They all had structural advantages over middle-class blacks (e.g., greater inheritances from parents and other transformative assets). However, even given these advantages, they view themselves as self-made.

Work by Shapiro, Heather Beth Johnson, and others demonstrates empirically that in reference to the different meritocratic metaphors we deploy, these assets translate into collectively different starting lines, different rules for success, different rewards for accomplishments. They enable white families to make many different decisions about where to live or send their children to school, or, in the case of contexts like Riverview, they give families different resources with which to advocate for their children within the same systems and schools. The very same processes simultaneously advantage most whites and disadvantage most blacks and Latina/os.

Opportunity hoarding historically was done quite explicitly (e.g., separate schools funded at different levels). Now it is done more subtly and in a seemingly less organized fashion. White families in Riverview are not getting together and organizing to keep students of color out of honors. But they don't have to. The historical pattern persists, with different mechanisms producing it. Between 40 and 50 years ago, the best education in Riverview was available primarily to white students—this is still the case. It was never otherwise. We miss key dimensions in trying to understand schooling outcomes today if we detach them from their historical trajectory. It has always been this way. We just now understand it to be meritocratic and a matter of individual choices (poor choices or lack of initiative/caring/right values for black or Latino families, and good choices for white families).

In the context of US history, the racialized social system has always depended in part on the actions of private individuals as one way that hierarchy gets defended, enshrined, developed. In the case of housing segregation and the emergence of large urban black belts (ghettos), a number of authors have shown that key to this development was public policy, organizational practices by realtors, and the strategic actions of whites acting alone and collectively (e.g., homeowners associations).[57] The same is true in the history of white behavior around schooling. Amy Stuart Wells and colleagues' recent book demonstrates just how this works at every turn in the battles around school desegregation—not just in the Deep South in 1955, but in the North and West in the 1980s and 1990s.[58]

The point in the case of Riverview is that the school itself contributes to the perpetuation of gaps in school outcomes, and white parents in their various roles as advocates for their individual children or activists in the community or school board members, defend and protect the system as it is. We are not arguing that racial antipathy is driving their actions—they do not appear to operate with an active dislike for blacks (or at least don't most of the time—except, perhaps, when trying to get out of a level 1 class). Whether out of *racial apathy*, lack of care for the other students, or just a vigorous attempt to provide advantages for their own kid (opportunity hoarding), collectively their efforts help maintain a status quo that benefits their kids more than others.

This pattern of opportunity hoarding in Riverview is noteworthy also because whites in Riverview are not "typical." Most whites with school-age children keep their distance from diversity or move away from it entirely.[59] On the surface, at least, Riverview white parents have made a different decision, opting to live in a relatively diverse community and to send their children to relatively diverse schools. They appear distinct from those described in other recent research who move to all-white districts.[60] However, their decisions and actions within the district are not so different, as they work to secure their children access to the best classes, teachers, and tracks. In other cases, scholars describe white parents avoiding schools and districts with "urban demographics," but in Riverview, parents are only avoiding classes and tracks with such demographics.[61] And the way school officials respond to white parents' desires within the

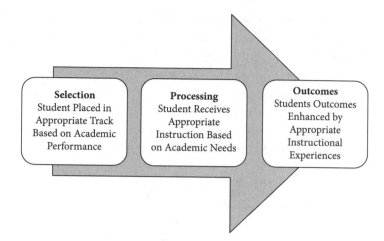

FIGURE 5.1. The Tracking Routine—The Ostensive Aspect

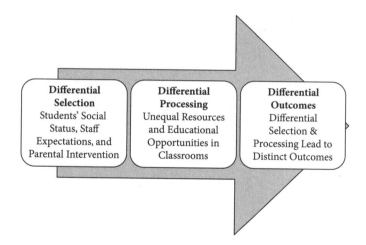

FIGURE 5.2. The Tracking Routine—The Performative Aspect

tracking routine enables white parents to be successful. It is in the performative aspect of the tracking routine through which advantages are generated and reinforced. It is the immediate promotions upon parents' requests, the teachers' encouragement to enroll in upper-level classes, the inflated grades due to both the assumption of active parent involvement and upper-level course placement itself. Even though, as others have noted, white parents' actions in these processes are often not organized, they are still effective and have broad consequences for what is possible within schools, within districts, and across districts nationally.[62]

All of these inequalities are generated through the performance of the tracking routine, which is perceived as a merit-based race-neutral process in its ostensive aspect. As Figures 5.1 and 5.2 demonstrate, the ostensive aspect of the tracking routine (the ideal of the routine) diverges dramatically from what actually transpires (the performative aspect). Yet the existence of the ideal is a key factor in providing legitimacy to the system overall and leading too few to challenge what happens in practice.

CONCLUSION

On the surface, white middle-class Riverview parents sometimes seem nonsensical and confusing. How could they want diverse schools but not care if their kids have actual contact with a diverse group of students or have diverse friendships? How could liberal parents who choose to live in this community at least in part because of the high-quality, desegregated schools be so untroubled by the structures that reproduce segregation and educational inequality in the school? In fact, their response to clearly inequitable distributions is to just try to get access to more resources for their kids. How do white parents who are using race as a proxy for quality of educational experience in a particular classroom, school, or community not perceive their own decision making to be "racial"?[63]

In a study of adults who grew up during the first wave of school desegregation, Amy Stuart Wells and her colleagues found that even as these desegregation veterans embraced the idea of diversity, as parents they often acted against that idea. Even liberal whites committed to the ideal of diversity, to living in a relatively diverse community, who had often themselves experienced the benefits of being in diverse schools, in the end acted in contradiction to these commitments. In the interest of making sure their own kids could get ahead, "[parents] are clear that in the current context, this commitment only goes so far, and once they have concerns about the perceived quality of the schools, they will opt out of a 'diverse' school to attend a 'better' school."[64] This chapter has shown that Riverview parents may not be so different.

One key dynamic here may be that white parents' commitment to diversity is a shallow one. These parents seemed to define their desire for diversity narrowly—while they would like their children to have diverse experiences, they are not willing to sacrifice any advantage to ensure that such experience is real and substantive. Parents' understandings and commitments feel contradictory, but as Joyce Bell and Douglas Hartmann point out in recent work, such contradictions might be more functional than they are illogical.[65] In writing about the limits of "diversity discourse," Bell and Hartmann argue that the "tensions and ambiguities" between people's optimistic discussion of their ideal selves and their limited actual commitments to practicing diversity should be understood less as "cracks and fissures" and more as the source of the discourse's real power. They argue that diversity discourse is a kind of "happy talk" that "allows Americans to engage race on the surface but disavow and disguise its deeper structural roots and consequences."[66] That is, embracing diversity allows those who express support for it to feel as if they are living out their ideals—supporting, welcoming, and engaging the differences that exists in a multicultural metropolis—even as they are largely avoiding dealing with the complicated racial reality of which they are a part. Their diversity discourse helps reassure Riverview's white middle-class families that they are living up to their liberal commitments. Combined with larger ideologies of meritocracy, these discourses help them to understand that while there might be uncomfortable patterns of inequality in their children's schools, these are not patterns for which they have any responsibility. Similar to the kind of racial apathy described in previous research, this includes a sense that racial disparities are "other people's problems." White Riverview parents have deliberately chosen to embrace racial and ethnic diversity rather than avoid it. And yet, theirs is a very loose embrace—an embrace of the idea of diversity combined with a limp handshake to the reality.

At the beginning of this chapter, we quoted philosopher Sandra Bartky, posing the following questions from her book *Sympathy and Solidarity*: "What does or does not go on in the minds of 'nice' white people which allows them to ignore the terrible effects of racism and, to the extent that these effects are recognized at all, to deny that they bear any responsibility for their perpetuation?" Later in the book she offers an answer to that question that resonates with much of what we found in Riverview. While most white people are complicit in the unjust system from which they benefit, this complicity is not chosen. Nor, however, is it typically acknowledged, "because there are powerful ideological systems in place that serve to reassure whites that the suffering of darker-skinned others is not of their doing and because the capacity of whites to live in denial of responsibility is very highly developed."[67] This ideological system includes the achievement ideology or ideology of meritocracy that, as Bartky puts it, denies the effects of race and class, as it saddles victims with the responsibility for those same effects. Any guilt, therefore, that privileged people might feel for others' disadvantaged position is alleviated if they believe that those others have been *justly* excluded because of their own moral or cultural or biological defects. Moreover, as Charles Payne and others have also noted, partly because they have at the ready alternate explanations for stratification, the haves in our society typically do not recognize meaningful connections between their own status at the top, and the situation of the have-nots at the bottom of societal or local hierarchies. They fail to see any relationship between their own privilege and the distress or suffering of others (e.g., the connections, for instance, between highly resourced high-track classes and underresourced lower-track classes). Similar to recent work by Amy Stuart Wells and others, Bartky talks about whites operating with a "double consciousness" that allows them to live in denial about larger racial realities, in part because they understand privilege to be earned rather than unearned.

As we show in this chapter, white parents are not just passive recipients of structural advantages. Individually and collectively they still participate, working to ensure that the rules, policies, and arrangements that are serving their children well do not change. Likely they do this not out of animosity toward others but out of a fierce interest in advocating for their own children. One response to this kind of opportunity hoarding would be to suggest that it is not fair to penalize or criticize parents for loving their children deeply and for advocating for them strongly. The problem here is that such logic implies somehow that other parents do not love their children as much or just need to advocate better. In fact, the problem is not the extent of parental love but the gaps in material, cultural, social, and symbolic resources that enable some to translate their care into more advantages for their children. These resource differences interact with school policies and practices that enable white and middle-class parents' resources to "pay off." Under current arrangements, this "working the system" to maximize opportunity for individual children will inevitably contribute to stratifying processes and have decidedly unmeritocratic effects. The answer, therefore, is not for all parents to do what these white parents do—the whole point is not everyone can. As the school social worker Mr. Morris implied earlier, responding to the regular demands of some families leaves little time to address the needs of others. There are only so many hours in the workday, so many spots in the high-track classes, so many award-winning teachers to go around.

Instead, we return to the words of John Dewey, quoted at the beginning of this chapter. How do we encourage folks to be committed to the common good and broader humanity? How do we encourage folks to act on the principle Dewey articulated—to get the community to advocate for all its children, not just their own children. For instance, what could be accomplished if all these highly resourced parents worked to ensure that a "high-track" stimulating and challenging curriculum was available to all students?

6

Conclusion

One can imagine a group of new first-year students approaching Riverview high school to start their freshman year—black, white, Latina/o, girl, boy, tall, short, graceful, strong, goofy. Their trajectories are complicated. Some love school, some are ambivalent. One is nervous about how to find the cafeteria, another worries about whether she will like her volleyball coach. One knows she wants to be an oncologist, another dreams of playing professional soccer, a third just wants to play guitar. They arrive at school with different skill sets—half have already taken algebra, three have already mastered a second language, one has learning challenges. They also arrive at school with different resources—some want for nothing while others already have part-time jobs, one child's father has the superintendent's cell phone number programmed into his iPhone, another child's father works as a school safety officer, some have a carefully mapped out plan to get into their college of choice (Yale, Duke, Stanford, Northwestern, Oberlin) while others are not sure how college admissions works much less how to pay for it. At Riverview many of these differences do not map easily or neatly onto racial categories; however, historic and contemporary racial dynamics are interwoven throughout these youths' biographies.

Imagine for a moment that you watch these teens walk into Riverview for their first day of school but envision yourself not as one of the teens themselves but as one of their parents. Imagine that you have faced obstacles others have not or that you have not always had the same advantages as others, but that you are doing okay for yourself and your family. Imagine that you know that your child, while not perfect, is perfectly maddening and delightful—clever, engaged, thoughtful, silly. You have used what resources you have to move into the Riverview district. Via the "broken record" technique, you have reinforced for your child over and over how important school is to her future. And yet, as you send her off to school for this important day, as you have sent her off to school since the first day of kindergarten, you worry. You worry about whether these "good schools" will do right by your child. Will her potential be recognized? Will her strengths be nurtured? Her weaknesses addressed? And while worrying might well be a prerogative of all parents, if you imagine yourself as the parent of one of the black or Latina/o children walking into the building, that worry is not only intensified but necessary.

That worry is not because of any inherent characteristics of black or Latina/o students. In fact, we've demonstrated that students' engagement, motivation, and effort are roughly the same across racial groups (and on most dimensions black students are more committed to education than whites). However, race is at work in many complicated ways as these students walk down the hallways of Riverview, move through the day to their assigned courses, are greeted by their third-period teachers, are or are not invited to join a study group, and decide where to eat lunch. While none of these students' lives and experiences are solely determined by their racial categorization, the history and present realities of race shape the parameters within which they operate. Long histories of formal and informal racism contribute to persistent racial stratification and play a role in what kinds of resources their families have. Racial ideologies and cultural belief systems set a context for how they and others understand racial difference. These systems of ideas also shape how school personnel interact with and respond to these youth and their families. These various racial dynamics set the context for action. In this way, understanding how race matters for achievement outcomes at Riverview and elsewhere involves paying attention to the many simultaneous levels, from the structural to the "mundane," on which race works on and through these youth.

As we have written about throughout this book, the very way different youths' and families' resources get understood and responded to has a racial valiance—like a distorted or corrupted version of "rose-colored glasses." On average, white families have more resources than black and Latina/o families; however, even those resources that black and Latina/o families have do not always pay off. And even when white families do not have abundant resources, the symbolic capital of whiteness means that they do not face the same kinds of penalties as members of other groups. Race thus matters not only for the black and Latina/o youth in that entering class of first-year students but for their white peers also. Many of the same school practices that put black and Latina/o students at a disadvantage actually help white students.

We have outlined how contemporary *patterns* of racial inequality are similar to those of the past, and yet the *mechanisms* that produce them are somewhat different. *Structural inequalities, institutional practices*, and *racial ideologies* mutually reinforce each other and collectively generate different educational trajectories, but today often appear to be "nonracial." School practices systematically create institutional advantages for some groups (i.e., whites) and disadvantages for other groups (i.e., blacks and Latina/os) by differentially responding to and rewarding parents' and students' social and cultural resources. These practices that create advantages and disadvantages are not explicit, nor are they generally intended to produce discrepant outcomes. They are the products of the hour-by-hour and moment-by-moment decisions and actions of typically well-meaning professionals who are trying to handle the situation immediately in front of them as best they can. When staff members respond to black and Latina/o students with lower performance expectations or more persistent disciplining and monitoring of behavior, or when they respond differently to parents' actual or anticipated interventions on their children's behalf, they do so in ways of which they are often not aware. Yet good intentions do not mitigate the disparate results. These patterns reinforce racial hierarchies and dominant racial belief systems. It is, we argue, in the daily interaction among school policy, everyday practice, and racial ideology that a disjuncture emerges between good intentions and bad outcomes.

The material and ideological aspects of racial hierarchies are a part of school. The differential processing and sanctioning we detailed in the realms of academics and discipline are partly about how resources are differentially distributed but also about how those resource differences interact with cultural belief systems to shape how students experience school. For, as we have also documented throughout this book, race itself serves as a resource for some with the symbolic capital of whiteness leading to different performance expectations in classrooms and different patterns of scrutiny within classrooms and beyond. Some kids (whites) are assumed to be less destructive, less in need of surveillance, and more in need of challenging curriculum, while others (blacks and Latina/os) are more likely to face scrutiny, be punished for minor transgressions, and face a reality of dampened expectations. While some students like Nia (the girl who set down her honor roll certificate at the beginning of our interview with her) have to make sure they are not judged "by their cover," for others, color provides cover.

A key point that we have tried to illustrate throughout this book is that schools play a key part in the translation of differential resources outside of school into actual advantages in school. Institutional and everyday forms of discrimination mean that while all kids come to school with social and cultural resources, only some of those "pay off" and translate into currency (i.e., capital) in the context of formal schooling. As Bourdieu and Passeron observed several decades ago: "By doing away with giving explicitly to everyone what it implicitly demands of everyone, the educational system demands of everyone alike that they have what it does not give."[1]

While the ostensive aspect of school organizational routines conveys the pretense of fairness and neutrality, too often the performance of those routines deviates significantly. These details of how things actually unfold on a daily basis help explain why we find disproportionate patterns in school discipline and racialized track placements. School practices lead to children being disciplined differently and tracked differently despite the school's stated goals to the contrary. Even if active parental intervention is partly to blame for generating differential outcomes, schools either need to be explicit that it is the school's *policy* to punish students differently depending on how ardently parents protest punishment and to track students differently based on their parents' assessments of their potential or need *to do things differently*. But the contradiction between the race neutrality of stated policies and how they are actually practiced is a core issue that contributes to the reproduction of racial inequality.

All these ways that we have documented that, in practice, social networks, cultural knowledge, and even skin color itself translate into advantages in schools need to be understood as *mechanisms of inequality*. The many daily moments when schools and school personnel, intentionally or inadvertently, reward such "non-meritocratic" resources through extra reminders to turn homework in, encouragement to try a higher-level class, a gentle reminder to have a hall pass next time, or lighter sanctions for rule breaking add up. These daily moments do not necessarily result from deliberate attempts to harm but rather from subtle and unconscious forms of discrimination and favoritism[2]—they may be inadvertent but they are powerful and consequential nevertheless. The point is that even those operating with the best intentions can contribute to negative consequences, particularly if they are operating without full awareness of and information about the ways that racial dynamics are a part of daily life in schools and beyond.

HOW TO INTERVENE?

To address persistent inequalities in educational opportunities and outcomes, district and school leaders as well as teachers need to first focus on the educational practices that contribute to these outcomes. For too long we have focused our energy in the wrong direction, either (a) emphasizing the individual or cultural dispositions of groups on the low end of academic hierarchies (e.g., Do black or Latina/o peer groups dampen motivation? Do black parents value education?) or (b) searching for intentional discrimination or racist school officials who willfully seek to advantage some students and disadvantage others. Surely there are intermittent moments of peer group discouragement or incidents of a teacher who utters a racist slur or school officials who advocate for some clearly discriminatory policies. However, what we have found is that it is school policies and practices that seem the most consequential and the racial dynamics in these processes are generally subtle and unintentional. The lesson here is that we need to focus far more on what schools are doing and focus far less on individual attitudes. It is good that overt discrimination is less acceptable and no longer enjoys the support of a majority of Americans. Unfortunately, however, many practices that maintain racial inequality continue—cloaked by the rhetoric of broadening equality and race neutrality.

As we have documented throughout this book, it is not enough to focus only on the ostensive component of organizational routines like tracking, discipline, or parent involvement because the practice of these routines does not always match their stated intentions. Therefore, those who are concerned with disparities in educational outcomes need to carefully analyze key organizational practices to assess how they are designed to work *as well as* how they actually work and unfold in the day-to-day. The ostensive and performative aspects of organizational routines will never be identical. Social interaction is by its very nature dynamic and improvisational. It is shaped by who interacts, the various resources they bring to these interactions, and the contexts in which they encounter each other. However, when the outcomes of the routines like course assignment and discipline seem to run counter to how these routines are designed, counter to the values that undergird them, a careful examination is in order. A key here is the collection of evidence to document disparities. When disparities in discipline emerge, for example, school officials need to unpack the discipline routine piece by piece from potential differential identification through teacher referrals to differential processing that may be influenced by parents' unequal resources. By doing this, interventions can focus on the actual sources of the discrepancies and modify the routine accordingly.

We believe that focusing on disparate impacts rather than intentional discrimination is helpful in at least two ways. First, contemporary racial inequality is reproduced through the accumulation of actions that do not necessarily require intent. In fact, we believe that this is one key dimension of contemporary racial inequality that is missed when we mistakenly focus too heavily on old-fashioned forms of racial animus.[3] Instead, our focus should be on how organizational policies and practices lead to disparate impacts on students. As Mica Pollock has shown in her study of discrimination cases brought before the United States Department of Education's Office of Civil Rights, cases were bogged down in trying to determine intentionality, which often led to no remedy at all for students of color who had clearly been harmed. As she writes:

> While analyzing educator bias is still essential ... arguments about harms to students and families of color inside schools and districts might be more productive if they focused on the unintended occurrence and consequential experiences of harm and opportunity denial, rather than seeking primarily to prove the harm's intentional causation.[4]

Discussion of disparate impacts needs to be combined with evidence about what led to the outcomes; together they provide a basis for changing practices in ways that directly address what contributed to the inequality in the first place.

Second, using evidence of differential impacts on students that arise from organizational processes can help shift the conversation away from individual blame (a potentially unproductive witch hunt for racists) and toward frank conversations about racial dynamics that can move beyond fights about who's at fault and toward a discussion of interventions and solutions. Conversations about race are hard to have within our current cultural milieu. With color-blind rhetoric suggesting that even talking about race is a problem or shallow diversity talk preventing us from being able or willing to grapple with what is and is not real about "race," it is challenging sometimes to even begin a conversation about what is really "racial" about "racial achievement gaps." Seeing that race works through the normal functioning of organizations, and that racism without racists[5] may best define our contemporary reality, may help alleviate at least some of the tension that characterizes discussions related to racial inequality. We believe that having evidence to ground these conversations can elevate them to a more substantive level (a point to which we return below).

To facilitate evidence-based discussions, policies requiring the collection of disaggregated racial data (e.g., special education, discipline, and tracking) remain important. Knowing what the patterns of disproportionality or inequity are is the first step in confronting them (i.e., focusing on "achievement gaps" and the disaggregation of data is perhaps one of the most agreed-upon positive aspects of the controversial No Child Left Behind Act). Having such data available may assist in encouraging districts and schools to implement policies that mitigate rather than exacerbate patterns of inequality. There is evidence that districts can successfully do so when committed to the endeavor. For example, in a recent study of racial disproportionality in special education referrals, scholars found that even when the referral process itself was riddled with racial bias, institutional safeguards could be instituted that remedied the tendency for inappropriate referral.[6] The authors contend:

> Teacher and student interactions that begin the processes that lead to disproportionality are mired in teachers' culture deficit thinking. ... although teachers' beliefs about students may change at rates that are slightly slower than glacial pace, effective school practices can interrupt the influence of deficit thinking.[7]

By focusing on data and disparate impacts, we do not mean to imply that it has become less important to interrogate racial dynamics directly. Instead, we believe that honest and frank discussions of racial dynamics are crucial but need to integrate a more sophisticated understanding of how race matters and how race works in the contemporary moment. We need to capitalize on the increasingly sophisticated understanding of race that is emerging from the social sciences and apply this evolving knowledge to our analysis of the implications of race in education. As we outlined in the Introduction, race is operating simultaneously on multiple levels, including shaping how we think about one another, what resources we have to engage with the world, and how institutions like schools reward those resources.

A major challenge in education is how, exactly, to have these frank conversations about race and what should be their focus. Organizationally, schools and those who work in them approach conversations about race in many ways. Some attempt to avoid the conversation altogether—working under the color-blind assumption that talking about race itself is potentially racist.[8] Other conversations introduce race only to show that racial disparities exist but wind up not really analyzing *how* race matters. Still other conversations provide modernized versions of essentialist interpretations of racial patterns (replacing biology with culture), suggesting that family or student "culture" drives differences in educational outcomes.[9]

Other, more useful conversations about race and education have focused on creating deeper cultural knowledge among educators. The push for culturally relevant pedagogy and similar frameworks that call on staff to appreciate the cultural repertoires and funds of knowledge[10] students bring to school are important. Often influenced by constructivist approaches to education, a key point raised in these frameworks is that all students bring important cultural resources to school, but schools need to do a much better job of recognizing, honoring, and celebrating such resources rather than treating them as deviant. Yet like traditional forms of multiculturalism, when narrowly construed, cultural frameworks can sometimes lead educators to adopt a delimited or fixed understanding of culture that "conflates culture and race in problematic ways,"[11] particularly given the rise of cultural arguments as a proxy for more biologically oriented ones. Not only is vast ethnic and cultural diversity within racialized groups too often ignored in an effort to easily capture "cultural difference," but a singular focus on culture itself does not address the full consequences of racialization for educational outcomes. We also need to have structural and institutional understandings of how and why race is relevant. Cultural frameworks will not, for instance, provide explanations for why black or

Latina/o students do not tend to have the same resources as other groups. Also, by interrogating the structural and institutional practices of schools (e.g., how they differentially reward cultural styles), we also can see how cultural differences translate into advantages and disadvantages in particular school settings.

Scholars such as Jonathan Metzl, discussing the consequences of racial dynamics for medical diagnoses, have recently begun to call for the development of *structural competency*. While developed originally in discussions of health and medicine, this framework has direct relevance for education. As Metzl and colleagues have argued, structural competency pushes us to understand how "racialized assumptions and biases are historically embedded into the very DNA [of our systems], and shape interactions and outcomes long before the participants appear on the scene."[12] Similar to calls for a more critical multiculturalism in schools, this orientation forces us to grapple not merely with what cultural understandings, skills, resources, or knowledge students may or may not bring to school, but also with the history and present realities of school structures, policies, and practices that help to frame and constrain how we understand students' knowledge and skills before they even walk in the door.

To some extent, this means that part of what we struggle with in schools is not of our own making. However, the claim (even if accurate) that we did not personally create the present situation does not remove us from responsibility for addressing it. Currently, schools are too often perpetuating structural violence on the very students they are meant to help.[13] This fact is disturbing but also points us toward change. In the words of philosopher Charles Mills, step one toward structural competency would mean shifting away from "racial opacity."[14] According to Mills, "the most obvious manifestations of racial opacity are sanitized histories of the United States ... The whitewashed history seems to confirm the validity of the deraced concepts; the deraced concepts orient us away from looking for disconfirming racial evidence."[15] As Mills argues, we too often operate with collective amnesia about even our recent racial history and such opacity makes it almost impossible to confront what we cannot even see or, in fact, what we deny.[16]

We have no doubt that most of those working in schools are operating with the best of intentions. Such good intentions, however, are not enough. The kind of impact broad cultural belief systems have on classroom dynamics are often at the level of the unconscious—only by bringing them to the surface can we begin to confront them. We have to recognize that status categories like race will impact how we read and interact with students and it is only by acting with opposing force that we can mitigate such effects.[17]

Our typical narratives, for example, about why things are the way they are in schools, why the AP and honors tracks are almost all white or why detention is filled with too many black and brown youth, point us away from the larger history and context of such realities and instead provide local and narrow explanations embedded in the bodies, minds, and intentions of individual youth, their families, or their immediate community. A focus on structural competency and racial transparency would instead encourage us to examine how the structures within which we operate developed and evolved and, in doing so, force us to reframe how we understand them today.

Looking at the phenomenon of tracking provides a great example of these dynamics and their consequences. As Jeannie Oakes and other scholars have captured, the history of tracking in American public schools is rife with racist strands, deeply connected to Social Darwinism and the eugenics movement.[18] According to Alan Stoskepf, "Eugenic ideology [worked] its way into the educational reform movements of the 1910s and 20s playing a key role in teacher training, curriculum development and school organization."[19] Social Darwinism provided the early scientific justification for offering children different kinds of educational experiences. The ideas that children from different racial/ethnic groups and social classes differed in essential ways combined with new theories of efficiency to generate the push to model schools after factories, with the idea that differentiated education would prepare students for their "proper" life's work.[20] "By about 1920 an integral aspect of comprehensive high schools became the separation of students within them for different kinds of instruction."[21] The new science of IQ testing legitimated these processes under the rubric of science and "objectivity," so that when children were sorted along racial/ethnic and class lines with certain groups consistently placed in low/vocational tracks, this was seen as reflecting underlying differences. The deep connections between racist ideas of the time and commitment to IQ tests as a sorting device are captured in the writing of one of the early proponents of testing, Lewis Terman, in his "The Measurement of Intelligence":

Among laboring men and servant girls there are thousands like them [feebleminded individuals]. They are the world's 'hewers of wood and drawers of water.' And yet as far as intelligence is concerned, the tests have told the truth. . . . No amount of school instruction will ever make them intelligent voters or capable voters in the true sense of the word . . . The fact that one meets this type with such frequency among Indians, Mexicans and negroes suggests quite forcibly that the whole question of racial differences in mental traits will have to be taken up anew and by experimental methods. . . . Children of this group should be segregated in special classes and be given instruction which is concrete and practical. They cannot master, but they can often be made efficient workers, able to look out for themselves. There is no possibility at present of convincing society that they should not be allowed to reproduce, although from a eugenic point of view they constitute a grave problem because of their unusually prolific breeding.[22]

Early IQ tests were used not only to track students into separate and unequal educational courses but to establish the first gifted and talented programs.

The ideas that school success is a product of ability and that ability is fixed and heritable emerged during this period. Tracking then made sense because if some have more intellectual talents than others, differentiated instruction should match these differences. Around this time Charles Eliot and others were arguing instead for high-level curriculum for all based on the belief in "the remarkable human potential for learning . . . It was Eliot's conviction that individual differences in intellect were not of such importance to require the designing of special programs to accommodate them."[23] In the battles that emerged for how to educate and Americanize a burgeoning population, Eliot and those arguing for college preparatory curriculum for all lost out. The intellectual foundation for the creation of special classes, academic tracks, and separate schools became firmly entrenched in U.S. public school systems. (In comparison, some of our peer nations like Japan have no tracking—students there are considered to be equally capable but differently motivated.[24])

Day to day in schools, we do not think of tracking in this broader historical context, but some of the very foundational ideas, the "common sense" that ground and justify the practice currently, emerged during this founding period. Surely no one today would make Terman's argument that "Children of [Indians, Mexicans and negroes] should be segregated in special classes and be given instruction which is concrete and practical." Yet that is, too often, what continues to transpire in actuality. Tracking is and has always been deeply racialized. The mechanisms that distribute students to different course levels may have shifted over time, but the structure itself has always had stratifying effects. As we have already discussed, abundant recent research shows that tracking has significant negative consequences for equity, exacerbating race and class learning gaps, and it is a matter of public policy. As Jeannie Oakes writes,

> Because public schools are governmental agencies, tracking is a governmental action. More specifically, tracking is a governmental action that classifies and separates students and thereby determines the amount, the quality, and even the value of the government service (education) that students receive. The classifications made are both durable and stigmatizing. Further, they do not appear to be essential to the process of providing educational services. In fact, for some students they may interfere with the educational process.[25]

There are abundant empirical, moral, and ethical grounds for questioning the continued use of the practice.[26]

While shifting how we think about and talk about race with regard to schooling matters, obviously key policy changes need to occur as well. At the school and district level, for example, the careful analysis of organizational routines is essential. For instance, if we examine the discipline routine at Riverview, we find a disconnection between the stated goal of impartiality in discipline selection and processing and the disproportional representation of black students in referrals to discipline and in the severity of punishment. Spillane and Coldren provide a useful framework for how school leaders can take on the work of school improvement.[27] They argue that these leaders need to engage in diagnosis and design work that can guide educational practices in their particular contexts. More specifically, they show how school leaders can carefully diagnose the causes of specific outcomes in their schools and engage in purposeful design and redesign of organizational routines to facilitate different outcomes. Such an approach helps us move beyond accusation and blame and toward equity-based practices that can transform educational outcomes.

Likewise (as discussed earlier), it is important to interrogate taken-for-granted organizational practices like tracking that exacerbate racial inequality. Abundant evidence from decades of research has shown the negative consequences of tracking for equity. Clearly, as our work has also shown, obstacles to detracking are multiple and varied. In addition to the resistance that often comes from the families of those in high-track classes, another powerful force is inertia—the tendency on the part of teachers and other school community members to want to keep doing things in familiar ways. As Welner and Burris put it, "educators are not immune to the human tendency to continue doing things the way they have always been done . . . the same holds true of principals, parents and students."[28]

In recent years, however, with courageous leadership from district and school administrators, some schools and districts have managed to successfully detrack, with positive results for achievement.[29] Where detracking efforts have found success, districts have used several strategies—"winning them over" or "taking them on"—depending on the amount of local resistance to reforms. As with the programs focused on addressing disproportionality in special education assignment, institutional changes are key to successful detracking. In their review of successful detracking efforts in two different districts, scholar Kevin Welner and school administrator Carol Burris outline some of the key components for success. These include stable and committed leadership, elimination of lower-track classes first to "level up" and expose all students to high-level and high-quality curriculum, providing support for struggling learners in newly heterogeneous classes and giving teachers time to transition slowly to the new teaching model. Successful districts monitored achievement consistently and communicated findings to the community regularly, in part to move the debate and discussion about changes "from opinion to fact."[30] Administrators also had to carefully choose and monitor staff to ensure that those who do not believe that all students can achieve did not sabotage efforts, regularly monitor classes to confirm that they were truly heterogeneous, and figure out how to respond without capitulating to parental concerns and/or fears. Where resistance from the "top" was particularly ardent, instituting detracking reform also required cultivating political support for reform from those who had historically been less vocal. As Welner and Burris point out, those who have been on the losing end of tracking in schools may not be as politically powerful as other constituencies, but their voices still need to be heard. "When parents of low-track students are politically invisible, they are too easily ignored."[31]

As the careful political maneuvering of districts that have success-fully detracked shows, there are also significant forces pushing against the equalization of educational resources and thus toward more strati-fication. Those forces (e.g., opportunity hoarding) mean that those with advantages are operating in what they see as their own best interests. They are focused on the private needs of their own children regardless of the consequences for others. The accumulated actions of Riverview's mostly middle-class white community members help sustain a set of educational practices and structures that benefit their children more than others.[32] In this way, school outcomes or "achievement gaps" need to be understood in the context of the historic and current actions of white racial actors to secure educational advantage. We have demonstrated how racial advan-tages play out in the performance of organizational routines like tracking and discipline, where whites (and a smaller number of African Americans and Latina/os) parlay their resource advantages into preferential treatment by school officials. Therefore, to address the gaps in educational outcomes, it is important to challenge the in-group favoritism, opportunity hoarding, and racial apathy of parents and encourage them to serve as allies in the struggle for racial justice. It is not enough to possess a shallow commit-ment to liberalism and racial justice that embraces racial and economic diversity at the school level, for example, while accepting (even encourag-ing) resegregation at the classroom level.

Our findings, along with many of those of our colleagues, indicate that it is also time to rethink the organization and practices of current disciplinary routines. Disciplinary practices are not merely about prevent-ing rule-breaking or maintaining order. They are not just about discipline. To the extent that such practices result in unequal patterns of surveillance and punishment, they perpetuate real and symbolic violence against too many of our children, conveying to them the message that they are not full members of the community. Weakening students' sense of belonging in the school also directly jeopardizes their academic outcomes.[33] In this way these processes are directly contrary to school's larger educational mission. In recent years some schools and districts have moved toward a model of restorative justice, shifting away from a focus on blame and punishment to a focus on repairing harm that violations to community norms do to rela-tionships and communities. Like efforts to detrack schools, these kinds of shifts will require commitment and courage, as they fundamentally chal-lenge things as they are and as they have been for too long. Minimally, we need to work toward school discipline routines that will address students' educational needs without replicating the criminalization of black and brown youth.

Central to making these kinds of changes is a full (re)commitment to providing all children with high-quality educational experiences. There are a number of excellent books written in recent years about what such schools might look like.[34] While providing important insights into what needs to be done, most also take time to make the case for why such efforts should be undertaken. For example, Linda Darling-Hammond writes, "Central to our collective future is the recognition that our capacity to survive and thrive ultimately depends on ensuring to all of our people what should be an unquestioned entitlement—a rich and inalienable right to learn."[35] Why it should be necessary to make such pleas is indicated exactly in Darling-Hammond's phrase "what *should be* an unquestioned entitlement." The impulse to think about a collective future comes up against contradictory impulses to just maximize the advantages for one's own child or family or community. As Forman and Bartky have argued, we will have to push back against the growing impulse toward apathy—the tendency not only to disown the recent past but to distance ourselves from the current suffering of others.[36]

These are lessons not just about schooling but also about racial dynamics in our society today writ large, and this case study of Riverview high school provides a window into the persistence of societal-level racial inequality. More specifically, it helps us understand that color-blind racial discourse, while, seemingly, at best progressive and at worst benign, is deeply corrosive to society's ability to attend to racial matters. Both within and outside Riverview, the maintenance of racial inequity does not happen because of raving racists, but rather (1) because of subtle processes emboldened by widespread cultural narratives that shape individual understandings of the social order and thus how they operate in the world, (2) equally important, because of the impact that these racialized norms have on organizational practices, so that even apparently "race-neutral" rules reproduce or create racialized outcomes. The mechanisms that generated and reproduced racial inequality in the past are not the same as those that operate today—but their legacies are still felt. Like at Riverview, in the United States in general many today claim to value diversity and yet live segregated lives, advocate for equality but strategize for personal advantage. While we have seen narrowing of racial gaps in some arenas, in far too many areas such gaps remain wide and continue to prevent all too many from living full and dignified lives.

The larger and obvious conclusion to be drawn from this work is that as long as deep racial inequality persists in the United States, it is likely to persist in schools. Racial ideology and the cultural belief systems about race that shape understandings and practices are deeply connected to the reality of entrenched economic inequalities and segregation writ large. When asked in public lectures for solutions to the challenges addressed in this book, we often begin with, "well, first, redistribute wealth." While this typically receives chuckles, it is only humorous because it is so unlikely. We agree with Bonilla-Silva that what is needed to address the core issues herein is a new "civil rights movement demanding equality of results."[37] One lesson from Riverview is that those with resources are unlikely to relinquish advantages voluntarily. Too many commitments to "diversity" or liberalism remain shallow and disconnected from a larger politics of social justice.[38]

Fundamentally, conversations about "racial achievement gaps" need to engage fully with the many complicated consequences of "race" and racialization for the educational experiences of youth today. If we focus on "blackness," for instance, we need to recognize that it is not, as often imagined, some set of delimited cultural dispositions that "black" students bring with them to school. Blackness is a historical and social construct that has shaped the experiences of those with African ancestry in the United States since before the country's founding. It has had substantial consequences for the experiences of those of African descent in every domain—economic, political, social, and educational—and despite regular pronouncements to the contrary, continues to today. Whether and how those racialized as black take up their blackness is less relevant for their schooling experiences than how others' ascription of blackness to them shapes those others' reading of and interactions with "black" youth.

While there is a great deal of reason for cynicism, as people who have worked in and around schools for all of our adult lives, we strongly believe that schools and school personnel can do a great deal more to reduce the amount that they currently contribute to such "gaps" and divisions. Schools are too often used as an excuse not to do more—they still play a key role in society in reassuring us all that everyone has a chance to make it, a chance to be Horatio Alger or Oprah Winfrey or Barack Obama and move from hardship to triumph through hard work in school. But they have much work to do before they can truly take up the mantle of "great equalizers," as places where every child is valued and embraced for all of his or her wonderful, quirky imperfection.

Our hope is that someday youth like those we describe at the beginning of this chapter will come to see themselves and each other as members of thriving democratic communities where all are called to contribute and all are provided with the opportunity to develop the power of mind and spirit to do so fully. Such a reality seems, at times, to reside within the realm of the fantastic, but here is where the widespread good intentions that we found in the Riverview community provide some sense of possibility. Our challenge is only to live up to our aspirations, to have the courage to proceed in the service of justice.

Appendix

Short Summary of Research Methods

INTERVIEWS

We began our data collection in the 2003–2004 school year shortly after our early conversations with assistant principal Mr. Webber. We started where he asked us to, by interviewing low-achieving black students. After interviewing 23 students, we then contacted their parents and interviewed 14 of them. After examining that data, we proceeded to seek out additional resources to do a broader examination of experiences of those across the institution. With support from our academic institutions and the Spencer Foundation, in 2006 we then expanded the project to interview a wider group of black students, white students, and Latino students, along with their parents.[1] We also interviewed teachers and staff from departments and units across the school. In total, between 2003 and 2007 we interviewed just over 170 members of the Riverview community (see Tables A.1 and A.2 for a breakdown of interviews by race and parental education, respectively). During this period we also spent regular time at the school participating in various formal and informal roles. For part of this period of time, one of us worked for an external organization that had a collaborative relationship with the district and was housed in the school building. While we did not conduct systematic participant

TABLE A.1. Riverview High School Interviews by Race and Status

Students	
Black	42
White	28
Latino	13
Parents	
Black	27
White	27[a]
Latino	7
Staff	
Black	15
White	12
Total	171

[a] These 27 parents represent 21 families as, in several cases, both parents participated in the interview. This was not the case for either Black or Latino families.

TABLE A.2. Descriptive Breakdown of Riverview Parents' Education Levels

Race[a]	HS or less	AA/some college	BA/BS/BFA	Advanced degree (MBA, MSW, PhD, JD, etc.)
White	1		6	13
Black	3	3	11	8

[a] These numbers represent the parent with the highest degree in the family. For one white family and two black families, they are not included because the highest educational level was not clear from interviews.

observation, our regular participation in and around the school undoubtedly assisted in our being able to secure participation in the research from such a wide swath of the school community.

To our surprise, throughout this process very few respondents we contacted refused to participate in the research. That is not to say that we were able to contact all potential respondents, but once we actually made contact with potential participants, most consented to be interviewed. For example, of the teachers, administrators, and staff we reached out to, less than 10 percent turned us down. Most of those explained that they were just too busy to make time for the interview. Given how hard it was to find a good time to meet with the folks we did interview, this time crunch seemed an honest reflection of the demands on Riverview staff's time rather than an avoidance strategy.

When trying to interview students, we faced some attrition waiting for them to return permission forms from parents. We would initially send home a letter describing the project, along with parental permission forms for students to return. Often, we would send this packet of information home several times before the forms were actually returned to school, but only about 20 percent of those were never returned (and thus students and families not included). We were not able to assess directly whether this non-response was about disinterest in the project or just adolescent disorganization, but we often suspected the latter, as many returned forms had clearly been sitting at the bottom of a crowded backpack for some time.

Parents, the one group we interviewed who are not physically present at the school, were the most challenging group to make contact with overall. In fact, the group we had the most challenges with in terms of participation was the initial group of parents we reached out to—parents of low-achieving black students. We eventually interviewed 14 of the 26 parents we contacted in the first round. Of the 12 we were not able to interview, about a third were people with whom we could never manage to actually make contact. Another six parents expressed interest in doing the interviews but were not willing to schedule a specific time for the interview, repeatedly rescheduled, or just did not show up for the scheduled interview on one or more occasions. We were relieved, then, in our next round of parent outreach that almost all of the parents contacted in the second round of interviews (black, white, and Latino) agreed to participate (though several who agreed to be interviewed rescheduled repeatedly or did not show up for scheduled interviews). We attributed this difference in response partly to an improved process of outreach as well as a set of research assistants who were particularly persistent in contacting families and providing regular reminders leading up to a scheduled interview.

The two authors of this book conducted the majority of interviews but were greatly assisted along the way by a group of trained research assistants, including four African American graduate students (Geoff Banks, Michelle Green, Mosi Ifatunji, and Carole Ayanlaja), two Latino students (Tomas Garret, a graduate student, and Matthew Rodriguez, an undergraduate), and two white graduate students (Julie Noveske and Michelle Manno). In almost every case we tried to match the race of interviewer and interviewee. Interviews were professionally transcribed and then a member of the research team would clean the transcript, listening to the original recording while reading the transcript to make sure nothing had been missed or miscaptured. We analyzed the data using several different qualitative data analysis software programs. Generally, we began with a process of open coding of data to identify initial themes. We then proceeded to do more thematic coding.

To select our sample, we used different selection strategies for students and parents vis-à-vis staff. We began by selecting students. We focused on 10th- and 11th-grade students and started our process with a list of sophomores and juniors listed by GPA, with student achievement falling into three large categories. High achievers were students with grade point averages (GPA) between 3.0 and 4.0 on a 4.0 scale (here we did not factor in weighted grades). Moderate achievers had GPAs between 2.0 and 2.9 and low achievers had GPAs below 2.0. We randomly selected students from these different achievement levels so that we could get a broad range of perspectives on the school, achievement hierarchies, and peer dynamics. We also collected data about respondents' parents' employment and educational backgrounds and used this information to categorize students by social class. We over-selected African American students because we were particularly interested in their educational experiences and because of the initial interest of school officials in obtaining a large sample of low-achieving black students. We then used this list of student interviewees to select parents, contacting those of all the student respondents.

We selected staff for interviews based on a range of recommendations we received from administrators, students, and other staff. We attempted to interview staff from all the major academic units (e.g., science, math, English, social studies) as well as all the different departments in the building (e.g., administrators, teachers, counseling, special education, administrative support staff, security, school board). We also tried to ensure that we interviewed both new and longtime staff, along with staff from different racial/ethnic groups. In addition to our formal interviews with staff, we had numerous informal interviews with a wider group of staff during our time at the school. These conversations often helped us to test out emerging themes, pointed us in new directions for further data collection, or provided background information about the school's history, policies, or politics.

Student interviews lasted between 45 and 90 minutes and were conducted at Riverview High School. They were semi-structured interviews conducted by the authors as well as by trained students using a standard interview protocol. We were interested in gaining an understanding of students' school experiences, their educational aspirations and expectations, their perceptions of race and opportunity, and the beliefs about peer dynamics that impacted their school achievement.[2] Formal interviews with adults (parents and staff) lasted anywhere from 60 minutes to three hours and took place in a location of their choosing (e.g., school, home, coffee shop). These were also semi-structured interviews conducted by the authors as well as by trained graduate students using a standard protocol. The parent interview guide included questions about family and educational background, educational aspirations for their children, their knowledge about Riverview policies and practices, their impressions of their children's social and academic experiences at Riverview, and their understandings about the racial achievement gap. Staff interviews also included questions about family and educational background, their experiences working at Riverview, their understandings of student learning dynamics at the school, and their understandings of factors that shape racial achievement gaps.

SURVEY

In additional to our data collection, we also secured access to survey data collected in Riverview and 14 similar districts (see Table A.3 for detailed survey information). Our survey evidence comes from the Assessment of Secondary School Student Culture (ASSSC, Ferguson 2002), which was collected from 101 secondary schools across 10 states during the school year of 2000–2001 (Ferguson 2002). The data for the analysis presented in this book come from nearly 25,000 7th- to 11th-grade students.[3] The dataset is particularly advantageous because of its focus on integrated suburban schools— the precise context that is speculated to be most fertile for the oppositional culture and acting white phenomena (Fryer and Torelli 2010; Tyson 2011). Surveys were administered by classroom teachers and school administrators, and were then compiled by independent researchers. Riverview middle and high school students participated in the survey. To ensure their anonymity, no identifying information was collected from students.

Measures for this study are taken from the ASSSC survey and are described next. Indicators of academic orientation were included in this study contingent on their being both representative of relevant theory and also significantly related to achievement in these data categories.

TABLE A.3. Means, Standard Deviations, Ranges, and Descriptions of Student-Level Independent and Dependent Variables

Variable	Mean	SD	Min	Max
Aspirations: What is the highest level that you would like to go in school? (Selected "Post-Graduate Degree")	0.338	0.473	0	1
Affect Toward School: Degree of agreement with the following statement: "I am happy to be at this school" ("Strongly Disagree" to "Strongly Agree")	3.015	0.713	1	4
Positive Peer Pressure: Degree of agreement with the following statement: "My friends want me to study harder than I do" ("Strongly Disagree" to "Strongly Agree")	2.150	0.728	1	4
Positive Peer Pressure: How important do your friends think it is to continue their education past high school? ("Not important at all" to "Very Important")	3.612	0.638	1	4
Academic Behaviors: On weekdays after school, how many hours per day on average are you studying and doing homework? ("No time" to "8 + hours")	3.618	1.200	1	7
Academic Behaviors: How often do you really pay attention in class? ("Never" to "Always")	4.538	1.036	1	6
Negative Peer Pressure: Think of times you did not study for a test or did not complete homework during the last year. Which of the following reasons were most important? (Selected "My friends wanted me to do something else")	0.115	0.319	0	1
Racial Composition of Friend Group: Are any of your six closest friends of a different race/ethnicity than yourself? ("None," "Some," or "Most")	2.041	0.630	1	3
GPA: What was your Grade Point Average last term? ("D–/F" to "A")	3.107	0.816	0.5	4
School Percent White	58.99	16.33	0	100

Descriptive statistics for the independent and dependent variables can be seen in Table A.1.

Academic Achievement. Academic achievement was captured through students' self-reported GPA from the last academic term, as measured by an 11-point Likert scale ranging from "A" to "D–/F." Grade reports were checked for validity using race-by-gender data from student transcripts. Comparisons revealed only moderate levels of inflation, with no significant differences in GPA rankings across race and gender groups (Ferguson 2002).

Academic Behaviors. Academic behaviors were assessed based on two indicators. The first is a question that asked, "On week days after school, how many hours per day on average are you studying and doing homework?" The response options were on a 7-point scale that ranged from "No time" to "8 + hours." The second was a question that asked, "How often do you really pay attention in class?" and the responses were on a 6-point Likert scale ranging from "Never" to "Always."

Negative Peer Pressure. Negative peer pressure was captured by a dichotomous indicator that asked whether at times one of the most important reasons that the student didn't complete school assignments or studies over the past year was because the student's friends wanted him or her to "do something else."

Positive Peer Pressure. Positive peer pressure was represented by two indicators. The first was an item that asked for the student's level of agreement with the statement "My friends want me to study harder than I do," with potential responses ranging from "Strongly Disagree" to "Strongly Agree" on a 4-point Likert scale. The second indicator was a question that asked how important the student's friends think it is to "continue their education past high school," which was also measured on a 4-point Likert scale ranging from "Very Important" to "Not Important at All."

Affect Toward School. Affect toward school was captured using the student's level of agreement with the statement "I am happy to be at this school" on a 4-point Likert scale ranging from "Strongly Agree" to "Strongly Disagree."

Academic Aspirations. Aspirations were measured by a dichotomous item that asked whether the highest level the students would like to go to in school was in the post-graduate range. This aspiration level was used because it was highly predictive of student GPA.

School Racial Composition. School racial composition was measured using the percent of a given school's student population that report their race as being white, which is consistent with extant literature on the impact of the percent of white students in a school on African American students' attitudes toward achievement (Fryer and Torelli 2010; Tyson, Darity, and Castellino 2005; Tyson 2011).

Friend Group Racial Composition. Friend group racial composition was captured by two dichotomous items indicating whether "most" or "none" of the students' closest friends were of other races.

Demographic Controls. Demographic controls include students' race, gender, whether they were in high school or middle school, and several proxies for socioeconomic background, including parents' highest level of education, number of parents in the home, number of siblings in the home, and indicators of home possessions.

PROCEDURES

We used multilevel hierarchical regression analyses to estimate the relationships between academic orientation indicators and achievement, as well as the associations between race and academic orientations among black and white students across secondary schools with a range of racial compositions. These analyses were then used to estimate the impact of achievement orientations on potential black-white differences in GPA. The modeling building sequence first considered the effects of the question predictors alone on outcome variables. We then incorporated the relevant demographic control variables into a second set of models with the question predictors, and finally we included theoretically relevant interaction terms into a set of final models. Finally, to assess whether the racial composition of black students' friend groups contributed to their academic orientations, we ran a fourth set of separate models for black students specifically. Missing data were addressed using multiple imputation and stochastic regression techniques.

Notes

1. While we refer to this desegregation as voluntary, the history of desegregation at Riverview was far from peaceful. Members of the black community and community-based civil rights organizations applied pressure to desegregate the schools, while disagreements marked the dialogue about what form that desegregation should take. This conflict notwithstanding, the community ultimately agreed to a desegregation process, and no court order was needed to bring it about.

2. The low-income percentage is based on students who are eligible for free and reduced-price lunches. In order to protect the confidentiality of the Riverview District and the people we interviewed, we report only approximate data for all district information that can be easily accessed online.

3. US Census Bureau, American Community Survey.

4. By way of comparison, in Metro—the major urban district located near Riverview—college attendance rates of high school graduates are about 60 percent. However, that district has much lower graduation rates than Riverview, meaning that a much smaller percentage of students who begin ninth grade in Metro schools attend college.

5. The survey data indicated similar findings across the 15 school districts surveyed.

6. Clotfelter (2004); Kozol (2005); Orfield and Eaton (1996).

7. King (1986), 118.

8. As with the educational levels at the high school, these educational levels are not the same as traditional educational tracks in which students' placement in mathematics led to rigid placement across all other subjects. See Samuel Lucas (2001) for a discussion of the changes in educational tracking over the past several decades.

9. These differences in track placement are very important. Students in lower educational tracks are typically taught by less qualified teachers using instructional materials and strategies that are less challenging and engaging (Oakes 1994, 2005). By being overrepresented in these tracks, black and Latina/o students are systematically placed in the school contexts least conducive to educational achievement. We will discuss the implications of tracking in Chapter 4.

10. Tyson (2011), 10.

11. Disparities in grade point averages are reported in larger-scale examinations of student achievement. Data from the US Department of Education/NAEP High School Transcript Study indicate that in 2005, 12th-grade Asian students averaged 3.16 GPAs on a 4.0 scale, whites 3.05, Latina/os 2.82, and blacks 2.69. In 2001, when 15 districts similar to Riverview were surveyed, comparable racial gaps in achievement existed in all of them. For example, Ferguson (2002) reports that 50 percent of white students across these districts had grade point averages of A or A–, while only 15 percent of African American students had grades in this range. Conversely, 44 percent of African American students had grade point averages of C+ or lower, while only 14 percent of whites reported grades in this range.

12. In comparison to national averages, white students at Riverview far exceed their peers nationally, while black and Latina/o students do slightly better than their same-race peers. The highest possible composite score is 36.

13. We ended up interviewing 14 parents in this first round. We made multiple phone calls to all households, but in some cases never managed to make contact. In other cases, we made contact and set up interviews, only to have them canceled or rescheduled multiple times. For complete details, see the Appendix.

14. For complete details, see the Appendix.

15. For complete details on the survey, see the Appendix.

16. Thanks to an anonymous reviewer for input on this point.

CHAPTER 1

1. There are literally hundreds of books, articles, and chapters in scholarly outlets about the racial achievement gap. These tackle documenting the current and historic parameters of "the gap," theoretical and empirical debates about causes, and discussions about how the "gap" should be conceptualized. Here we list just a *few* recent examples: Anderson (2004); Carter and Welner (2013); Condron (2009); Harris (2011); Jencks and Phillips (1998); Ladson-Billings (2006); Lee (2002, 2009); Mickelson (2003); O'Connor, Hill, and Robinson (2009); Ogbu (2003); Perry, Steele, and Hilliard (2003); Tyson (2011).

2. Asian students have largely been absent from the achievement gap discussion. This is in part because, on average, Asian students perform at a higher level than blacks, Latina/os, or whites, a fact which prompts some to refer to this group as a "model minority." However, there are large differences in performance among Asian subgroups. For instance, South East Asian students (e.g., Laotian, Cambodian, and Hmong) tend to perform less well on average than Chinese, Japanese, and East Indian students. For a discussion of differences in academic performance among Asian American students and its implications for the model minority argument, see Stacey Lee (2009); Louie (2004). Our discussion focuses primarily on the black/white gap

because of the small number of Asian American and Latina/o students at Riverview and the small number of Asian American students in our overall sample.

3. While racial differences in standardized test scores have been studied since the early 1900s, interest intensified during the 1990s. This was in part due to a widening of the gap on the National Assessment of Education Progress (NAEP) after it had narrowed for nearly 20 years (Grissmer, Flanagan, and Williamson 1998). From the early 1970s through 1988, the black-white gap in reading and mathematics scores closed substantially. However, in 1988 these gaps began to widen before narrowing again more recently. The Latina/o-white gap closed in both of these subjects between 1975 (when data began being collected on Latino/s as a group) and 2004.

4. Asian students have the highest average mathematics scores, averaging 578. Asian students score below whites but above Latina/o and black students in the verbal test (510). The data reported here come from Kobrin, Sathy, and Shaw (2006).

5. For an in-depth discussion of these patterns, see Mickelson (2003). For a discussion of differences in placement in educational tracks in desegregated schools, see Mickelson (2001). For a discussion of racial differences in placement in educational tracks, see Hallinan (1994); Lucas (2001); Mickelson (2003); Oakes (1994, 2005).

6. US Census Bureau, Current Population Survey (noninstitutionalized population, excluding members of the Armed Forces living in barracks).

7. Phillips, Crouse, and Ralph (1998). One exception to this general pattern is the work on gaps in early childhood or at school entry. For example, Fryer and Levitt (2006) found that after controlling for related covariates, the entire black-white gap in reading and math performance in kindergarten is erased. That gap, however, then grows over the next four years of schooling, with blacks falling further behind.

8. Fryer and Levitt (2006). For more on this, see O'Connor, Hill, and Robinson (2009).

9. Roscigno and Ainsworth-Darnell (1999), 159.

10. Condron (2009), 700.

11. For example, even in an otherwise really useful review piece in the *Annual Review of Sociology* entitled "Racial and Ethnic Stratification In Educational Achievement And Attainment," Kao and Thompson (2003) discuss the competing paradigms that "explain" achievement differences as ranging from research on parental SES to those that focus on cultural beliefs. There is almost no mention of within-school dynamics that might contribute to differential outcomes.

12. See Lewis (2014); Noguera and Wing (2006); Ogbu (2003) for notable exceptions to this.

13. Important exceptions to this include Prudence Carter's book *Keeping It Real* (2005), which looked at variations in attitudes toward school among black and Latina/o low-income students, and Horvat and O'Connor's (2006) edited volume *Beyond Acting White*, which examined variations in black students' educational orientations.

14. See O'Connor, Lewis, and Mueller (2007).

15. Zuberi (2001).

16. There is abundant historical and sociological writing about the social (rather than genetic or biological) origins of race. For some excellent examples, see Almaguer (1994); Cornell (1988); Davis (1991); Espiritu (1992); Frederickson (1981); Gossett (1965); Gross (2008); Guglielmo (2003); Haney Lopez (1996); Hirschman (2004); Jordan (1974); Loewen (1971); Montagu (1962); Montejano (1987); Omi and Winant (1994); Pascoe (2009); Smedley (2012); Thompson (1975); Thornton (1987).

17. For more on this, see Koenig, Lee, and Richardson (2008).

18. As Omi and Winant (1994:55) explain in their book *Racial Formation in the United States*, "Although the concept of race invokes biologically based human characteristics (so-called 'phenotypes'), selection of these particular human features for purposes of racial signification is always necessarily a social and historical process." Just one example of writing about the instability of race comes from the critical race scholarship chronicling shifting definitions of race in legal battles (e.g., Gross 2008; Haney Lopez 1996; Pascoe 2009).

19. In fact, those who teach and learn about race on college campuses often continue to treat race as a biological construct. For a discussion of racial conceptualization or how people conceptualize race, see Morning (2011).

20. There are, of course, important exceptions. See, for example, Harris (2011); Lewis (2003); Noguera and Wing (2006); Perry, Hilliard, and Steele (2003); Pollock (2004); Tyson (2011).

21. Guglielmo (2003), 50. Similarly, Eduardo Bonilla-Silva's (2001:37) work on *racialized social systems* (RSS) outlines how in racialized societies "economic, political, social and ideological levels are partially structured by the placement of actors in racial categories or races."

22. Hughey (2012), 4.

23. For a good example of an historiography of some of these ideas, see Muhammed (2011) and Smedley (2012).

24. Mills (1959), 3–4.

25. See, for example, Ridgeway et al. (1998).

26. Ridgeway and Erickson (2000), 580.

27. Ibid. Historically, sociologists ranging from Max Weber in discussing status groups, W. E. B. DuBois (1962) in discussing racial groups and the "wages of whiteness," Michele Lamont in discussing social boundaries, Pierre Bourdieu in discussing cleavages within social classes, and Patricia Hill Collins in discussing "controlling images" have all highlighted the importance of such beliefs in reinforcing social stratification.

28. Clearly one can imagine a context in which such belief systems are not necessary to maintaining hierarchy. As Gramsci (1971) discusses at length in *The Prison Notebooks*, the existence of ideologies that help both those at the top and the bottom of social hierarchies make sense of such hierarchies is partly what distinguishes societies that are ruled by coercion from those that are ruled by consent.

29. Montejano (1987) and Takaki (1993).

30. Anderson (2004), 11.

31. Boykin and Noguera (2011); Carter and Welner (2013); Darity and Jolla (2009).

32. Bobo, Kluegel, and Smith (1997); Bonilla-Silva (2001, 2003); Bonilla-Silva and Lewis (1999); Dovidio et al. (1997); Forman (2004); Krysan and Lewis (2004); Mills (2003); Sears (1988); Sears et al. (2000).

33. Johnson (2006), 20.

34. Ibid., 21.

35. The racial cost of being African American has been documented in terms of income and earnings, occupational mobility, labor market participation, home loan approvals, various interactions with the legal system (including exploding rates of incarceration), and everyday forms of racial discrimination (for a comprehensive discussion, see Bonilla-Silva 2001, 2003).

36. For more on these issues, see Bobo et al. (1997); Bonilla-Silva (2003); Forman (2004); Lewis (2003).

37. US Census Bureau 2009–2011, American Community Survey. We give only approximations here to ensure the community is not easily identifiable. Also, note that these median family income differences do not even begin to capture the likely patterns in wealth differences between these groups that we discussed earlier.

38. Such differences are lost in categorical comparisons of social class across racial groups.

39. Pattillo-McCoy (1999).

40. Beyond kindergarten, taking social class into account reduces the black-white and Latina/o-white gaps substantially but does not eliminate them. For a discussion of the implications of social class for the black-white achievement gap, see Rothstein (2004). For an examination of the role of social class in reducing the black-white achievement gap, see Fryer and Levitt (2006) and Jencks and Phillips (1998). For differing explanations for the persistence of the black-white gap among the middle class, see Gosa and Alexander (2007) and Ogbu (2003).

41. Anderson (2010).

42. Mickelson (2003), 1076.

43. See Mickelson (2001); Noguera and Wing (2006); Ogbu (2003); Tyson (2011).

44. Holt (1995).

45. Ridgeway (2011), 40.

46. Ibid.

47. For an in-depth discussion of expectations in schooling, see Weinstein (2002).

48. Aronson and Steele (2005), 438. For a discussion of the development and awareness of racial stereotypes in childhood, see Hirschfeld (2012); Mckown and Weinstein (2003); Van Ausdale and Feagin (2003).

49. Kao (2000).

50. George W. Bush acceptance speech at the 2004 Republic National Convention. http://www.washingtonpost.com/wp-dyn/articles/A57466-2004Sep2.html.

51. It is important to recognize that such perceptions and behaviors need not be conscious. Part of the power of status beliefs is that they provide a shorthand for interpreting and responding to others across a broad range of situations. In just one example from a recent study on implicit bias, researchers found that medical residents behave differently toward black and white emergency room patients based on their own unconscious racial beliefs. Medical residents who reported no explicit racial biases were presented with narratives describing an emergency room patient complaining of chest pains. Along with the narrative, the residents were shown either a black or white male patient with a neutral facial expression. They were asked if they would make a heart attack diagnosis and then asked whether or not they would provide commonly used "clot-busting" drugs (that can save the lives of people experiencing heart attacks). After this, the residents took an implicit association test (IAT), which measured the extent to which the residents made positive or negative associations to blacks and whites. The researchers found that doctors who were least likely to provide blacks the clot-busting medicine were also those who made the most negative associations with blacks in the implicit association test. See Green et al. (2007).

52. Bonilla-Silva (2001); Collins (2000); Hall (1991).

53. Ridgeway and Erickson (2000), 580.

54. Aronson and Steele (2005); Weinstein (2002).

55. For discussions of the research on stereotype threat, see Aronson and Steele (2005); Steele (2003, 2010).

56. Carter (2008).

57. Goffman (1959).

58. Feldman and Pentland (2003); Pentland and Feldman (2005); Sherer (2007).

59. Sherer (2007), 108. While we can talk about the ostensive aspect of organizational routines as the ideal or generalized narrative of the routine, that does not mean everyone in the organization agrees with the identical ostensive meaning of the routine (Pentland and Feldman, 2005).

60. Feldman and Pentland (2003), 101 Pentland and Feldman (2005) also discuss the distinction between the ostensive and performative aspects of organizational routines in the faculty hiring process at a university. The ostensive aspect of the routines would include the creation of a job announcement, the review of applications, interviews with top candidates, extending an offer to the most qualified person, and negotiating the terms of the employment relationship. This seems like a fair and legitimate process that will lead to equitable outcomes. However, in practice, this process leads to highly unequal hiring and compensation outcomes for different status groups because the performance of this routine is carried out by real people with real biases in unequal power positions interacting with each other to make multiple decisions. Status categories like race matter in the performance of routines.

61. Feldman and Pentland (2003), 103.

62. In what follows we have done our best to address the experiences of all students at Riverview. However, we clearly give far more attention to the experiences of black and white students at the school than we do to Latina/o and Asian American students. This is in part because of the demographics of the school, which was predominantly black and white. While Latina/os were a small but growing demographic, Asian Americans remain a very small minority at the school. We did interview a sample of Latina/o students and parents and incorporate wider literature on Latina/o students herein, but we recognize that we do not fully do justice to capturing their experiences at Riverview.

63. Fordham and Ogbu (1986); Ogbu (1978, 1987).

64. While the work of scholars such as Ogbu and Fordham in this area attend to the societal and school forces that they suggest lead to oppositional orientations among some students, the popular discussion that has grown out of their work has focused almost entirely on students' attitudes and educational orientations.

65. Anderson (2004), 360–361.

CHAPTER 2

1. This chapter borrows passages from John B. Diamond, Amanda E. Lewis, and Lamont Gordon (2007), "Race, Culture, and Achievement Disparities in a Desegregated Suburb: Reconsidering the Oppositional Culture Explanation." *International Journal of Qualitative Studies in Education,* 20(6), 655–679; Diamond, J. B. and J. Huguley (2011), "Black/White Disparities in Educational Outcomes: Rethinking Issues of Race, Culture, and Context." In N. E. Hill, T. L. Mann, and H. E. Fitzgerald (Eds.), *African American Children's Mental Health: Development and Context.* New York: Praeger; and Diamond, J. B. and J. Huguley (2008), "Testing the Oppositional Culture Explanation

for Racial Disparities in Educational Outcomes in Desegregated Schools." Paper presented at the Annual Meeting of the American Educational Research Association, New York, NY; and Diamond, John B. (2013), "The Resource and Opportunity Gap: The Continued Significance of Race for African American Student Outcomes."

2. Herbert (1995).

3. Lewin (2000).

4. Ainsworth-Darnell and Downey (1998); Carter (2005); Diamond, Lewis, and Gordon (2007); Downey and Ainsworth-Darnell (2002); Farkas et al. (2002); Fordham and Ogbu (1986); Harris (2011); Horvat and O'Connor (2006); Ogbu (1974, 1978, 2003); Warikoo (2011).

5. Fordham and Ogbu (1986); Ogbu (1974, 1978, 2003, 2008), among others.

6. This pattern of opportunity and social position intermingling to shape students' academic motivation is echoed in studies of class dynamics among whites in the United Kingdom, France (Bourdieu and Passeron 1990), and the United States. Paul Willis (1977) demonstrates that some working-class boys in England valorize their male working-class culture and define school as a domain in which they should invest little energy. Jay Macleod (2009) argues that working-class white males lower their education and employment aspirations partially because they doubt that educational investment will pay off for them in the long run. Finally, Pierre Bourdieu (1990) argues that a social class–based habitus—a set of beliefs about what is possible for people of one's social class—can lead to a set of behaviors that reinforce patterns of class inequality. However, an important distinction exists between the social class resistance models of MacLeod and Willis and Ogbu's. For Willis and MacLeod, subgroups within the *working-class or poor* population adopt distinct responses to constraints on opportunity. For a more recent discussion of this social class pattern in the United Kingdom, see Harris (2011), chapter 8. Ogbu's theory seeks to explain the cultural adaptations of the entire African American population, a perspective that has led him to be criticized by other writers (see Carter 2005). While Bourdieu has been criticized for presenting a structurally deterministic argument in discussing class-based habitus (Swartz 1998), he does examine variations within classes by focusing on class fractions. However, his work is largely silent on racial inequality.

7. Fordham and Ogbu (1986).

8. Carter (2005); Farkas, Lleras, and Maczuga (2002); Fordham and Ogbu (1986); Fryer and Levitt (2006b); Horvat and Lewis (2003); Ogbu (2003); Rodriguez (2002); Tyson, Darity, and Castellino (2005).

9. Horvat et al. (2006).

10. Ibid. Even though there has been much debate on this issue within the scholarly literature, Tyson (2011:4) writes: "The popularity of the notion that black students reject achievement as acting white and that this accounts for the black-white achievement gap has helped turn this hypothesis into an accepted fact."

11. Herbert (1995).

12. Harris (2011).

13. Ainsworth-Darnell and Downey (1998); Carter (2005); Diamond and Huguley (2014); Harris (2011); Horvat and O'Connor (2006); O'Connor (1997, 1999); Tyson (2002); Tyson et al. (2005).

14. Harris (2011).

15. Ibid.

16. Cook and Ludwig (1998).

17. Ainsworth-Darnell and Downey (1998); Downey, von Hippel, and Hughes (2008), Downey, Ainsworth, and Qian (2009); Harris (2008, 2011). See Farkas et al. (2002) for an alternative interpretation.

18. Diamond and Huguley (2014).

19. Harris (2011); Robinson and Harris (2013).

20. Carter (2005); Tyson et al. (2005).

21. Buck (2010); Fryer and Levitt (2006b); Tyson (2011); Tyson et al. (2005).

22. Tyson's (2011) argument is not that oppositional culture is pervasive in integrated schools. She writes that "Only a small number of participants in any study reported on in this book experienced ostracism or taunts of acting white because of their academic achievement or achievement-related behaviors" (166). In fact, the acting white accusation related to achievement-related behaviors was reported by only 13 of 65 (20 percent) black students. Instead, she argues that when students connect race and achievement, this results from the racialization of school achievement by schools through racialized tracking. In an earlier study, Tyson and her colleagues argue that "[racialized oppositionality] is more likely to be part of the local school culture of schools in which socio-economic status differences between blacks and whites are stark and perceived as corresponding to patterns of placement and achievement" (Tyson et al. 2005: 601).

23. Ogbu (2003).

24. Fryer and Levitt (2006a); Fryer and Torelli (2010).

25. Fryer and Levitt (2006a); Fryer and Torelli (2010); Tyson (2011); Tyson et al. (2005); O'Connor et al. (2011).

26. Harris (2011) provides a particularly comprehensive and convincing analysis of oppositional culture explanations drawing evidence from six datasets from the United States and the United Kingdom.

27. Proponents of oppositional culture explanations tend to emphasize that these responses are but one of several potential responses to minority status and limited opportunity. See Ogbu (2008).

28. See the discussion of the Assessment of Secondary School Student Culture Survey in the Appendix.

29. As we will report later in the chapter, for all of these indicators except for one (students reporting that they liked being at their current schools) black students were as pro-school as their white counterparts and in most cases more so once socio-economic status is taken into consideration.

30. Harris (2011).

31. As we have discussed, contemporary racial inequality has largely transformed from overt racial policies and practices to covert patterns that are more difficult to identify. See Bonilla-Silva (2001, 2003); Coates et al. (2011); Payne (1984).

32. Bertrand and Mullainathan (2004); Harris (2011).

33. Pager, Western, and Bonikowski (2009). Some researchers have critiqued audit studies of this type because there is no way to fully account for behavioral differences that might exist between the field testers. However, similar findings using resumes suggest similar patterns.

34. Bertrand and Mullainathan (2004).

35. Bonilla-Silva (2006), 3.

36. In this survey, conducted in 2004 (during the period when the majority of our interviews were conducted), the comparable number for whites was 27 percent (Krysan 2011).

37. Washington Post/ABC News telephone poll, random sample of 1,079 people in the United States cited by Harris (2011), 43.

38. Harris (2011), 43.

39. Coleman, Darity, and Sharpe (2008).

40. Cohen et al. (2007).

41. At Riverview, students receive a GPA boost for taking honors and advanced placement classes. An honors student who receives an "A" is given 4.5 on a 4.0 scale and AP students are given 5.0 on a 4.0 scale for an "A" grade. Ostensibly this is to encourage students to challenge themselves by taking more difficult classes without the threat of hurting their overall GPA.

42. Ogbu (2003, 2008).

43. NCES (2012).

44. Harris (2011). See also Mangino (2010); Mason (1997).

45. Of the four students who were not planning to go to college, three were considering going into filmmaking, culinary arts, and music. The other student was undecided about what she wanted to do after high school.

46. The data reported in this chapter are drawn from the Assessment of Secondary School Student Culture (ASSSC, Ferguson 2002), which was collected from 101 secondary schools across 10 states during the school year of 2000–2001. The data were collected from over 36,000 7th- to 11th-grade students. For the tables in this chapter (n = 36,894), values were obtained from multilevel hierarchical regression analyses. Socio-economic measures included parents' highest level of education, family composition (number of parents and siblings in the home), and measures of home possessions (number of books and computers).

47. For instance, in the survey, black students were more likely than white students to report that their friends thought it is important to go to one of the best colleges in the United States (Ferguson 2002).

48. Anderson (1988); Neckerman (2007). Neckerman's account of Chicago school history does suggest that in the period from the 1960s going forward discipline and student engagement issues arose resulting from school policy failures.

49. In using counternarrative here, we are borrowing from the work of Theresa Perry (2003), 49. She argues that African Americans developed a counternarrative "that stands in opposition to the dominant society's notions about the intellectual capacity of African Americans, the role of learning in their lives, the meaning and purpose of school, and the power of their intellect."

50. Harris (2011).

51. Theresa Perry argues that this tension has been fundamental to the education of African Americans historically and served as the basis for the development of an African American philosophy of education that was not dependent on economic rewards to educational investment. See Perry, Steele, and Hilliard (2003).

52. Harris (2011). Several authors find that conceptions of black achievement that incorporate ideas of collective struggle, resistance, and critical race understandings are important tools in the success of high achievers (Akom 2003; Carter 2008; O'Connor 1997; Perry 2003; Ward 1996). Similarly, Brown and colleagues (2009) find that parents who use cultural socialization practices—parenting practices that teach children their cultural history and promote cultural traditions and pride (Hughes et al. 2006)—tend to have children who achieve at higher levels in schools. Also see Wang and Huguley (2011).

53. Harris (2008) argues that in their analysis of students' beliefs about schooling, scholars have conflated the "value of schooling and perceived barriers despite schooling." In other words, students' beliefs about whether or not school has some value have been conflated with their ideas about whether or not labor market discrimination exists. As our analysis here shows, his work also demonstrates that the recognition of discrimination can coexist with the belief in the instrumental value of education.

54. For similar findings, see Tyson et al. (2005).

55. While the majority of students do not see such negative peer pressure as an issue that undermines their performance, for those students who are targets this could be an important point of intervention. However, the reader should note that there are no major racial differences in the experience of negative peer pressure and that black students are in fact *less likely* to experience negative peer pressure once we control for social class background.

56. This is similar to what Tyson finds in her interviews with high-achieving black students in North Carolina. See Tyson (2011).

57. For more on this, see O'Connor et al. (2011) and Tyson (2011).

58. See Kinney (1993) for more on the phenomenon of kids being labeled as "nerds."

59. Because these students attended integrated schools, we also took the composition of their peer groups into account. In other words we compared black students with mostly black friends, some black friends, and mostly white friends. We found that the composition of students' friendship groups did not matter. The patterns remained the same. What did emerge was that the sex of the student mattered. Boys were twice as likely as girls to experience negative peer pressure. For further discussion of this gender pattern, see Lundy (2003).

60. They were also more likely than non-black students to report that their friends believed that it was important to study hard and get good grades, to participate actively in class (among high school students), and to continue their education past high school.

61. Tyson (2002); Ferguson, personal communication.

62. Fordham and Ogbu (1986); Horvat and Lewis (2003).

63. Ogbu (1994), 289.

64. Ogbu (2003).

65. Mickelson (1990).

66. Using data from eight Los Angeles high schools, Mickelson (2008) makes important distinctions between abstract attitudes (idealized beliefs about education and opportunity) and concrete attitudes (students' "realistic assessment of future opportunities"). While black students had higher abstract attitudes than white students, they possessed lower concrete attitudes and these concrete attitudes predicted educational effort and outcomes. Therefore, it may be black students' concrete (as opposed to abstract) attitudes account for the apparent attitude-achievement paradox. Mickelson's argument depends on concrete attitudes (e.g., beliefs about discrimination) predicting educational outcomes and abstract attitudes not predicting those outcomes. More recent work challenges both of these components of Mickelson's argument. It turns out that black students' positive attitudes toward school predict their outcomes in ways that are comparable to white students. When black students have positive school attitudes, their achievement is higher. Moreover, black students' concrete attitudes do not affect their school outcomes. Black students who believe that discrimination will affect them do just as well in school as those who discount the

impact of discrimination. For further discussion of these issues, see Downey et al. (2009) and Harris (2011).

67. It is worth noting that unlike the abstract attitudes Mickelson (1990) considered and found to be unassociated with achievement, the indicators highlighted in our survey study do in fact predict student performance. Thus, even before considering behaviors, these achievement attitudes are in and over themselves associated with improved academic outcomes.

68. Family background here refers to the educational resources found in the homes of black students. In his book *Kids Don't Want to Fail*, Angel Harris (2011) makes a similar argument. He suggests that black students possess more pro-school attitudes than their white counterparts but that there are skill deficits among black students that account for racial differences in school outcomes. These skill deficits arise from lack of educational opportunities that are likely a product of the interaction of their racial categorization and schools' educative processes.

69. Ainsworth-Darnell and Downey (1998); Coleman (1961); Downey (2008).

70. Thanks to an anonymous reviewer for the reminder to make this point explicitly.

71. Diamond and Huguley (2014).

72. Thanks to an anonymous reviewer for the reminder to make this point explicitly.

CHAPTER 3

1. In fact, most students from all racial groups report having at least one close friend from another racial group (though most of the groups are somewhat racially homogenous).

2. Feldman and Pentland (2003).

3. Gregory, Skiba, and Noguera (2010), 63. See also Morrison and Skiba (2001).

4. Gregory et al. (2010); Piquero (2008); Skiba et al. (2011).

5. For at least the last 30 years, abundant research has documented the patterns across school level, showing much higher rates of suspension and expulsion for black students. See Ferguson (2000); Losen and Gillespie (2012); McCarthy and Hoge (1987); Raffaele Mendez and Knoff (2003); Reyes (2006); Rocque (2010); Skiba et al. (2000); Skiba and Rasch (2006); Skiba et al. (2006); US Department of Education Office of Civil Rights (2012); Wu et al. (1982).

6. Latina/o students, while not overrepresented among in-school suspensions, are represented in out-of-school suspensions at 1.5 times their representation among the student body overall US Department of Education, Office of Civil Rights (2012).

7. Increasingly, studies are finding that these large differences in suspension and expulsion rates originate in large differences in referral rates for minor offenses. See Skiba et al. (2002); Skiba et al. (2011).

8. Pentland and Feldman (2005) distinguish between the ostensive aspect of organizational routines and artifacts. As they write, "It would be more appropriate to describe standard operating procedures as indicators of the ostensive aspect or, from another perspective, as efforts to codify the ostensive aspect" (797). This is the sense in which we discuss the discipline code and other rules and standard operating procedures here.

9. Vavrus and Cole (2002).

10. Carter (2012), 4.

11. Ibid., 5.

12. Recent research has shown that relationships with teachers and other school personnel are particularly important for black and Latina/o student engagement. See Ferguson (1998); Gregory et al. (2010); Valenzuela (1999).

13. Walton and Cohen (2007, 2011).

14. Inzlicht and Good (2006), 131.

15. As Steele discusses in his book *Whistling Vivaldi*, identity threat raises self-doubt and leads to performance anxiety. Experiencing self-doubt has a negative affect on our ability to complete challenging academic work, partly because it is distracting and leads us to use the wrong part of our brains. Ironically, it has the most impact when the work is difficult and when we *care* about how we do. Steele (2010) states, "caring about doing well in areas where your group is disadvantaged, discriminated against and negatively stereotyped can extract a price" (131).

16. See, for example, Ferguson (2000); Lewis (2003); Morris (2003).

17. Abundant literature discusses the tendency to read black and brown bodies, particularly male bodies, as suspect and potentially criminal. Recent examples include Dance (2002); Eberhardt (2005); Eberhart et al. (2004); Eberhardt et al. (2006); Graham and Lowery (2004); Gyimah-Brempong and Price (2006); Hurwitz and Peffley (1997); Lopez (2002); Rios (2011); Russell-Brown (1998). Much of this work implicitly, if not explicitly, discusses the related concept of "white innocence." Other recent research in critical race studies and critical whiteness studies has explored the idea further (Gotanda 2003–2004; Hunt 2005–2006; Lewis 2004).

18. In her work, Annette Lareau (2003) found similar patterns of parental intervention and negotiation to be true of both white and black middle-class families. At Riverview, we found that middle-class black parents did try to intervene on behalf of their children, at least with regard to academic issues, but that their intervention was not received in the same way as from white parents. We discuss these patterns further in the next chapters.

19. A counterargument could be made that rather than a tight alignment between ostensive and performative aspects of disciplinary routines, a more consistent looseness in enforcement of the rules with *all* students would be better. One could argue, for example, that school personnel should retain discretion to ignore rules when behavior is not interfering with school activities. Given abundant evidence in both our research and in that of previous studies, we are cynical about whether such "looseness" would be applied equally for all students. We will explore variations of these possibilities in the conclusion to the chapter.

20. There is substantial research on authority relations in schools and the important roles these play in conveying status within the school environment.

21. Just because rules are written in "race-neutral" language does not mean that they are race-neutral in design or practice. For example, US drug laws have long been argued to have racial bias built into them in the different penalties resulting from possession of crack versus powder cocaine (see Alexander 2010).

22. Ferguson (2000), 52.

23. Collins (2009).

24. See Lareau (2003).

25. See, for example, Lareau and Horvat (1999).

26. Gregory et al. (2010), 61. See also McCarthy and Hoge (1987); Skiba et al. (2002); Wallace et al. (2008).

27. As Evelyn Higginbotham (1992:256–257) writes, the conflation of race and class has roots in the history of the emergence of race and racial categories: "The social context for the construction of race as a tool for black oppression is historically rooted in the context of slavery." Barbara Fields reminds us: 'The idea one people has of another, even when the difference between them is embodied in the most striking physical characteristics, is always mediated by the social context within which the two come in contact.' Race came to life primarily as the signifier of the master/slave relation and thus emerged superimposed upon class and property relations."

28. Hallett (2007); Lewis (2003).

29. Horvat and Lewis (2003).

30. Heath (1983); Lewis (2003); Rist (1970).

31. Calarco (2010); Lareau (2003).

32. Connolly (1998); Lewis (2003).

33. Connolly (1998), 21. Also see Downey and Pribesh (2004).

34. Lewis (2003).

35. Morris (2006).

36. Eberhart (2005); Eberhardt et al. (2004); Eberhardt et al. (2006); Graham and Lowery (2004).

37. Hughey (2012); Russell-Brown (2008).

38. Quillian (2008).

39. Quillian (2008), 8.

40. Ridgeway (2011), 40.

41. Ridgeway (2011), 12.

42. For a similar finding in another institution, see Morris (2003).

43. We found similar language in school discipline codes from around the country by doing an Internet search. These expectations about appropriate dress seem to be common in many high schools.

44. As Patricia Hill Collins (2000) discusses in *Black Feminist Thought*, there is a long history of regulating black women's bodies. See also Glenn (1992); Higginbotham (1992).

45. Gregory et al. (2010); Skiba et al. (2002); Skiba et al. (2009/10); Skiba et al. (2011); Vavrus and Cole (2002); Wallace et al. (2008).

46. Lewis (2003) discusses a similar phenomenon.

47. As the students describe, sometimes the "discipline" meted out is only a verbal admonishment. However, these interactions all serve as the kind of "cues" social psychologists discuss as contributing to identity threat.

48. Forman (2004), 44. See also Forman and Lewis (2006).

49. Some might suggest that school officials are acting on historical data regarding discipline infractions, a statistical form of discrimination rooted in evidence rather than bias. The result is nonetheless that black students, whether or not they are violating the rules, are more closely scrutinized. The impact of these patterns on students, and the meaning they attach to them, does not differ based on the intentions.

50. Here we borrow from Weber's (1968) work on status groups.

51. McIntosh (1990:31) argues "white privilege is like an invisible weightless knapsack of special provisions, assurances, tools, maps, guides, codebooks, passports,

visas, clothes, compass, emergency gear, and blank checks." These advantages are supported by institutional structures and practices that reinforce inequality.

52. Gregory et al. (2010).

53. Smith's (2007) work builds off the original work of Charles Pierce, who coined the term. A number of others have written about microaggressions in recent years, including Daniel Solorzano, Tara Yosso, and Debra Wing Sue. For more see Smith, Allen, and Danley (2007); Solorzano (1998); Sue (2010); Yosso et al. (2009).

54. Smith, Allen, and Danley (2007) list some of the implications of racial microaggressions that are cumulative and constant, discussing what they refer to as racial battle fatigue. The cumulative symptoms of racial battle fatigue are both physiological and psychological (Smith 2004). Examples of physiological symptoms include, but are not limited to, (a) tension headaches and backaches, (b) elevated heart beat, (c) rapid breathing in anticipation of racial conflict, (d) an upset stomach or "butterflies," (e) extreme fatigue, (f) ulcers, (g) loss of appetite, and (h) elevated blood pressure. The psychological symptoms of racial battle fatigue include (a) constant anxiety and worrying, (b) increased swearing and complaining, (c) inability to sleep, (d) sleep broken by haunting, conflict-specific dreams, (e) intrusive thoughts and images, (f) loss of self-confidence, (g) difficulty in thinking coherently or being able to articulate (confirming stereotype), (h) hypervigilance, (i) frustration, (j) denial, (k) *John Henryism*, or prolonged, high-effort coping with difficult psychological stressors, (l) emotional and social withdrawal, (m) anger, anger suppression, and verbal or nonverbal expressions of anger, (n) denial, (o) keeping quiet, and (p) resentment. For more information on the effects of racial stressors, see Clark et al. (1999); Feagin and McKinney (2003); Feagin and Sikes (1994); James (1994); Pierce (1974, 1975, 1995); Prillerman et al. (1989); Turner and Myers (2000); Williams et al. (1997).

55. Kupchik and Ellis (2008). See also Ruck and Wortley (2002).

56. Hill Collins (2009), 65–66.

57. In the essay "Do you live in this neighborhood," Paul Butler (2010) discusses being followed by police as he walked home in his posh DC neighborhood. A professor of criminal procedure, Butler recollects the experience of harassment as part of a larger set of experiences that black men, even law professors, regularly contend with in interactions with law enforcement.

58. Bobo (2011).

59. Gregory et al. (2010), 62. In fact, there is evidence that white students are more likely to break the rules (e.g., skipping class and vandalism).

60. Vavrus and Cole (2002), 87. See also Gregory and Weinstein (2008) and Skiba et al. (2008).

61. See also Goff et al. (2014). A number of scholars have written about the connection between race and crime, what Kathryn Russell (1998) wrote about as the idea of "criminal blackman."

62. Further, other related research suggests that even if what they were actually doing was similar to white students' actions, black students' behavior would still be read as more threatening. For example, recent research by Goff et al. (2014) found in multiple experiments that black boys were seen as older and less innocent than their white peers.

63. Dance (2002), 128.

64. In his book, McBride (2005) talks about the brand's widespread identification with a kind of whiteness that is both normative and exclusive. See also Greenhouse (2004).

65. Bourdieu (1984:43) argues: "When habitus encounters a social world of which it is the product, it finds itself 'as a fish in water,' it does not feel the weight of the water and takes the world about itself for granted."

66. See, for example, Carter (2005) and Lareau and Horvat (1999).

67. Abercrombie & Fitch seems to have embraced whiteness as a value. In *González v. Abercrombie & Fitch* (2004) the company agreed to pay $45,000 in an out-of-court settlement of a class action lawsuit claiming that minority employees were excluded from desirable positions. The company also agreed to address its nearly-all-white advertising campaigns. In addition, the company has a history of outfitting elite whites, including many former presidents and celebrities.

68. There are certain behaviors and styles that can also signal trouble for white students. For instance, identification with a school's burnout culture of drug users can lead students to be scrutinized. However, as a general rule, it is black and Latina/o students who are often subject to quick cultural assessments that can place them under more intense surveillance.

69. Morris (2005), 41.

70. Ferguson (2000).

71. Weber (1968).

72. Julius's parents are both lawyers. Therefore, he is an individual exception to the race and class pattern he identifies. His general point is that teachers and administrators conflate class and race, and enact discipline in ways that assume white parents have the resources to make more vigorous interventions.

73. Lewis (2004); Morris (2006).

74. Vavrus and Cole (2002), 109.

75. For more on status construction theory, see Ridgeway (2006, 2011).

76. Lewis (2003).

77. Bobo, Kluegel, and Smith (1997); Bonilla-Silva (2006); Forman (2004); Forman and Lewis (2006).

78. Fraser (2000), 113–114.

79. Antonia Randolph (2012) discusses what she refers to as ethnic credits and racial penalties that teachers give students when they talk about them in interviews. In her work, she examines how teachers construct white and Asian immigrants as ethnic students and assess them more favorably than black students.

80. Here we borrow from Pierre Bourdieu's work on symbolic power and draw on previous work by Amanda Lewis (2003) in which she discusses race as symbolic power.

81. Staples (2010), 6.

82. For more on this, see Steele (2010).

83. See Bowman and Howard (1985); Harris (2011); Wang and Huguley (2012) for discussion of the role of race related socialization and student achievement.

84. Harris (2011), 138.

85. For more on the question of decoupling race, crime, and punishment, see Bobo (2011).

86. Recent research by Greg Walton, Geoff Cohen, Claude Steele, and colleagues has shown that facilitating a sense of student belonging can have dramatic effects on students' school performance. See Logel et al. (2012); Walton and Carr (2012); Walton et al. (2012); Yeager and Walton (2011); Yeager, Walton, and Cohen (2013).

87. Kennedy as quoted in Butler (2010), 122.

88. This movement is about trying to develop responses to violations of community norms that are not focused on punishment. Such policies are gaining traction nationwide, with some cities implementing district-wide policies (see http://greatergood. berkeley.edu/article/item/can_restorative_justice_keep_schools_safe). For great examples of restorative justice at the school level, see Maria Hantzopoulo's (2006) article on the "fairness committee" at Humanities Prep and Kazu Haga's (2011–2012) piece on training Peace Warriors at Chicago North Lawndale Charter School, both in *Rethinking Schools*. See also Haft (1999–2000); Hopkins (2002); Karp and Breslin (2001).

CHAPTER 4

1. O'Connor and colleagues (2011) have labeled these patterns "Racially Stratified Academic Hierarchies." See also Clotfelter (2004); Lucas and Berends (2002); Mickelson (2001); Oakes (2005); Tyson (2011).

2. Darity and Jolla (2009) discuss the widespread adoption of tracking in the period right after desegregation as a way of mitigating (for whites) the effects of desegregation at the facility level.

3. Tyson (2011).

4. Fischer et al. (1996); American Anthropological Association (1994, 1998).

5. Aronson and Steele (2005), 437.

6. A number of psychologists have recently been writing about the fluid and constructed nature of intelligence. In addition to Aronson and Steele (2005), see, for example, Resnick (1995) and Walton (2013).

7. For a longer discussion about the problems with a "cultural" framing of school outcomes, see Darity and Jolla (2009); Gould (1999); Lewis (2013); O'Connor, Hill, and Robinson (2009); O'Connor, Lewis, and Mueller (2007).

8. Orfield and Gordon (2001); Orfield and Lee (2005); Orfield and Yun (1999).

9. Harris (2011) speaks to the importance of skills gaps in his book *Kids Don't Want to Fail*.

10. O'Connor et al. (2009); Roscigno and Ainsworth-Darnell (1999).

11. O'Connor et al. (2009), 8. However, some research suggests that out-of-school time and differences in summer learning might also play a role in increased differences in outcomes across demographic groups (Downey, von Hippel, and Hughes, 2008).

12. Clotfelter (2004); Lucas and Berends (2002); Mickelson (2001); Noguera and Wing (2006); Oakes (2005); O'Connor et al. (2011); Tyson (2011).

13. Lewis (2003); Lewis-McCoy (2014); Posey-Maddox (2014); Shapiro (2004).

14. Aronson and Steele (2005); Steele (2010).

15. Bobo et al. (1997), 23.

16. Tyson (2011). See also Perry (2002).

17. For a discussion of discrimination in its various forms, see Blank, Dabady, and Citro (2004). See also the abundant writing of William A. Darity.

18. Pager and Shepherd (2008), 2.

19. Pager and Shepherd (2008), 20.

20. Deitch et al. (2003), 1299.

21. Oliver and Shapiro (1995); Patillo-McCoy (1999); Shapiro (2004); Shaprio, Meschede, and Sullivan (2010); Shapiro, Meschede, and Osoro (2013); Wolff (2010).

22. US Census Bureau, American Community Survey (2007).

23. Ibid.

24. These dissimilarity indices were calculated using Census 2000 data. See Frey and Myers's (2000) analysis.

25. The exception here is clearly for the small Asian/Pacific Islander population in Riverview.

26. Correll and Ridgeway (2003); Ridgeway (2006, 2011).

27. Greenwald and Banaji (1995); Greenwald and Krieger (2006).

28. Correll and Ridgeway (2003).

29. Here the point is that people of color recognize that others likely have low expectations for them. Thus, while they might be highly confident in their own abilities, in the context of realizing that others likely think they are less competent, they are more likely to act tentatively, to defer more often to others, and so on.

30. Correll and Ridgeway (2003).

31. This also speaks to the way those with low-status characteristics are challenged more when in leadership positions. It is clearly true that despite performance expectations and disadvantage in interaction, some from low-status groups achieve success and high-ranking positions—often by acquiring other advantaging status characteristics (e.g., education) and through their high-level performance. But when they try to wield power, they often run into the problem of *legitimation*. Status beliefs associated with status characteristics not only affect performance expectations but also provide cultural support for status hierarchies in which leaders tend to be those from advantaged groups—this helps make the hierarchy seem "right." Leaders from low-status groups who achieve a leadership position despite barriers don't have added cultural support that makes their position seem natural and thus are likely to encounter more challenges to legitimacy of leadership.

32. Weinstein (2002), 7.

33. Steele (2010).

34. Steele (1997), 46.

35. Walton and Cohen (2003).

36. Abundant research on tracking shows poor and minority students disproportionately in bottom groups/lower tracks.

37. Diamond et al. (2004); Downey and Pribesh (2004); Ferguson (1998); Weinstein (2002).

38. Tyson (2011).

39. Ibid.

40. See, for example, Condron (2007, 2008); Hallinan and Sorenson (1983); Oakes (2005); Sorenson and Hallinan (1986); Wheelock (1982).

41. Scholars who study tracking processes refer to this pattern of teacher placement—placing the least experienced teachers with the lowest performing students—teacher tracking. For a discussion of this process, see Sean Kelly (2004).

42. Recent research by Timothy Diette (2005) in North Carolina shows that (1) minority students are more likely to attend schools that either do not offer Algebra I or that enroll a lower percentage of students in the course, and (2) low-income students, African American students, and students with less-well-educated parents are less likely to take Algebra I in middle school than are other students with equal academic achievement.

43. Wilson, Roscigno, and Huffman (2012).

44. Codjoe (2001); Diamond, Randolph, and Spillane (2004); Ferguson (2000); Ferguson (2002); Graybill (1997); Lewis (2003); Monroe (2005).

45. Tyson (2011), 159–60.

46. Darity and Jolla (2009), 109.

47. Blank et al. (2004), 226.

48. Ibid., 225.

49. http://www.npr.org/blogs/health/2012/09/18/161159263/teachers-expectations-can-influence-how-students-perform. For more on these dynamics, see Rosenthal and Jacobson (1992); Weinstein (2002).

50. Ferguson (1998), 313.

51. See Lewis (2003); Pollock (2004).

52. Steele (2010).

53. Resnick as quoted in Tyson (2011), 160.

54. Ridgeway (2011), 27. Here she offers an elaboration of these dynamics with regard to gender.

55. Oakes (2005), 134.

CHAPTER 5

1. Dewey (1915); Kohn (1998).

2. Bartky (2002), 151.

3. O'Connor et al. (2011); Tyson (2011).

4. As we will talk about further, a few parents were at least somewhat critical of current school structures. However, most were complacent about current arrangements or actively defended them.

5. Unless we noted otherwise, the parents we discuss in this chapter are white.

6. Note: Students were selected for interviews based on GPAs (stratified sampling of high, medium, and low GPAs), not based on the level of their course enrollment.

7. Wells and Serna (1996) find similar patterns of parents encouraging their children to remain in honors course in their research on detracking.

8. There were a few exceptions. Parents of a couple of kids with learning disabilities felt that "regular" classes were the appropriate place for them, and at least one other father we spoke to was comfortable with the idea that his kids were in regular classes and had no issues with the placement.

9. As we discuss later, intervening and being an "articulate" advocate are both forms of cultural capital that have been attributed to middle-class parents and seen as enhancing the success of their involvement (Lareau 1989, 2003).

10. In her research on high schools in California, Perry (2002: 58) also found a pattern of white parents pressuring counselors to put their children into accelerated tracks—pressure counselors often "succumbed to" partly because of the "difficulty of placing so many students."

11. This was not specific to Riverview. For example, a 2010 New York Times story reported that "A 2000 audit of California test takers showed a disproportionate number of white, affluent students receiving accommodations, igniting suspicions of exaggerated or nonexistent disabilities." See Abigail S. Moore (2010), "Accommodations Angst," http://www.nytimes.com/2010/11/07/education/edlife/07strategy-t.html?pagewanted=all&_r=2&.

12. Scholars refer to the process through which more experienced teachers are assigned to higher-performing students as "teacher tracking." See Sean Kelly (2004).

13. Oakes (2005); Sorensen and Hallinan (1986).

14. This pattern is not wholly surprising. Scholars of racial attitudes have documented a similar trend of a contradiction in public opinion polls between respondents' answers to questions about principles (e.g., should people be able to attend any school?) versus questions about policy (e.g., should the government make interventions to ensure integrated schools?). In their book *Racial Attitudes in America*, Schuman et al. (1997) state, "As we and others have found repeatedly, support for principles of equal treatment is often accompanied by opposition to government implementation of such principles" (i.e., support for the principle of integration but little support to change things to actualize the principle).

15. In a somewhat similar vein, Mechanic (2002) discusses how public health efforts developed to improve overall health can actually worsen health *disparities*, as those who are already advantaged are in a better position to be able to take advantage of interventions more quickly. Thus, while overall health may be improved, the health of those already in advantaged positions improves more and more quickly.

16. Again, this pattern is not entirely surprising, as it echoes a finding in public opinion research over the last few decades—the so-called principles/policy paradox. For more, see Krysan (2012); Schuman et al. (1997). Similarly, Bell and Hartmann (2007) find that while many of the folks they interviewed spoke positively and optimistically about diversity, few were able to live up to their ideals and actually *practice* diversity.

17. Brantlinger (2003), 188.

18. Wells and Serna (1996).

19. Bonilla-Silva (2003), 8.

20. Forman and Lewis (2006), 177–178. For more on this, see Bonilla-Silva, Lewis, and Embrick (2004); Forman (2004); Gallagher (2003); Lewis (2001, 2004); Lewis, Chesler, and Forman (2000).

21. Darity (2002), 1.

22. For example, see Bonilla-Silva (2003); Bush (2004); Eliasoph (1999); Myers (2005); and Pollock (2004). In her book *Colormute*, educational researcher Mica Pollock (2004:9) argues that adults in the California school she studied avoided race words, particularly when they discussed "inequitable patterns potentially implicating themselves."

23. Perry (2002), 171.

24. See also Lamont (2000).

25. Bobo et al. (2012).

26. See Macleod (1995).

27. Brantlinger (2003); Wells and Serna (1996).

28. Recent work has, in fact, focused on the creation of elite status through the impact of the college admissions process of elite colleges on family life and education at earlier levels (Stevens 2007) and the generation of elite status at boarding schools (Gaztambide-Fernández 2009) and how middle-class parents rationalize their privilege in public high schools (Brantlinger 2003). See also Khan (2012).

29. For a discussion of the construction of deserving and underserving students, see Wells and Serna (1996). See also Katz (1989).

30. We borrow the language "people above" and "people below" from Michele Lamont (2000).

31. Lamont and Molnar (2002), 186.

32. Ibid.

33. Tilly (1999).

34. Forman (2004), 44.

35. Forman (2004), 51. See also Michael Katz's (1989) discussion of the undeserving poor.

36. See Payne (1984).

37. Jackman (1994), 8.

38. Harris (2011) discusses the critical role of prior educational experiences in contributing to the black/white gap in school outcomes.

39. Anderson (2010), 9.

40. See Darity and Jolla (2009); Tyson (2011).

41. Allport (1954).

42. Leonardo (2009); Lewis (2003).

43. Bobo and Tuan (2006), 32.

44. Bonilla-Silva (2001).

45. Anderson (2010); DiTomaso (2012); Tilly (1999); Walters (2007).

46. See Anderson (2010); Massey (2007); Tilly (1999); Walters (2007).

47. Anderson (2010), 8.

48. Anderson (2010), 19.

49. DiTomaso (2012), 8.

50. Walters (2007), 25.

51. Walters (2007), 17.

52. Wells and Serna (1996), 100–101.

53. Shapiro (2004), 2. Walters (2007) refers to this practice as opportunity prying.

54. Shapiro (2004), 2–3.

55. Shapiro (2004), 75.

56. Ibid.

57. Massey and Denton (1993); Sugrue (1995).

58. Wells et al. (2009).

59. Shapiro (2004).

60. Johnson (2006); Shapiro (2004); Walters (2007); Wells et al. (2009).

61. Shapiro (2004).

62. Walters (2007); Wells et al. (2009).

63. Saporito (2003); Saporito and Lareau (1999); Shapiro (2004); Wells et al. (2005); Wells et al. (2009).

64. Stuart Wells (2005), 2171.

65. Bell and Hartmann (2007).

66. Bell and Hartmann (2007), 910.

67. Bartky (2002), 154.

CHAPTER 6

1. Bourdieu and Passeron (1990), 494.

2. DiTomaso (2012) has recently written extensively about the pernicious effects of intraracial favoritism among whites.

3. Imani Perry (2011) has discussed contemporary racial inequality as a "post-intentional" racism that is not based on traditional biological conceptions of race or intentional discrimination. For more, see recent social psychological research on racial attitudes, including Bobo, Kluegel, and Smith (1997); Dovidio et al. (1997); Forman (2004); Sears et al. (2000). Recently, legal scholars have also pushed for a shift away from focus on intent in legal discussions of discrimination. For example, see the work of Susan Sturm and Jerry Kang.

4. Pollock (2008), 178.

5. Bonilla-Silva (2003).

6. Ahram, Fergus, and Noguera (2011).

7. Ibid., 2256.

8. See Lewis (2003) and Pollock (2004).

9. One example of this kind of argument is the oppositional culture perspective that we reviewed and critiqued in Chapter 2.

10. Moll et al. (1992).

11. Metzl (2009), 201. See also Metzl (2013); O'Connor, Lewis, and Mueller (2007); Olneck (1990); Sleeter and Grant (1988). Certainly, cultural frameworks presented by scholars like Gloria Ladson-Billings, Geneva Gay, and Carol Lee appreciate this broader context and provide powerful tools for shaping instructional and organizational practices. However, it is still important to guard against the potential for interpretations that downplay or ignore institutional and structural dynamics.

12. Metzl (2009), 202.

13. "*Structural violence* is the term often used to describe how even seemingly benevolent social institutions can dominate, oppress, or exploit minority populations . . . . The invisible processes that separate a person's actual realizations from their potential realizations" (Metzl 2009:202). For more discussion of structural violence, see Farmer (2001); Metzl (2009).

14. Mills (2011) writing about the supposed liberalism of the American state asserts: "We are supposed to see others as our moral equals, expect to be seen by them the same way, and should conduct our interactions in the light of the norm of reciprocal respect . . . [but] what if disrespect for nonwhites is not contingent but structurally built in to the political system? It would mean that transparency cannot be the regulating ideal for government, because it would reveal too much. Instead, the actual norm, whether admitted or not, must be an opacity that is not the result of happenstance but epistemically and morally linked to the reproduction of the polity. The whitewashing, the whiting-out, of crucial aspects of the origins and routine workings of government becomes an organic part of the smooth functioning of the white racial state" (33).

15. Mills (2011), 34–35.

16. This opacity or denial is partly a consequence of what scholars have variously labeled "hegemony" or "doxa"—what Moon-Kie Jung (2004:109) describes as the way "our mental structures internalize social structures through gradual inculcation rendering them unconscious"; the way that unequal arrangements become intelligible and even logical to both those who benefit and those who suffer.

17. Ridgeway (2006); Steele (2010).

18. Oakes (2005).

19. Stoskepf (1999).

20. Oakes (2005), 27–30.

21. Ibid., 33.

22. Terman (1916), 91–92.

23. Oakes (2005), 18.

24. Ansalone (2006).

25. Oakes (2005).

26. Clearly, many continue to, however. Recently, Chester Finn (2012) has rehashed a familiar argument about protecting the needs of the gifted. This is based on the faulty premise that those in high-track classes have academic talents that are superior to those not in such classes.

27. Spillane and Coldren (2011).

28. Welner and Burris (2006), 90.

29. For more information about resistance to detracking and successful efforts to detrack, see Burris (2010); Burris, Welner, and Bezoza (2009); Burris and Welner (2005); Hattie (2009); Mathis (2013); Oakes (2005); Oakes et al. (1997); Welner and Burris (2006); Welner and Oakes (2000); Wells and Serna (1996).

30. Welner and Burris (2006), 94.

31. Ibid., 97.

32. Saporito and Lareau (1999); Wells and Serna (1996); Wells et al. (2009).

33. Inzlicht and Good (2006); Walton and Cohen (2007).

34. For just a few examples, see Carter and Welner (2013); Collins (2009); Darling-Hammond (2010); Ladson-Billings (2009); Meier (2002a, 2002b); Michie (2009).

35. Darling-Hammond (2010), 328.

36. Forman (2004); Bartky (2002).

37. Bonilla-Silva (2006), 212.

38. Bell and Hartmann (2007).

APPENDIX

1. We received support from the University of Illinois at Chicago (Office of Social Science Research, Departments of Sociology and African American Studies, and Institute for Research on Race and Public Policy), Emory University, Harvard School of Education (The Dean's Dissemination Fund at HGSE), The Radcliffe Institute for Advanced Study at Harvard, The University of Wisconsin School of Education (Wisconsin Center for Educational Research, and Department of Educational Leadership and Policy Analysis), and The Center for Advanced Studies in the Behavioral Studies at Stanford University. Segments of text summarizing quantitative methods in this appendix also appear in Diamond and Huguley (2014).

2. Because we were interested in exploring the impact of peer relationships, specifically the ways that peers might discourage students from educational engagement, we asked questions about such influences. However, we chose not to interject the term "acting white" into the interview. While others have asked students directly about the "acting white" accusation in order to unpack the meaning that students attach to it (e.g., Mickelson 2006; Neal-Barnett 2001), we argue that, in our case, asking students if they or their friends avoid doing well in school because they might be accused of acting white could potentially lead students to overestimate the impact of

the accusation and to connect the accusation to academic achievement because this is suggested by the question. In the context of other studies, it makes sense to ask this question directly. Even though we made this decision, we thought that the students we interviewed might raise the term "acting white." Surprisingly, they did not. However, our study is not about the "acting white" accusation. It is an examination of *school dynamics associated with academic achievement.*

References

Ahram, Roey, Edward Fergus, and Pedro Noguera. 2011. "Addressing Racial/ Ethnic Disproportionality in Special Education: Case Studies of Suburban School Districts." *Teachers College Record* 113(10):2233–2266.

Ainsworth-Darnell, James and Douglas B. Downey. 1998. "Assessing the Oppositional Culture Explanation for Racial/Ethnic Differences in School Performance." *American Sociological Review* 63(4):536–553.

Akom, A. A. 2003. "Reexamining Resistance as Oppositional Culture: The Nation of Islam and the Creation of a Black Achievement Ideology." *Sociology of Education* 76:305–325.

Alexander, Michelle. 2010. *The New Jim Crow: Mass Incarceration in the Age of Colorblindness*. New York: The New Press.

Allport, Gordon Willard. 1954. *The Nature of Prejudice*. Cambridge, MA: Perseus Book Publishing.

Almaguer, Tomas. 1994. *Racial Fault Lines: The Historical Origins of White Supremacy in California*. Berkeley, CA: University of California Press.

American Anthropological Association. 1994. "Statement on 'Race' and Intelligence." Retrieved January 8, 2013 (http://www.aaanet.org/stmts/ race.htm).

American Anthropological Association. 1998. Statement on "Race." Retrieved January 8, 2013 (http://www.aaanet.org/stmts/racepp.htm).

Anderson, Elizabeth. 2010. *The Imperative of Integration*. Princeton, NJ: Princeton University Press.

Anderson, James D. 1988. *The Education of Blacks in the South, 1860–1935*. Chapel Hill, NC: University of North Carolina Press.

Anderson, James D. 2004. "Crosses to Bear and Promises to Keep: The Jubilee Anniversary of Brown v. Board of Education." *Urban Education* 39(4):359–373.

Ansalone, George. 2006. "Tracking: A Return to Jim Crow." *Race, Gender, & Class* 13:144–153.

Aronson, Joshua and Claude M. Steele. 2005. "Stereotypes and the Fragility of Academic Competence, Motivation, and Self-Concept." Pp. 436–456 in *Handbook of Competence and Motivation*, edited by A. Elliott and C. Dweck. New York: Guilford Press.

Bartky, Sandra Lee. 2002. *"Sympathy and Solidarity" and Other Essays*. Oxford: Rowman & Littlefield Publishers, Inc.

Bell, Joyce M. and Douglas Hartmann. 2007. "Diversity in Everyday Discourse: The Cultural Ambiguities and Consequences of 'Happy Talk.'" *American Sociological Review* 72(6):895–914.

Bertrand, Marianne and Sendhil Mullainathan. 2004. "Are Emily and Greg More Employable Than Lakisha and Jamal? A Field Experiment on Labor Market Discrimination." *American Economic Review* 94(4):991–1013.

Blank, Rebecca M., Marilyn Dabady, and Constance F. Citro, Editors. 2004. *Measuring Racial Discrimination*. Panel on Methods for Assessing Discrimination. Committee on National Statistics, Division of Behavioral and Social Sciences and Education. Washington, DC: The National Academies Press.

Bobo, Lawrence D. June 20, 2011. "On De-Coupling Race, Crime and Punishment" Remarks and Presentation. National Institute of Justice Annual Conference. Arlington, VA.

Bobo, Lawrence and Mia Tuan. 2006. *Prejudice in Politics: Group Position, Public Opinion, and the Wisconsin Treaty Rights Dispute*. Cambridge, MA: Harvard University Press.

Bobo, Lawrence, Camille Z. Charles, Maria Krysan, and Alicia D. Simmons. 2012. "The *Real* Record on Racial Attitudes." Pp. 38–83 in *Social Trends in American Life: Findings from the General Social Survey*, edited by Peter V. Marsden. Princeton, NJ: Princeton University Press.

Bobo, Lawrence, James R. Kluegel, and Ryan A. Smith. 1997. "Laissez Faire Racism: The Crystallization of a 'Kinder, Gentler' Anti-Black Ideology." Pp. 15–42 in *Racial Attitudes in the 1990s: Continuity and Change*, edited by S. Tuch and J. Martin. Westport, CT: Praeger.

Bonilla-Silva, Eduardo. 2001. *White Supremacy and Racism in the Post-Civil Rights Era*. Boulder, CO: Lynne Rienner.

Bonilla-Silva, Eduardo. 2003. *Racism Without Racists: Color-Blind Racism and the Persistence of Racial Inequality in the United States*. Lanham, MD: Rowman & Littlefield.

Bonilla-Silva, Eduardo. 2006. *Racism Without Racists: Color-Blind Racism and Racial Inequality in Contemporary America* (2nd edition). Lanham, MD: Rowman & Littlefield.

Bonilla-Silva, Eduardo and Amanda Lewis. 1999. "The New Racism: Racial Structure in the United States, 1960s–1990s." Pp. 55–101 in *Race, Ethnicity, and Nationality in the USA: Toward the Twenty-First Century*, edited by Paul Wong. Boulder, CO: Westview.

Bonilla-Silva, Eduardo, Amanda Lewis, and David G. Embrick. 2004. "I Did Not Get That Job Because of a Black Man . . .": The Story Lines and Testimonies of Color-Blind Racism." *Sociological Forum* 19(4):555–581.

Bourdieu, Pierre. 1984. *Distinction: A Social Critique of the Judgment of Taste.* London: Routledge and Kegan Paul.

Bourdieu, Pierre. 1990. *The Logic of Practice.* Stanford, CA: Stanford University Press.

Bourdieu, Pierre and Jean Claude Passeron. 1990. *Reproduction in Education, Society, and Culture.* Newbury Park, CA: Sage.

Bowman, Philip and Cleopatra Howard. 1985. "Race-Related Socialization, Motivation, and Academic Achievement: A Study of Black Youth in Three-Generation Families." *Journal of the American Academy of Child Psychiatry* 24:134–141.

Boykin, A. Wade and Pedro Noguera. 2011. *Creating the Opportunity to Learn: Moving from Research to Practice to Close the Achievement Gap.* Alexandria, VA: ASCD.

Brantlinger, Ellen. 2003. *Divided Classes: How the Middle Class Negotiates and Rationalizes School Advantage.* New York: Routledge Falmer.

Brown, Tiffany L, Miriam R. Linver, Melanie Evans, and Donna DeGennaro. 2009. "African-American Parents' Racial and Ethnic Socialization and Adolescent Academic Grades: Testing Out the Role of Gender." *Journal of Youth and Adolescence* 38:214–227.

Buck, Stuart. 2010. *Acting White: The Ironic Legacy of Desegregation.* Grand Rapids, MI: Yale University Press.

Burris, Carol Corbett and Kevin G. Welner. 2005. "Closing the Achievement Gap by Detracking." *The Phi Delta Kappan* 86(8):594–598.

Burris, Carol Corbett, Kevin G. Welner, and J. W. Bezoza. 2009. *Universal Access to a Quality Education: Research and Recommendations for the Elimination of Curricular Stratification.* Boulder, CO: National Education Policy Center. Retrieved June 15, 2003 (http://nepc.colorado.edu/publication/universal-access).

Burris, Carol Corbett. 2010. "Detracking for Success." *Principal Leadership.* 10(5):31–34.

Bush, Melanie. 2004. *Breaking the Code of Good Intentions: Everyday Forms of Whiteness.* Lanham, MD: Rowman & Littlefield.

Butler, Paul. 2010. "Do You Live in this Neighborhood?" Pp. 111–124 in *Twelve Angry Men: True Stories of Being a Black Man in America Today,* edited by Gregory S. Parks and Matthew W. Hughey. New York: The New Press.

Calarco, Jessica McCrory. 2010. "'I Need Help!' Social Class and Children's Help-Seeking in Elementary School." *American Sociological Review* 76:862–882.

Carter, Dorinda. J. 2008. "On Spotlighting and Ignoring Racial Group Members in the Classroom. Pp. 230–234 in *Everyday Antiracism: Getting Real about Race in School,* edited by Mica Pollock. New York: New Press.

Carter, Prudence. 2005. *Keepin' It Real: School Success Beyond Black and White.* New York: Oxford University Press.

———. 2012. *Stubborn Roots: Race, Culture, and Inequality in U.S. and South African Schools.* New York: Oxford University Press.

Carter, Prudence and Kevin Welner, eds. 2013. *Closing the Opportunity Gap: What America Must Do to Give Every Child an Even Chance.* New York: Oxford University Press.

The Center for Civil Rights Remedies at The Civil Rights Project at UCLA. August 2012. Retrieved May 6, 2014 (http://civilrightsproject.ucla.edu/resources/projects/center-for-civil-rights-remedies/school-to-prison-folder/federal-reports/upcoming-ccrr-research/losen-gillespie-opportunity-suspended-2012.pdf).

Clark, Rodney, Norman B. Anderson, Vernessa R. Clark, and David R. Williams. 1999. "Racism as a Stressor for African Americans: A Biopsychosocial Model." *American Psychologist* 54(10):805.

Clotfelter, Charles. 2004. *After "Brown:" The Rise and Retreat of School Desegregation.* Princeton, NJ: Princeton University Press.

Coates, Adam, Blake Carpenter, Carl Case, Sanjeev Satheesh, Bipin Suresh, Tao Wang, David J. Wu, Andrew Y. Ng. 2011. "Text Detection and Character Recognition in Scene Images with Unsupervised Feature Learning." Paper presented at International Conference on Document Analysis and Recognition.

Codjoe, Henry M. 2001. "Fighting a 'Public Enemy' of Black Academic Achievement—the Persistence of Racism and the Schooling Experiences of Black Students in Canada." *Race, Ethnicity and Education* 4(4):343–375.

Cohen, Cathy J., Jamila Celestine-Michener, Crystal Holmes, Julie Lee Merseth, and Laurence Ralph. 2007. *The Attitudes and Behavior of Young Black Americans: Research Summary.* Chicago: University of Chicago Center for the Study of Race, Politics, and Culture.

Coleman, M. G., Darity Jr., W. A., Sharpe, R. V., 2008. "Are Reports of Discrimination Valid? Considering the Moral Hazard Effect." *American Journal of Economics and Sociology* 67(2):149–175.

Coleman, James. 1961. *The Adolescent Society: The Social Life of the Teenager and Its Impact on Education.* Hartford, CT: Greenwood Press.

Collins, Patricia Hill. 2000. *Black Feminist Thought: Knowledge, Consciousness, and the Politics of Empowerment* (Second Edition). New York: Routledge.

Collins, Patricia Hill. 2009. *Another Kind of Public Education: Race, Schools, the Media, and Democratic Possibilities.* Boston: Beacon Press.

Condron, Dennis. 2007. "Stratification and Educational Sorting: Explaining Ascriptive Inequalities in Early Childhood Reading Group Placement." *Social Problems* 54:139–160.

———. 2008. "An Early Start: Skill Grouping and Unequal Reading Gains in the Elementary Years." *The Sociological Quarterly* 49:363–394.

———. 2009. "Social Class, School and Non-School Environments, and Black/White Inequalities in Children's Learning." *American Sociological Review* 74:683–708.

Connolly, Paul. 1998. *Racism, Gender Identities and Young Children: Social Relations in a Multi-Ethnic, Inner-City Primary School.* London: Routledge.

Cook, Phillip J. and Jens Ludwig. 1998. "The Burden of 'Acting White:' Do Black Adolescents Disparage Academic Achievement?" Pp. 375–400 in *The Black-White Test Score Gap*, edited by Christopher Jencks and Meredith Philips. Washington, DC: Brookings Institution Press.

Cornell, Stephen. 1988. *The Return of the Native: American Indian Political Resurgence.* New York: Oxford University Press.

Correll, Shelley J. and Cecelia Ridgeway. 2003. "Expectation States Theory." Pp. 29–51 in *Handbook of Social Psychology*, edited by John Delamater. New York: Kluwer Academic Publishers.

Dance, L. Janelle. 2002. *Tough Fronts: The Impact of Street Culture on Schooling.* New York: Routledge.

Darity, William A. 2002. *Intergroup Disparity: Why Culture Is Irrelevant.* Unpublished manuscript, Chapel Hill, NC.

Darity, William A. and Alicia Jolla. 2009. "Desegregated Schools with Segregated Education." Pp. 99–117 in *Integration Debate: Competing Futures for America's Cities*, edited by Chester Hartman. Florence, KY: Routledge.

Darling-Hammond, Linda. 2010. *The Flat World and Education: How America's Commitment to Equity Will Determine Our Future*. New York: Teachers College Press.

Davis, F. James. 1991. *Who Is Black? One Nation's Definition*. University Park, PA: Pennsylvania State University Press.

Deitch, Elizabeth A., Adam Barsky, Rebecca M. Butz, Suzanne Chan, Arthur P. Brief, and Jill Bradley. 2003. "Subtle Yet Significant: The Existence and Impact of Everyday Racial Discrimination in the Workplace." *Human Relations* 56(11):1299–1324.

Dewey, John. 1915. *The School and Society*. Chicago: University of Chicago Press.

Diamond, John B. 2013. "The Resource and Opportunity Gap: The Continued Significance of Race for African American Student Outcomes." Pp. 97–111 in *Contesting the Myth of a Post-Racial Era: The Continued Significance of Race in Education*, edited by D. C. Andrews and F. Tuitt. New York: Peter Lang Publishers.

Diamond, John B. and James P. Huguley. 2008. "Testing the Oppositional Culture Explanation for Racial Disparities in Educational Outcomes in Desegregated Schools." Paper presented at the Annual Meeting of the American Educational Research Association, New York, NY.

———. 2011. "Black/White Disparities in Educational Outcomes: Rethinking Issues of Race, Culture, and Context." Pp. 63–94 in *African American Children's Mental Health: Development and Context*, edited by Nancy E. Hill, Tammy L. Mann, and Hiram E. Fitzgerald. New York: Praeger.

Diamond, John B. and James P. Huguley. 2014. "Testing the Oppositional Culture Explanation in Desegregated Suburban Schools: The Impact of Racial Differences in Achievement Orientations on Academic Performance" *Social Forces*. 93(2): 747–777.

Diamond, John B., Amanda E. Lewis, and Lamont Gordon. 2007. "Race, Culture, and Achievement Disparities in a Desegregated Suburb: Reconsidering the Oppositional Culture Explanation." *International Journal of Qualitative Studies in Education* 20(6):655–679.

Diamond, John B., Antonia Randolph, and James P. Spillane. 2004. "Teachers' Expectations and Sense of Responsibility for Student Learning: The Importance of Race, Class, and Organizational Habitus." *Anthropology and Education Quarterly* 35(1):75–98.

Diette, Timothy. 2005. "The Algebra Obstacle: Access, Race and the Math Achievement Gap." PhD Dissertation, University of North Carolina, Chapel Hill.

DiTomaso, Nancy. 2012. *The American Non-Dilemma: Racial Inequality Without Racism*. New York: Russell Sage Foundation.

Dovido, John F., Kerry Kawakame, Craig Johnson, Brenda Johnson, and Adaiah Howard. 1997. "On the Nature of Prejudice: Automatic and Controlled Responses." *Journal of Experimental Social Psychology* 33:510–540.

Downey, Douglas B. 2008. "Black/White Differences in School Performance: The Oppositional Culture Explanation." *Annual Review of Sociology* 34:107–126.

Downey, Douglas B. and James Ainsworth-Darnell. 2002. "The Search for Oppositional Culture Among Black Students." *American Sociological Review* 67:156–164.

Downey, Douglas, James Ainsworth, and Zhenchao Qian. 2009. "Rethinking the Attitude Achievement Paradox Among Blacks." *Sociology of Education* 82:1–19.

Downey, Douglas B. and Shana Pribesh. 2004. "When Race Matters: Teachers' Evaluations of Students' Classroom Behavior." *Sociology of Education* 77(4):267–282.

Downey, Douglas B., Paul T. von Hippel, and Melanie Hughes. 2008. "Are 'Failing' Schools Really Failing? Using Seasonal Comparison to Evaluate School Effectiveness." *Sociology of Education* 81(3):242–270.

DuBois, W. E. B. 1962. *Black Reconstruction in America: 1860–1880*. Cleveland, OH: Meridian Books.

Eberhardt, Jennifer L. 2005. "Imaging Race." *American Psychologist* 60:181–190.

Eberhardt, Jennifer L., Davies, Paul. G., Purdie-Vaughns, Valerie. J., and Johnson, S. L. 2006. "Looking Deathworthy: Perceived Stereotypicality of Black Defendants Predicts Capital-Sentencing Outcomes." *Psychological Science* 17:383–386.

Eberhardt, Jennifer L., Goff, P. A., Purdie, V. J., and Davies, P. G. 2004. "Seeing Black: Race, Crime, and Visual Processing. *Journal of Personality and Social Psychology* 87:876–893.

Eliasoph, Nina. 1999. "'Everyday Racism' in a Cultural of Political Avoidance: Civil Society, Speech, and Taboo." *Social Problems* 46(4):479–502.

Espiritu, Yen. 1992. "Pan-Asian American Ethnicity: Retrospect and Prospect." Pp. 161–176 in *Asian American Panethnicity: Bridging Institutions and Identities*. Philadelphia, PA: Temple University Press.

Farkas, George, Christy Lleras, and Steve Maczuga. 2002. "Does Oppositional Culture Exist in Minority and Poverty Peer Groups?" *American Sociological Review* 67:148–155.

Farmer, Paul. 2001. *Infections and Inequalities: The Modern Plagues*. Berkeley, CA: University of California Press.

Feagin, Joe and Karyn D. McKinney. 2003. *The Many Costs of Racism*. Lanham, MD: Rowman & Littlefield.

Feagin, Joe and Melvin Sikes. 1994. *Living with Racism: The Black Middle Class Experience*. Boston: Beacon Books.

Feldman, Martha S. and Brian T. Pentland. 2003. "Reconceptualizing Organizational Routines as a Source of Flexibility and Change." *Administrative Science Quarterly* 48(1):94–118.

Ferguson, Anne. 2000. *Bad Boys: Public Schools in the Making of Black Masculinity*. Ann Arbor, MI: University of Michigan Press.

Ferguson, Ronald F. 1998. "Teacher Perceptions and Expectations and the Black–White Test Score Gap." Pp. 273–317 in *The Black–White Test Score Gap*, edited by Christopher Jencks and Meredith Philips. Washington, DC: Brookings Institution Press.

———. 2001. "Test-Score Trends Along Racial Lines 1971 to 1996: Popular Culture and Community Academic Standards." Pp. 348–390 in *America Becoming: Racial Trends and Their Consequences*, edited by Neil Smelser, William Julius Wilson, and Faith Mitchell. Washington, DC: National Academy Press.

———. 2002. "What Doesn't Meet the Eye: Understanding and Addressing Racial Disparities in High-Achieving Suburban Schools." *Special Edition Policy Issues Report*. North Central Regional Educational Laboratory (NCREL).

Finn, Chester E. 2012. "Young, Gifted, and Neglected." *The New York Times*, September 19, A29.

Fischer, Claude S., Michael Hout, Martin Sanchez Jankowski, Samuel R. Lucas, Ann Swidler, and Kim Voss. 1996. *Inequality by Design*. Princeton, NJ: Princeton University Press.

Fordham, Signithia and John U. Ogbu. 1986. "Black Students' School Success: Coping with the 'Burden of Acting White.'" *Urban Review* 18:176–206.

Forman, Tyrone. 2004. "Color-Blind Racism and Racial Indifference: The Role of Racial Apathy in Facilitating Enduring Inequalities." Pp. 43–66 in *The Changing Terrain of Race and Ethnicity*, edited by Maria Krysan and Amanda Lewis. New York: Russell Sage.

Forman, Tyrone and Amanda Lewis. 2006. "Racial Apathy and Hurricane Katrina: The Social Anatomy of Prejudice in the Post-Civil Rights Era." *Du Bois Review* 3(1):175–202.

Fraser, Nancy. 2000. "Rethinking Recognition." *New Left Review*. 3 May/June.

Frederickson, George. 1981. *White Supremacy: A Comparative Study in American and South African History*. New York: Free Press.

Frey, William H. and Dowell Myers. 2000. "Dissimilarity Index Analysis of Census 2000." *Social Science Data Analysis Network (SSDAN)*.

Fryer, Roland and Steven D. Levitt. 2006a. "Testing for Racial Differences in the Mental Ability of Young Children." NBER Working Paper #12066. Cambridge, MA: National Bureau of Economic Research.

Fryer, Roland and Steven D. Levitt. 2006b. "Acting White." *Education Next*, Winter.

Fryer, Roland and Paul Torelli. 2010. "An Empirical Analysis of 'Acting White.'" *Journal of Public Economics* 94(5–6):380–396.

Gallagher, Charles. 2003. "Color-Blind Privilege: The Social and Political Functions of Erasing the Color Line in Post-Race America." *Race Gender and Class* 10(4):22–37.

Gaztambide-Fernández, Rubén A. 2009. *The Best of the Best: Becoming Elite at an American Boarding School*. Cambridge, MA: Harvard University Press.

Glenn, Evelyn Nakano. 1992. "From Servitude to Service Work: Historical Continuities in the Racial Division of Paid Reproductive Labor." *Signs: Journal of Women in Culture and Society* 18:1–43.

Goffman, Erving. 1959. *The Presentation of Self in Everyday Life*. New York: Doubleday.

Gosa, Travis and Karl Alexander. 2007. "Family (Dis)Advantage and the Educational Prospects of Better Off African American Youth: How Race Still Matters." *Teachers College Record* 109(2):285–321.

Gossett, Thomas F. 1965. *Race: The History of an Idea in America*. New York: Shocken.

Gotanda, Neil. 2003–04. "Reflections on Korema Tsu, Brown and White Innocence." *Temple Political and Civil Rights Law Review* 13:663–674.

Gould, Mark. 1999. "Race and Theory: Culture, Poverty, and Adaptation to Discrimination in Wilson and Ogbu." *Sociological Theory* 17:171–200.

Graham, Sandra and Brian S. Lowery. 2004. "Priming Unconscious Racial Stereotypes about Adolescent Offenders." *Law and Human Behavior* 28(5):483–504.

Gramsci, Antonio. 1971. *Selections from the Prison Notebooks*. New York: International Publishers.

Graybill, Susan W. 1997. "Questions of Race and Culture: How They Relate to the Classroom for African American Students." *Clearing House* 70:311–319.

Green, Alexander R., Dana R. Carney, Daniel J. Pallin, Long H. Ngo, Kristal L. Raymond, Lisa I. Iezzoni, and Mahzarin R. Banaji. 2007. "Implicit Bias among

Physicians and Its Prediction of Thrombolysis Decisions for Black and White Patients." *Journal of General Internal Medicine* 22(9):1231–8.

Greenhouse, Steven. 2004. "Abercrombie & Fitch Bias Case Is Settled." *The New York Times*. National Section. November 17, 2004.

Greenwald, Anthony and Mahzarin Banaji. 1995. "Implicit Social Cognition: Attitudes, Self-Esteem, and Stereotypes." *Psychological Review* 102(1):4–27.

Greenwald, Anthony and Linda H. Krieger. 2006. "Implicit Bias: Scientific Foundations." *California Law Review* 94:945–967.

Gregory, Anne, Russell J. Skiba, and Pedro A. Noguera. 2010. "The Achievement Gap and the Discipline Gap: Two Sides of the Same Coin?" *Educational Researcher* 39(1):59–68.

Gregory, Anne and Rhona S. Weinstein. 2008. "The Discipline Gap and African Americans: Defiance or Cooperation in the High School Classroom." *Journal of School Psychology* 46:455–475.

Grissmer, David, Ann Flanagan, and Stephanie Williamson. 1998. "Does Money Matter for Minority and Disadvantaged Students: Assessing the New Empirical Evidence." Pp. 98–212 in *Developments in School Finance: 1997*, edited by William Fowler. U.S. Department of Education, NCES.

Gross, Ariela Julie. 2008. *What Blood Won't Tell: A History of Race on Trial in America*. Cambridge, MA: Harvard University Press.

Guglielmo, Thomas A. 2003. "No Color Barrier." Pp. 29–43 in *Are Italians White? How Race Is Made in America*, edited by Jennifer Guglielmo and Salvatore Salerno. New York: Routledge.

Gyimah-Brempong, Kwabena and Gregory Price. 2006. "Crime and Punishment: And Skin Hue Too?" *American Economic Review* 96:246–250.

Haft, William. 1999–2000. "More than Zero: The Cost of Zero Tolerance and the Case for Restorative Justice in Schools." *Denver University Law Review* 77:795–812.

Haga, Kazu. 2011–2012. "Chicago's Peace Warriors." *Rethinking Schools* 26(2). Retrieved March 18, 2013 (http://www.rethinkingschools.org//cmshandler.asp?archive/26_02/26_02_haga.shtml).

Hall, Stuart. 1991. "The Local and the Global: Globalization and Ethnicity." Pp. 19–39 in *Culture, Globalization and the World System*, edited by A. King. London: Macmillan.

Hallett, Tim. 2007. "Between Deference and Distinction: Interaction Ritual Through Symbolic Power in an Educational Institution." *Social Psychology Quarterly* 70(2):148–171.

Hallinan, Maureen T. 1994. "Tracking: From Theory to Practice." *Sociology of Education* 67(2):79–91.

Hallinan, Maureen T. and Sorensen, A. B. 1983. "The Formation and Stability of Instructional Groups." *American Sociological Review* 48(6):838–851.

Haney Lopez, Ian. 1996. *White by Law: The Legal Construction of Race*. New York: New York University Press.

Hantzopoulos, Maria. 2006/2011. "Deepening Democracy: Rethinking Discipline in Schools." In *Rethinking Schools in Schools: Studies in Education*. Chicago: University of Chicago Press.

Harris, Angel L. 2008. "Optimism in the Face of Despair: Black/White Differences in Beliefs about School as a Means for Upward Social Mobility." *Social Science Quarterly* 89:629–651.

———. 2011. *Kids Don't Want to Fail: Oppositional Culture and the Black-White Achievement Gap*. Cambridge, MA: Harvard University Press.

Hattie, John. 2009. *Visible Learning: A Synthesis of over 800 Meta-Analyses Related to Achievement*. New York: Routledge.

Heath, Shirley Brice. 1983. *Ways with Words: Language, Life, and Work in Communities and Classrooms*. Cambridge: Cambridge University Press.

Herbert, Bob. 1995. "In America; A Nation of Nitwits." *The New York Times*, Opinion Section. March 1. Retrieved October 19, 2012 (http://www.nytimes.com/1995/03/01/opinion/in-america-a-nation-of-nitwits.html).

Higginbotham, Evelyn Brooks. 1992. "African-American Women's History and the Metalanguage of Race." *Signs* 17:251–274.

Hirschfeld, Lawrence. 2012. "Seven Myths of Race and the Young Child." *Du Bois Review* 9(1):17–39.

Hirschman, Charles. 2004. "The Origins and Demise of the Concept of Race." *Population and Development Review*. 30(3):385–415.

Holt, Thomas C. 1995. "Marking: Race, Race-making, and the Writing of History." *American Historical Review* 100(1):1–20.

Hopkins, Belinda. 2002. "Restorative Justice in Schools." *Support for Learning* 17(3):144–149.

Horvat, Erin. M. and Kristine S. Lewis. 2003. "Reassessing the "Burden of 'Acting White'": The Importance of Peer Groups in Managing Academic Success." *Sociology of Education* 76(4):265–280.

Horvat, Erin and Carla O'Connor. 2006. *Beyond Acting White: Reassessments and New Directions in Research on Black Students and School Success*. Boulder, CO: Rowman & Littlefield.

Hughes, Diane, James Rodriguez, Emilie P. Smith, Deborah J. Johnson, Howard C. Stevenson, Paul Spicer. 2006. "Parents' Ethnic–Racial Socialization Practices: A Review of Research and Directions for Future Study." *Developmental Psychology* 42(5):747–770.

Hughey, Matthew. 2012. *White Bound: Nationalists, Antiracists, and the Shared Meanings of Race*. Stanford, CA: Stanford University Press.

Hunt, Cecil J. 2005–06. "The Color of Perspective: Affirmative Action and the Constitutional Rhetoric of White Innocence." *Michigan Journal of Race and Law* 11:477.

Hurwitz, Jon and Mark Peffley. 1997. "Public Perceptions of Race and Crime: The Role of Racial Stereotypes." *American Journal of Political Science* 41:375–401.

Inzlicht, Michael and Catherine Good. 2006. "How Environments Can Threaten Academic Performance." Pp. 129–150 in *Stigma and Group Inequality: Social Psychological Perspectives*, edited by Shana Levin and Colette van Laar. Mahwah, NJ: Lawrence Erlbaum Associates, Inc.

Jackman, Mary R. 1994. *The Velvet Glove: Paternalism and Conflict in Gender, Class, and Race Relations*. Berkeley: University of California Press.

James, Sherman A. 1994. "John Henryism and the Health of African-Americans." *Culture, Medicine, and Psychiatry* 18:163–182.

Jencks, Christopher and Meredith Phillips. 1998. *The Black-White Test Score Gap*. Washington, DC: Brookings Institution Press.

Johnson, Heather Beth. 2006. *The American Dream and the Power of Wealth: Choosing Schools and Inheriting Inequality in the Land of Opportunity*. New York: Routledge.

Jordan, Winthrop. 1974. *The White Man's Burden: Historical Origins of Racism in the United States*. New York: Oxford University Press.

Jung, Moon-Kie. 2004. "Symbolic and Physical Violence: Legitimate State Coercion of Filipino Workers in Prewar Hawai'i." *American Studies* 45:107–137.

Kao, Grace. 2000. "Group Images and Possible Selves Among Adolescents: Linking Stereotypes to Expectations by Race and Ethnicity." *Sociological Forum*. 15(3):407–430.

Kao, Grace and Jennifer S. Thompson. 2003. "Racial and Ethnic Stratification in Educational Achievement and Attainment." *Annual Review of Sociology* 29:417–442.

Karp, David R. and Beau Breslin. 2001. "Restorative Justice in School Communities." *Youth and Society* 33(2):249–272.

Katz, Michael B. 1989. *The Undeserving Poor: From the War on Poverty to the War on Welfare*. New York: Random House.

Kelly, Sean. 2004. "Are Teachers Tracked? On What Basis and with What Consequences." *Social Psychology of Education* 7:55–72.

King, Martin Luther. 1986. *A Testament of Hope: The Essential Writings and Speeches of Martin Luther King, Jr*. San Francisco: Harper and Row.

Kinney, David A. 1993. "From Nerds to Normals: The Recovery of Identity among Adolescents from Middle to High School." *Sociology of Education* 66:21–40.

Kobrin, Jennifer L., Viji Sathy, and Emily J. Shaw. 2006. "A Historical View of Subgroup Performance Differences on the SAT Reasoning Test." *College Board Report* No. 2006-5.

Koenig, Barbara, Sandra Soo-Jin Le, and Sarah S. Richardson. 2008. *Revisiting Race in the Genomic Age*. New Brunswick, NJ: Rutgers University Press.

Kohn, Alfie. 1998. "Only for My Kid: How Privileged Parents Undermine School Reform." *Phi Delta Kappan* 79(8):569–577.

Kozol, Jonathan. 2005. *The Shame of the Nation: The Restoration of Apartheid Schooling in America*. New York: Crown Publishers.

Krysan, Maria. 2011. "Racial Attitudes in America: Trends and Interpretations, 2011 Update." Retrieved June 19, 2012 (http://igpa.uillinois.edu/system/files/Trends%20 in%20Racial%20Attitudes_5-4A.pdf).

———. 2012. "From Color Caste to Color Blind, Part III: Contemporary Era Racial Attitudes, 1976–2004." Pp. 235–275 in *The Oxford Handbook of African American Citizenship, 1865–Present*, edited by Henry Louis Gates Jr., Claude Steele, Lawrence D. Bobo, Michael C. Dawson, Gerald Jaynes, Lisa Crooms-Robinson, and Linda Darling-Hammond. New York: Oxford University Press.

Krysan, Maria and Amanda E. Lewis, eds. 2004. *The Changing Terrain of Race and Ethnicity*. New York: Russell Sage Foundation.

Ladson-Billings, Gloria. 2006. "From the Achievement Gap to the Education Debt: Understanding Achievement in U.S. Schools." *Educational Researcher* 35:3–12.

———. 2009. *The Dreamkeepers: Successful Teachers of African American Children*. San Francisco: John Wiley and Sons.

Lamont, Michele. 2000. *The Dignity of Working Men: Morality and the Boundaries of Race, Class, and Immigration*. Cambridge, MA: Harvard University Press and New York: Russell Sage Foundation.

Lamont, Michele and Virág Molnár. 2002. "The Study of Boundaries in the Social Sciences" *Annual Review of Sociology* 28:167–195.

Lareau, Annette. 1989. *Home Advantage: Social Class and Parental Intervention in Elementary Education*. Lanham, MD: Rowan and Littlefield.

———. 2003. *Unequal Childhoods: Race, Class, and Family Life*. Berkeley: University of California Press.

Lareau, Annette and Erin McNamara Horvat. 1999. "Moments of Social Inclusion and Exclusion: Race, Class, and Cultural Capital in Family-School Relationships." *Sociology of Education* 72(1):37–53.

Lee, Jaekyung. 2002. "Racial and Ethnic Achievement Gap Trends: Reversing the Progress Toward Equity?" *Educational Researcher* 31:3–12.

———. 2009. "Multiple Facets of Inequity in Racial and Ethnic Achievement Gaps." *Peabody Journal of Education* 79:51–73.

Lee, Stacey J. 2009. *Unraveling the "Model Minority" Stereotype: Listening to Asian American Youth* (2nd edition). New York: Teachers College Press.

Leonardo, Zeus. 2009. *Race, Whiteness, and Education*. New York: Routledge.

Lewin, Tamar. 2000. Growing Up, Growing Apart. *The New York Times*, June 25, 2000.

Lewis, Amanda E. 2001. "There Is No "Race" in the Schoolyard: Colorblind Ideology in an (Almost) All White School." *American Educational Research Journal* 38(4):781–812.

———. 2003. *Race in the Schoolyard: Negotiating the Color Line in Classrooms and Communities*. New Brunswick, NJ: Rutgers University Press.

———. 2004. "What Group?: Studying Whites and Whiteness in the Era of Colorblindness." *Sociological Theory* 22(4):623–646.

———. 2013. "The Nine Lives of 'Oppositional Culture': A Review of Angel Harris' 'Kids Don't Want to Fail' and Karolyn Tyson's 'Integration Interrupted.'" *Du Bois Review* 10(1):279–289.

Lewis, Amanda E., Mark Chesler, and Tyrone Forman. 2000. "The Impact of Color-Blind Ideologies on Students of Color: Intergroup Relations at a Predominantly White University." *Journal of Negro Education* 69(1/2):74–91.

Lewis-McCoy, R. L'Heureux. 2014. *Inequality in the Promised Land: Race, Resources, and Suburban Schooling*. Stanford, CA: Stanford University Press.

Loewen, James. 1971. *The Mississippi Chinese: Between Black and White*. Cambridge, MA: Harvard University Press.

Logel, C., Walton, G. M., Peach, J., Spencer, S. J., and Zanna, M. P. 2012. "Unleashing Latent Ability: Implications of Creating Stereotype-Safe Environments for College Admissions." *Educational Psychologist* 47:42–50.

Lopez, Nancy. 2002. *Hopeful Girls, Troubled Boys: Race and Gender Disparity in Urban Education*. New York: Routledge.

Losen, Daniel J. and Jonathan Gillespie. 2012. Opportunities Suspended: The Disparate Impact of Disciplinary Exclusion from School. UCLA: The Civil Rights Project/Proyecto Derechos Civiles. Retrieved July 15, 2014 (http://escholarship.org/uc/item/3g36n0c3).

Louie, Vivian. 2004. *Compelled to Excel: Immigration, Education, and Opportunity among Chinese Americans*. Stanford, CA: Stanford University Press.

Lucas, Samuel R. 2001. "Effectively Maintained Inequality: Education Transitions, Track Mobility, and Social Background Effects." *American Journal of Sociology* 106:1642–1690.

Lucas, Samuel R. and Mark Berends. 2002. "Sociodemographic Diversity, Correlated Achievement, and De Facto Tracking." *Sociology of Education* 75:328–348.

Lundy, Garvey F. 2003. "School Resistance in American High Schools: The Role of Race and Gender in Oppositional Culture Theory." *Evaluation and Research in Education* 17(1):6–30.

MacLeod, Jay. 1995. *Ain't No Making It: Leveled Aspirations in a Low-Income Neighborhood*. Boulder, CO: Westview.

Mangino, William. 2010. "Race to College: The "Reverse Gap." *Race and Social Problems* 2(3–4):164–178.

Mason, Patrick L. 1997. Race, Culture, and Skill: Interracial Wage Differences among African Americans, Latinos, and Whites." *Review of Black Political Economy* 25:5–40.

Massey, Douglas S. 2007. *Categorically Unequal: The American Stratification System*. New York: Russell Sage Foundation.

Massey, Douglas S. and Nancy A. Denton. 1993. *American Apartheid: Segregation and the Making of the Underclass*. Cambridge, MA: Harvard University Press.

Mathis, William. 2013. "Research-Based Options for Educational Policymaking: Moving Beyond Tracking." National Educational Policy Center. Retrieved June 15, 2013 (http://nepc.colorado.edu/publication/options).

McBride, Dwight. 2005. *Why I Hate Abercrombie & Fitch: Essays on Race and Sexuality*. New York: NYU Press.

McCarthy, John D. and Dean R. Hoge. 1987. "The Social Construction of School Punishment: Racial Disadvantage Out of Universalistic Process." *Social Forces* 65(4):1101–1120.

McIntosh, Peggy. 1990. "Unpacking the Knapsack of White Privilege." *Independent School* 49:31–36.

Mckown, Rhona S. and Clark Weinstein. 2003. "The Development and Consequences of Stereotype-Consciousness in Middle Childhood." *Child Development* 74(2):498–515.

Mechanic, David. 2002. "Disadvantage, Inequality, and Social Policy. *Health Affairs* 21(2):48–59.

Meier, Deborah. 2002a. *The Power of Their Ideas: Lessons for America from a Small School in Harlem*. Boston: Beacon Press.

Meier, Deborah. 2002b. *In Schools We Trust: Creating Communities of Learning in an Era of Testing and Standardization*. Boston: Beacon Press.

Metzl, Jonathan. 2009. *The Protest Psychosis: How Schizophrenia Became a Black Disease*. Boston: Beacon Press.

———. 2013. "Structural Health and the Politics of African American Masculinity." *American Journal of Men's Health* 7(4 Suppl):68S–72S.

Michie, Gregory. 2009. *Holler if You Hear Me: The Education of a Teacher and His Students* (2nd edition). New York: Teachers College Press.

Mickelson, Roslyn Arlin. 1990. "The Attitude-Achievement Paradox among Black Adolescents." *Sociology of Education* 63:44–61.

———. 2001. "Subverting Swann: First and Second-Generation Segregation in the Charlotte-Mecklenburg Schools." *American Educational Research Journal* 38:215–252.

———. 2003. "When Are Racial Disparities in Education the Result of Racial Discrimination? A Social Science Perspective." *Teachers College Record* 105(6):1052–1086.

———. 2008. "Twenty-First Century Social Science on School Racial Diversity and Educational Outcomes." *Ohio State Law Journal* 69:1173.

Mills, C. Wright. 1959. *The Sociological Imagination*. New York: Oxford University Press.

Mills, Charles. 2003. "White Supremacy as a Sociopolitical System: A Philosophical Perspective." Pp. 35–48 in *White Out: The Continuing Significance of Racism*, edited by Ashley Doane and Eduardo Bonilla-Silva. New York: Routledge.

———. 2011. "Liberalism and the Racial State." Pp. 27–46 in *State of White Supremacy: Racism, Governance and the United States*, edited by Moon-Kie Jung, Joao H. Costa Vargas, and Eduardo Bonilla-Silva. Stanford, CA: Stanford University Press.

Moll, Luis C., Cathy Amanti, Deborah Neff, and Norma Gonzalez. 1992. "Funds of Knowledge for Teaching: Using a Qualitative Approach to Connect Homes and Classrooms." *Qualitative Issues in Educational Research* 31(2):132–141.

Monroe, Carla R. 2005. "Understanding the Discipline Gap Through a Cultural Lens: Implications for the Education of African American Students." *Intercultural Education* 16(4):317–330.

Montagu, Ashley. 1962. "The Concept of Race." *American Anthropologist* 64(5), part 1:919–928.

Montejano, David. 1987. *Anglos and Mexicans in the Making of Texas, 1836–1986*. Austin, TX: University of Texas Press.

Moore, Abigail S. 2010. "Accommodations Angst," *The New York Times*, November 7, ED12.

Morning, Ann. 2011. *The Nature of Race: How Scientists Think and Teach about Human Difference*. Berkeley and Los Angeles: University of California Press.

Morris, Edward. 2003. *The Majority Minority: Academic Experiences of White Students in a Predominantly Racial/Ethnic Minority School*. PhD diss., University of Texas at Austin.

———. 2005. "'Tuck in That Shirt!': Race, Class, Gender, and Discipline in an Urban School." *Sociological Perspectives* 48(1):25–48.

———. 2006. *An Unexpected Minority*. New Brunswick: Rutgers University Press.

Morrison, Gale M. and Russell Skiba. 2001. "Predicting Violence from School Misbehavior: Promises and Perils." *Psychology in the Schools* 38(2):173–184.

Muhammed, Khalil. 2011. *Condemnation of Blackness: Race, Crime and the Making of Modern Urban America*. Cambridge, MA: Harvard University Press.

Myers, Kristen A. 2005. *Racetalk: Racism Hiding in Plain Sight*. Lanham, MD: Roman and Littlefield.

National Center for Education Statistics. 2012. "The Condition of Education." Retrieved March 12, 2013 (http://nces.ed.gov/programs/coe/).

Neckerman, Kathryn M. 2007. *Schools Betrayed: Roots of Failure in Inner-City Education*. Chicago: University of Chicago Press.

Noguera, Pedro and Jean Yonemura Wing. 2006. *Unfinished Business: Closing the Racial Achievement Gap in Our Schools*. San Francisco: Jossey-Bass.

Oakes, Jeannie. 1994. "Ability Grouping, Tracking and Within-School Segregation in New Castle County Schools." *Report to the US District Court for the District of Delaware in the Case of Coalition to Save Our Children v. State Board of Education*, et al.

———. 2005. *Keeping Track: How Schools Structure Inequality* (Second Edition). New Haven, CT: Yale University Press.

Oakes, Jeannie, Amy Stuart Wells, Makeba Jones, and Amanda Datnow. 1997. "Detracking: The Social Construction of Ability, Cultural Politics, and Resistance in Reform." *Teachers College Record* 98:482–510.

Obama, Barack. 2004. Keynote Address—Democratic National Convention. Transcript. Retrieved April 12, 2013 (http://www.washingtonpost.com/wp-dyn/articles/A19751-2004Jul27.html).

O'Connor, Carla. 1997. "Dispositions Toward (Collective) Struggle and Educational Resilience in the Inner City: A Case of Six African American High School Students." *American Educational Research Journal* 34(4):593–629.

———. 1999. "Race, Class, and Gender in America: Narratives of Opportunity among Low-Income African American Youths." *Sociology of Education* 72(3):137–157.

O'Connor, Carla, Lori Diane Hill, and Shanta R. Robinson. 2009. "Who's at Risk in School and What's Race Got to Do with It?" *Review of Research in Education* 33(1):1–33.

O'Connor, Carla, Erin Horvat, and Amanda E. Lewis. 2006. "Framing the Field: Past and Future Research on the Historic Underachievement of Black Students." Pp. 1–24 in *Beyond Acting White: Reassessments and New Directions in Research on Black Students and School Success*, edited by Erin Horvat and Carla O'Connor. Boulder, CO: Rowman & Littlefield.

O'Connor, Carla, Amanda E. Lewis, and J. Mueller. 2007. "Researching African Americans' Educational Experiences: Theoretical and Practical Considerations." *Educational Researcher* 36:541–552.

O'Connor, Carla, Jennifer Mueller, R. L'Heureux Lewis, and Seneca Rosenberg. 2011. "'Being' Black and Strategizing for Excellence in a Racially Stratified Academic Hierarchy." *American Educational Research Journal* 48:1232–1257.

Ogbu, John U. 1974. *The Next Generation: An Ethnography of Education in an Urban Neighborhood*. New York: Academic Press.

———. 1978. *Minority Education and Caste*. New York: Academic Press.

———. 1994. "Racial Stratification and Education in the United States: Why Inequality Persists." *The Teachers College Record* 96(2):264–298.

———. 1987. "Variability in Minority School Performance: A Problem in Search of an Explanation." *Anthropology and Education Quarterly* 18:312–334.

———. 2003. *Black American Students in an Affluent Suburb: A Study of Academic Disengagement*. Mahwah, NJ: Lawrence Erlbaum Associates.

———. 2008. *Minority Status, Oppositional Culture, and Schooling*. New York: Routledge.

Oliver, Melvin and Thomas Shapiro. 1995. *Black Wealth/White Wealth: A New Perspective on Racial Inequality*. New York: Routledge.

Olneck, Michael R. 1990. "The Recurring Dream: Symbolism and Ideology in Intercultural and Multicultural Education. *American Journal of Education*." 98:147–174.

Omi, Michael and Howard Winant. 1994. *Racial Formation in the United States: From the 1960s to the 1990s* (2nd edition). New York: Routledge.

Orfield, Gary and Susan E. Eaton. 1996. *Dismantling Desegregation: The Quiet Reversal of Brown v. Board of Education*. New York: The New Press.

Orfield, Gary and Nora Gordon. 2001. *Schools More Separate: Consequences of a Decade of Resegregation*. Cambridge, MA: Civil Rights Project, Harvard University.

Orfield, Gary and Chungmei Lee. 2005. *Why Segregation Matters: Poverty and Educational Inequality*. Cambridge, MA: Civil Rights Project, Harvard University.

Orfield, Gary and John T. Yun. 1999. *Resegregation in American Schools*. Cambridge, MA: Harvard University

Pager, Devah and Hana Shepherd. 2008. "The Sociology of Discrimination: Racial Discrimination in Employment, Housing, Credit, and Consumer Markets." *Annual Review of Sociology* 34:181–209.

Pager, Devah, Bruce Western, and Bart Bonikowski. 2009. "Discrimination in a Low-Wage Labor Market: A Field Experiment." *American Sociological Review* 74(5):777–799.

Pascoe, Peggy. 2009. *What Comes Naturally: Miscegenation Law and the Making of Race in America*. New York: Oxford University Press.

Patillo-McCoy, Mary. 1999. *Black Picket Fences*. Chicago: University of Chicago Press.

Payne, Charles M. 1984. *Getting What We Ask For: The Ambiguity of Success and Failure in Urban Education*. Westport, CT: Greenwood Press.

Pentland, Brian T. and Martha S. Feldman. 2005. "Organizational Routines as a Unit of Analysis." *Industrial and Corporate Change* 14(5):793–815.

Perry, Imani. 2011. *More Beautiful and More Terrible: The Embrace and Transcendence of Racial Inequality in the United States*. New York: NYU Press.

Perry, Pamela. 2002. *Shades of White: White Kids and Racial Identities in High School*. Durham, NC: Duke University Press.

Perry, Theresa, Claude Steele, and Asa Hilliard. 2003. *Young, Gifted, and Black: Promoting High Achievement among African-American Students*. Boston: Beacon Press.

Perry, Theresa. 2003. "Up from the Parched Earth: Toward a Theory of African-American Achievement." Pp. in *Young, Gifted, and Black: Promoting High Achievement among African-American Students*, edited by Theresa Perry, Claude Steele, and Asa Hilliard. Boston: Beacon Press.

Phillips, Meredith, James Crouse, and John Ralph. 1998. "Does the Black-White Test Score Gap Widen after Children Enter School?" Pp. 229–272 in *The Black-White Test Score Gap*, edited by Christopher Jencks and Meredith Phillips. Washington, DC: Brookings Institution Press.

Pierce, Charles M. 1974. "Psychiatric Problems of the Black Minority." Pp. 512–523 in *American Handbook of Psychiatry*, edited by Gerald Caplan and Silvano Arieti. New York: Basic Books.

———. 1975. "The Mundane Extreme Environment and Its Effect on Learning. Pp. 111–119 in *Learning Disabilities: Issues and Recommendations for Research*, edited by Suzanne G. Brainard. Washington, DC: National Institute of Education, Department of Health, Education, and Welfare.

———. 1995. "Stress Analogs of Racism and Sexism: Terrorism, Torture, and Disaster." Pp. 277–293 in *Mental Health, Racism, and Sexism*, edited by Charles Vert Willie, Patricia Perri Rieker, Bernard M. Kramer, and Bertram Brown. Pittsburgh, PA: University of Pittsburgh Press.

Piquero, Alex R. 2008. "Taking Stock of Developmental Trajectories of Criminal Activity over the Life Course." Pp. 23–78 in *The Long View of Crime: A Synthesis of Longitudinal Research*, edited by Akiva M. Liberman. New York: Springer.

Pollock, Mica. 2004. *Colormute: Race Talk Dilemmas in an American School*. Princeton, NJ: Princeton University Press.

Pollock, Mica. 2008. *Because of Race: How Americans Debate Harm and Opportunity in our Schools*. Princeton, NJ: Princeton University Press.

Posey-Maddox, Linn. 2014. *When Middle-Class Parents Choose Urban Schools: Class, Race, & the Challenge of Equity in Public Education.* Chicago: University of Chicago Press.

Prillerman, Shelly L., Hector F. Myers, and Brian D. Smedley. 1989. "Stress, Well-Being, and Academic Achievement in College." Pp. 198–217 in *Black Students: Psychological Issues and Academic Achievement,* edited by Gordon L. Berry and Joy K. Asamen. Newbury Park, CA: Sage.

Quillian, Lincoln. 2008. "Does Unconscious Racism Exist?" *Social Psychology Quarterly* 71:6–11.

Raffaele Mendez, Linda M. and Howard M. Knopf. 2003. "Who Gets Suspended from School and Why: A Demographic Analysis of Schools and Disciplinary Infractions in a Large School District." *Education and Treatment of Children* 26(1):30–51.

Randolph, Antonia. 2012. *The Wrong Kind of Difference: Challenging the Meaning of Diversity in American Classrooms.* New York: Teachers College Press.

Resnick, Lauren. 1995. "From Aptitude to Effort: A New Foundation for Our Schools." *Deadalus* 124:55–62.

Reyes, Augustina H. 2006. *Discipline, Achievement, and Race.* Lanham, MD: Rowman & Littlefield.

Ridgeway, Cecelia. 2006. "Status Construction Theory." Pp. 301–323 in *Contemporary Social Psychological Theories,* edited by Peter Burke. Stanford, CA: Stanford University Press.

———. 2011. *Framed by Gender.* New York: Oxford University Press.

Ridgeway, Cecilia L. and Kristan Glasgow Erickson. 2000. "Creating and Spreading Status Beliefs." *American Journal of Sociology* 106(3):579–615.

Ridgeway, Cecilia, Elizabeth H. Boyle, Kathy J. Kuipers, and Dawn T. Robinson. 1998. "How Do Status Beliefs Develop? The Role of Resources and Interactional Experience." *American Sociological Review* 63(3):331–350.

Rios, Victor. 2011. *Punished: Policing the Lives of Black and Latino Boys.* New York: NYU Press.

Rist, Ray C. 1970. "Student Social Class and Teacher Expectations: The Self-Fulfilling Prophecy in Ghetto Education." *Harvard Educational Review* 40:411–451.

Rocque, Michael. 2010. "Office Discipline and Student Behavior: Does Race Matter?" *American Journal of Education* 116:557–581.

Roscigno, Vincent J. and James W. Ainsworth-Darnell. 1999. "Race, Cultural Capital, and Educational Resources: Persistent Inequalities and Achievement Returns." *Sociology of Education* 72:158–178.

Rosenthal, Robert and Lenore Jacobson. 1992. *Pygmalion in the Classroom: Teacher Expectations and Pupil's Intellectual Development* (2nd edition). Norwalk, CT: Crown House Publishing.

Rothstein, Richard. 2004. *Class and Schools: Using Social, Economic, and Educational Reform to Close the Black-White Achievement Gap.* New York: Economic Policy Institute and Teachers College Columbia.

Ruck, M. and S. Wortley. 2002. "Racial and Ethnic Minority High School Students' Perceptions of School Disciplinary Practices: A Look at Some Canadian Findings." *Journal of Youth and Adolescence* 31:185–195.

Russell-Brown, Kathryn. 2008. *Color of Crime* (2nd edition). New York: NYU Press.

Saporito, Salvatore. 2003. "Private Choices, Public Consequences: Magnet School Choice and Segregation by Race and Poverty." *Social Problems* 50:181–203.

Saporito, Salvatore and Annette Lareau. 1999. "School Selection as a Process: The Multiple Dimensions of Race in Framing Educational Choice." *Social Problems* 46(3):418–439.

Schuman, Howard, Charlotte Steeh, Lawrence Bobo, and Maria Krysan. 1997. *Racial Attitudes in America*. Cambridge, MA: Harvard University Press.

Sears, David O. 1988. "Symbolic Racism." Pp. 53–84 in *Eliminating Racism*, edited by Phyllis A. Katz and Dalmas A. Taylor. New York: Plenum Press.

Sears, David O, John J. Hetts, Jim Sidanius, and Lawrence Bobo. 2000. "Race in American Politics." Pp. 1–43 in *Racialized Politics: The Debate about Racism in America*, edited by David O. Sears, Jim Sidanius, and Lawrence Bobo. Chicago: University of Chicago Press.

Shapiro, Thomas. 2004. *The Hidden Cost of Being African American: How Wealth Perpetuates Inequality*. New York: Oxford University Press.

Shapiro, Thomas M, Tatjana Meschede, and Laura Sullivan. 2010. "Racial Wealth Gap Increases Fourfold." *Boston Institute on Assets and Social Policy*.

Shapiro, Thomas M, Tatjana Meschede, and Sam Osoro. 2013. "The Roots of the Widening Racial Wealth Gap: Explaining the Black-White Economic Divide." *Institute on Assets and Social Policy Research and Policy Brief*. Waltham, MA: Brandeis University. Retrieved February 28, 2013 (http://iasp.brandeis.edu/pdfs/Author/shapiro-thomas-m/racialwealthgapbrief.pdf).

Sherer, Jennifer Z. 2007. "The Practice of Leadership in Mathematics and Language Arts: The Adams Case." Pp. 106–138 in *Distributed Leadership in Practice*, edited by James Spillane and John B. Diamond. New York: Teachers College Press.

Skiba, Russell J., Suzanne E. Eckes, and Kevin Brown. 2009/2010. "African American Disproportionality in School Discipline: The Divide Between Best Evidence and Legal Remedy." *New York Law School Law Review* 54:1071–1112.

Skiba, Russell J., Robert H. Horner, Choong-Geun Chung, M. Karega Rausch, Seth L. May, and Tary Tobin. 2011. "Race Is Not Neutral: A National Investigation of African American and Latino Disproportionality in School Discipline." *School Psychology Review* 40(1):85–107.

Skiba, Russell J., Robert S. Michael, Abra Carroll Nardo, and Reece L. Peterson. 2002. "The Color of Discipline: Sources of Racial and Gender Disproportionality in School Punishment." *The Urban Review* 34(4):317–342.

Skiba, Russell J., Reece Peterson, Kimberly Boone, and Angela Fontanini. 2000. "Preventing School Violence: A Practical Guide to Comprehensive Planning." *Reaching Today's Youth* 5(1):58–62.

Skiba, Russell J. and M. Karega Rausch. 2006. "School Disciplinary Systems: Alternatives to Suspension and Expulsion." Pp. 87–102 in *Children's Needs III: Understanding and Addressing the Developmental Needs of Children*, edited by George Bear and Kathleen Minke. Washington, DC: National Association of School Psychologists.

Skiba, Russell J., Ada B. Simmons, Shana Ritter, Ashley C. Gibb, M. Karega Rausch, Jason Cuadrado, and Choong-Geun Chung. 2008. "Achieving Equity in Special Education: History, Status, and Current Challenges." *Exceptional Children* 74:264–288.

Skiba, Russell J., Ada B. Simmons, Shana Ritter, Kristin Kohler, Michelle Henderson, and Tony Wu. 2006. "The Context of Minority Disproportionality: Practitioner Perspectives on Special Education Referral." *Teachers College Record* 108:1424–1459.

Sleeter, Christine and Carl Grant. 1987. "An Analysis of Multicultural Education in the United States." *Harvard Educational Review* 57:421–444.

Smedley, Brian D. 2012. "The Lived Experience of Race and Its Health Consequences." *American Journal of Public Health* 102(5):933–935.

Smith, William A., Walter R. Allen, and Lynette L. Danley. 2007. "Assume the Position … You Fit the Description: Psychosocial Experiences and Racial Battle Fatigue among African American Male College Students." *American Behavioral Scientist* 51(4): 551–578.

Smith, W. A. 2004. "Black Faculty Coping with Racial Battle Fatigue: The Campus Racial Climate in a Post–Civil Rights Era." Pp. ???–??? in *Broken Silence: Conversations about Race by African Americans at Predominately White Institutions*, edited by D. Cleveland. New York: Peter Lang.

Smith, William. A., Allen, Walter. R., and Danley, Lynette. L. 2007. "Assume the Position … You Fit the Description": Campus Racial Climate and the Psychoeducational Experiences and Racial Battle Fatigue among African American Male College Students. *American Behavioral Scientist*, 51(4):551–578 (formally cited as Smith 2007).

Solórzano, Daniel G. 1998. "Critical Race Theory, Race and Gender Microaggressions, and the Experience of Chicana and Chicano Scholars." *International Journal of Qualitative Studies in Education* 11(1):121–136.

Sorenson, A. and Maureen Hallinan. 1986. "Effects of Ability Grouping on Growth in Achievement." *American Educational Research Journal* 23(4):519–542.

Spillane, James P. and Amy Franz Coldren. 2011. *Diagnosis and Design for School Improvement*. New York: Teachers College Press.

Steele, Claude. 1997. "A Threat in the Air. How Stereotypes Shape Intellectual Identity and Performance." *American Psychologist* 52(6):613–629.

Steele, Claude. 2003. "Stereotype Threat and African-American Student Achievement." Pp. 109–130 in *Young, Gifted, and Black: Promoting High Achievement Among African-American Students*, edited by Theresa Perry, Claude Steele, and Asa Hilliard. Boston: Beacon Press.

Steele, Claude. 2010. *Whistling Vivaldi: And Other Clues to How Stereotypes Affect Us*. New York: W. W. Norton.

Stevens, Mitchell L. 2007. *Creating a Class: College Admissions and the Education of Elites*. Cambridge, MA: Harvard University Press.

Stoskepf, Alan. 1999. "The Forgotten History of Eugenics." *Rethinking Schools* 13(3). Retrieved January 28, 2009 (http://www.rethinkingschools.org/archive/13_03/eugenic.shtml).

Swartz, David. 1998. *Culture and Power: The Sociology of Pierre Bourdieu*. Chicago: University of Chicago Press.

Sue, Debra Wing. 2010. *Microaggressions in Everyday Life: Race, Gender, and Sexual Orientation*. Hoboken, NJ: Wiley.

Sugrue, Thomas J. 1995. "Crabgrass-Roots Politics: Race, Rights, and the Reaction Against Liberalism in the Urban North, 1940–1964." *The Journal of American History* 82(2):551–578.

Takaki, Ronald. 1993. *A Different Mirror: A History of Multicultural America*. Boston: Little, Brown and Company.

Terman, Louis. 1916. *The Measure of Intelligence*. New York: Houghton-Mifflin.

Thompson, E. P. 1975. "The Plantation as a Race-Making Situation." In B. Eugene Griessman, *Minorities*. New York: Dryden.

Thornton, Russell. 1987. *American Indian Holocaust and Survival: A Population History Since 1492*. Norman, OK: University of Oklahoma Press.

Tilly, Charles. 1999. *Durable Inequality*. Berkeley and Los Angeles: University of California Press.

Turner, Caroline Sotello Viernes and Samuel L. Myers. 2000. *Faculty of Color in the Academe: Bittersweet Success*. Needham Heights, MA: Allyn and Bacon.

Tyson, Karolyn. 2002. "Weighing In: Elementary-Age Students and the Debate on Attitudes toward School among Black Students." *Social Forces* 80(4):1157–1189.

———. 2011. *Integration Interrupted: Tracking, Black Students, & Acting White After Brown*. New York: Oxford University Press.

Tyson, Karolyn, William Darity, and Domini R. Castellino. 2005. "It's Not 'a Black Thing': Understanding the Burden of Acting White and Other Dilemmas of High Achievement." *American Sociological Review* 24:582–605.

U.S. Census Bureau. American Community Survey. 2007(?). Generated by John Diamond using American FactFinder. Retrieved.

U.S. Census Bureau. American Fact Finder. Figure 4.1.

U.S. Department of Education Office of Civil Rights. 2012. "Civil Rights Data Collection." Retrieved March 12, 2013 (http://ocrdata.ed.gov/). U.S. Census Bureau, Current Population Survey.

Valenzuela, Angela. 1999. *Subtractive Schooling: U.S.-Mexican Youth and the Politics of Caring*. New York: SUNY.

Van Ausdale, Debra and Joe Feagin. 2003. *The First R: How Children Learn Race and Racism*. Lanham, MD: Rowman & Littlefield Publishers.

Vavrus, Frances and Kim Marie Cole. 2002. "'I Didn't Do Nothin': The Discursive Construction of School Suspension." *The Urban Review* 34(2):87–111.

Wallace Jr., John M., Sara Goodkind, Cynthia M. Wallace, and Jerald G. Bachman. 2008. "Racial, Ethnic, and Gender Differences in School Discipline among US High School Students: 1991–2005." *The Negro Educational Review* 59(1–2):47.

Walters, Pamela Barnhouse. 2001. "Educational Access and the State: Historical Continuities and Discontinuities in Racial Inequality in American Education." *Sociology of Education* 74(extra issue):35–49.

———. 2007. "Explaining the Durable Racial Divide in American Education: Policy Development and Opportunity Hoarding from Brown to Vouchers." Paper presented at the Social Dimensions of Inequality Conference, Russell Sage Foundation and Carnegie Corporation, University of California, Los Angeles, January.

Walton, G. M. and P. B. Carr. 2012. Social Belonging and the Motivation and Intellectual Achievement of Negatively Stereotyped Students. Pp. in *Stereotype Threat: Theory, Processes, and Application*, edited by M. Inzlicht and T. Schmader. New York: Oxford University Press.

Walton, Gregory M. (2013). The Myth of Intelligence: Smartness Isn't Like Height. Pp. 155–172 in *Education, Justice, and Democracy*, edited by D. Allen and R. Reich. Chicago: The University of Chicago Press.

Walton, Gregory M. and Geoffrey L. Cohen. 2007. "A Question of Belonging: Race, Social Fit, and Achievement." *Journal of Personality and Social Psychology* 92:82–96.

———. 2011. "A Brief Social-Belonging Intervention Improves Academic and Health Outcomes of Minority Students." *Science* 331:1447–1451.

Walton, Gregory M., Geoff L. Cohen, D. Cwir, and S. J. Spencer. 2012. "Mere Belonging: The Power of Social Connections." *Journal of Personality and Social Psychology* 102:513–532.

Ward, Janie Victoria. 1996. "Raising Resisters: The Role of Truth Telling in the Psychological Development of African American Girls." Pp. 85–99 in *Urban Girls: Resisting Stereotypes, Creating Identities*, edited by Niobe Way. New York: NYU Press.

Warikoo, Natasha. 2011. *Balancing Acts: Youth Culture in the Global City*. Berkeley: University of California Press.

Weber, Max. 1968. *Economy and Society*. New York: Bedminster Press.

Weinstein, Rhona. 2002. *Reaching Higher: The Power of Expectations in Schooling*. Cambridge, MA: Harvard University Press.

Wells, Amy Stuart, Jennifer Jellison Holme, Anita Tijerina Revilla, and Awo Korantemaa Atanda. 2005. "How Society Failed School Desegregation Policy: Looking Past the Schools to Understand Them." *Review of Research in Education* 28(Special Issue for the Brown Anniversary):47–99.

———. 2009. *Both Sides Now: The Story of School Desegregation's Graduates*. Berkeley and Los Angeles: University of California Press.

Wells, Amy Stuart and Irene Serna. 1996. "The Politics of Culture: Understanding Local Political Resistance to Detracking in Racially Mixed Schools." *Harvard Educational Review* 66(1):93–119.

Welner, Kevin and Carol Corbett Burris. 2006. "Alternative Approaches to the Politics of Detracking." *Theory into Practice* 45(1):90–99.

Welner, Kevin Grant and Jeannie Oakes. 2000. *Navigating the Politics of Detracking*. Arlington Heights, IL: Skylight.

Wheelock, Anne. 1992. *Crossing the Tracks: How "Untracking" Can Save America's Schools*. New York: New Press.

Williams, David R., Yan Yu, James S. Jackson, and Norman B. Anderson. 1997. "Racial Differences in Physical and Mental Health: Socioeconomic Status, Stress and Discrimination." *Journal of Health Psychology* 2:335–351.

Willis, Paul E. 1977. *Learning to Labor: How Working Class Kids Get Working Class Jobs*. New York: Columbia University Press.

Wilson, George, Vincent Roscigno, and Matthew Huffman. 2012. "Public Sector Transformation, Racial Inequality and Downward Occupational Mobility." *Social Forces* 91(3):975–1006.

Wolff, Edward. 2010. "Recent Trends in Household Wealth in the United States: Rising Debt and the Middle-Class Squeeze—an Update to 2007." Levy Economics Institute of Bard College, Working Paper No. 59. Retrieved March 1, 2013 (http://www.levyinstitute.org/pubs/wp_589.pdf).

Wu, David J. and Andrew Y. Ng. 2011. "Text Detection and Character Recognition in Scene Images with Unsupervised Feature Learning." Paper presented at International Conference on Document Analysis and Recognition.

Wu, Shi-Chang, William Pink, Robert Crain, and Oliver Moles. 1982. "Student Suspension: A Critical Reappraisal." *The Urban Review* 14(4):245–303.

Yeager, David and Greg Walton. 2011. "Social-Psychological Interventions in Education: They're Not Magic." *Review of Educational Research* 81(2):267–301.

Yeager, D., Walton, G., and Cohen, G. L. 2013. "Addressing Achievement Gaps with Psychological Interventions." *Phi Delta Kappa* 94:62–65.

Yosso, T. J., W. A. Smith, M. Ceja, and D. G. Solórzano. 2009. "Critical Race Theory, Racial Microaggressions, and Campus Racial Climate for Latina/o Undergraduates." *Harvard Educational Review* 79(4):659–690.

Zuberi, Tukufu. 2001. *Thicker Than Blood: How Racial Statistics Lie.* Minneapolis, MN: University of Minnesota Press.

About the Authors

Amanda Lewis is an Associate Professor of African American Studies and Sociology and a Visiting Scholar in the Institute on Government and Public Affairs at the University of Illinois at Chicago. Her research focuses on how race shapes educational opportunities and how our ideas about race get negotiated in everyday life.

John Diamond is the Hoefs-Bascom Associate Professor of Education in the Department of Educational Leadership and Policy Analysis and a faculty affiliate in the Departments of Afro-American Studies and Educational Policy Studies at the University of Wisconsin—Madison. He studies the relationship between social inequality and educational opportunity, examining how educational leadership, policies, and practices shape students' educational opportunities and outcomes.

A NOTE ON AUTHORSHIP

This book has been a truly collaborative project from start to finish. The authors should be considered co–first authors.

Index

Figures are indicated by f and tables by t following the page number. Endnotes are indicated by n and the note number following the page number, e.g., 191n4.